Praise for

DINNER *with the* SMILEYS

"Uplifting."
—*O, the Oprah Magazine*

"A delicious diversion...Sarah Smiley is all heart...She's honest to a fault, filled with self-doubt, and frequently, perilously, vulnerable. And many people will see her as a hero for being so frank about it." —*USA Today*

"*Dinner with the Smileys* made me want to invite this family to dinner at my house. It made me want to gather my own family together for a meal."

—Lisa Belkin, author of *Life's Work: Confessions of an Unbalanced Mom*

"Sarah Smiley writes in such a very intimate and frank style that the reader feels like a fly on the wall in the Smiley home. Her humor is quiet and wry, and at times she is painfully honest."

—BookReporter.com

"It is both a joy and an inspiration...If you ever doubted the basic goodness of Americans, this book will restore your faith."

—Sue Halpern, author of *A Dog Walks into a Nursing Home*

"[The] st to hilarious."

—*Maine* Magazine

"Classic S ny and smart."

—Alex Witchel, "The 6th Floor," NYTimes.com

DINNER
with the
SMILEYS

SARAH SMILEY

PHOTOGRAPHS BY ANDREA HAND

New York Boston

Hachette Books
Hachette Book Group
237 Park Avenue
New York, NY 10017
www.HachetteBookGroup.com

Printed in the United States of America

RRD-C

First Hachette Books trade edition: September 2014
10 9 8 7 6 5 4 3 2 1

Hachette Books is a division of Hachette Book Group, Inc.

The publisher is not responsible for websites (or their content) that are not owned by the publisher.

The Library of Congress has catalogued the hardcover edition as follows:

Smiley, Sarah.
  Dinner with the Smileys: one military family, one year of heroes, and lessons for a lifetime/Sarah Smiley.—First edition.
    pages cm
  ISBN 978-1-4013-2487-2
  1. Smiley, Sarah.   2. Navy spouses—United States—Biography.   3. Families of military personnel—United States—Biography.   4. Dinners and dining—Social aspects.   5. Parent and child—United States—Anecdotes.   6. Smiley, Dustin.   7. Separation (Psychology).   8. Wives—Maine—Bangor—Biography.   9. Bangor (Me.)—Social life and customs.   10. Bangor (Me.)—Biography.   I. Title
  V736.S648 2013
  359.0092—dc23
                                                                    2013003152
ISBN 978-0-316-40894-3 (pbk.)

To every guest who filled Dustin's seat
at the dinner table.

And to my boys. All of them.

Contents

Preface

September 2014

When the boys and I started inviting guests to dinner after Dustin left for deployment, we had a simple reason: We didn't want to be alone. Especially not at dinner. What began with selfish motivations, however, quickly evolved to become something else entirely.

As early as our seventeenth dinner, with Frank and Anita at the assisted living facility, we knew that our endeavor had become less about us—even less about military families in general—and more about all the people in our community who eat alone at dinner. They are alone because they are widows and widowers, empty nesters, divorcees, single, or living away from home for the first time. They might even be alone with other people in the house. They are eating in the kitchen while their spouses eat in front of the television in the living room. They are eating with strangers at a nursing home. They are alone and ordering pizza in their apartments.

Indeed, there are many different ways to be "lonely."

And so, toward the end of the year, Dinner with the Smileys

became more about building a community that could help every-one be less alone at the dinner table. We realized our invitations didn't hold benefits solely for us; they offered something for our guests as well. As blessed as we were by people filling Dustin's empty seat, it turned out, our guests felt just as blessed for having been invited.

These connections often extended beyond the dinner. A year later, many of our dinner guests were still very much a part of our lives. They had become like family, and it is difficult for us to re-member a time when we didn't know them.

Ben Sprague and Malorie, who went to Boston with us to meet the Red Sox, are a great example. They got married a month later, and the boys and I were at the wedding. After the vows, as Ben and Malorie walked by us in the pews to exit the church, Ben reached out a hand to pat Ford's shoulder. Ford beamed.

Ben continued to take Ford to Middle School Youth Group at church, and any time he saw the boys playing basketball at the park, he walked over to join them. A year later, Ben became the mayor of our city, and he and Malorie had a son of their own.

Frank and Anita also made a profound, lasting impact on our family. When the hardcover version of *Dinner with the Smileys* came out about five months after Dustin returned home, one of the first people to whom I wanted to give a book was Frank. We had been back to visit Frank and Anita with Dustin in January, and we planned to have dinner with them again to present Frank with the book. When I called to set up the meeting, however, I learned that Frank had died shortly before the book's release. We considered visiting with Anita alone, but relatives told us her health had declined and she definitely would not remember us.

Instead, I met with Frank and Anita's daughter. She came to our house to share stories of Frank and to talk about our dinner. Lindell and Owen, then seven and eleven years old, passed through the living room on their way outside and were nearly oblivious to the stranger sitting on the couch. But when I said, "Boys, this is Frank and Anita's daughter," they both stopped and turned around with softened faces.

"How is Anita?" Owen asked.

"Didn't Frank go to Heaven?" Lindell said.

To this day, whenever we pass by the assisted living facility, the boys mention Frank and Anita, and now they include the couple's daughter, too.

Another dinner favorite was Maine Congressman Mike Michaud. Photographer Andrea Hand's photographs eloquently captured the immediate and intense affection my youngest son felt for the congressman. The picture of Lindell riding on Mike's shoulders continues to be a reader favorite.

Mike still sends each of the boys a handwritten letter every Christmas, and he has told many acquaintances that his Dinner with the Smileys was among the best days of his life. We visited Mike in his DC office a year later, and Lindell couldn't wait to give him an update. "I can read now," Lindell said. "Remember how I couldn't read before?"

For Lindell especially, who was only four years old when Dinner with the Smileys began, these friends in our community—from Melissa Huston, who still stops by to say hello, to Gibran at the bookstore, who always knows what the boys are reading—are as much a part of our family as cousins, aunts, and uncles. There is virtually nowhere Lindell goes in town without running into a dinner guest. What an incredible gift to be greeted by a loving community of adults who don't just know his name but have been to his house, met his dog, and have shared a dinner table with his family.

This lesson about community and dinners has become so ingrained in my boys that even today, when we meet someone interesting, they say, "Can we have that person to dinner?" For the boys, an invitation to dinner is a special language. It conveys a desire to welcome someone into our lives in a way that isn't possible outside of the kitchen table.

So, after a year hiatus and after much pleading from the boys, we started Dinner with the Smileys again on a monthly basis and with Dustin in his seat at the head of the table. These dinners—with a blind man and his Seeing Eye dog; with a man from Djibouti, Africa, who worked with Dustin on deployment; with an entomologist who once kept pet bed bugs—are less about abating loneliness and more about building our community, and the boys' horizons, even further.

Some people have called Dinner with the Smileys "homeschooling on steroids." I never saw it that way, because what happened wasn't planned. Instead, I view Dinner with the Smileys as a difficult and sad situation that, through the generosity of our community and the magic of the dinner table, turned into something beautiful.

"Magic of the dinner table"?

Yes. Nothing compares to sharing a dinner table with someone. Our guests entered as strangers, but they left as friends and family. Even the ones with which we don't agree.

Our most controversial guest was Governor Paul LePage, a politician who is despised by many in our state. Indeed, people claim to "hate" him. I don't agree with all of Governor LePage's politics or public statements, but I have shared a dinner table with the man, and therefore, I see him as a three-dimensional human being—a flawed and imperfect human like the rest of us. It is difficult to hate people (which is different than disagreeing with them) when you know them in this way.

And I wonder: What good could happen in our world—with politics, war, bullying, violence—if more people shared a dinner table?

The guests, the love, and the opportunities are limitless.

DINNER
with the
SMILEYS

CHAPTER ONE

An Old Farm Table

I don't like to cook, and I hate small talk. When I host a dinner party, there is a moment right before the guests show up when I wish I could disappear to the basement. The first few minutes of a party—with one or two early guests and awkward conversation—are the worst. I smile and struggle to talk about the weather, but inside I'm thinking, *Why did I think this was a good idea?* My natural tendency is to want to be alone. I constantly resist the urge, and I've trained myself to be sociable. It doesn't always work: I forget to offer our guests drinks. I leave too many silent pauses. And I eat too many appetizers.

So why did I volunteer to host fifty-two weekly dinners in a year? The answer lies in a warm spring day in 2011.

The snow was gone, and the muck of mud season had retreated into the soil. I was in the kitchen boiling noodles for dinner. Steam rose from the pot and left a wet trail across the stainless steel hood. Our old, yellowed wood floors creaked beneath my feet as I moved from the refrigerator to the stove. Despite the cooler (high fifties) weather, all the windows in the house were open. In Maine, in the spring, fifty degrees is warm. The new seasonal air moved through the house, carrying with it the smell of neighbors' barbecues, burning charcoal, and the dusty wire of the window screens. Through the front windows, I heard echoes of neighborhood children laughing up and down the sidewalk. They had each grown at least two inches since I last saw them at the sledding hill on Thirteenth Street back in November.

Through the back patio door, just outside the kitchen, my husband, Dustin, and our three boys, ages eleven, nine, and four, were quiet. The only sound was the rhythmic *thump* of a baseball going from glove to glove. This wasn't completely unusual. Dustin and Ford are often quiet when they play ball. They don't need to talk; they just throw and catch. And Owen doesn't talk when he thinks his older brother might. He'll stop midsentence if Ford interrupts. But Lindell, the youngest, is seldom quiet. The absence of his laugh, which is always one slight annoyance away from being a mad scream, made the new spring day seem as empty and cold as January.

Without looking, I knew Owen was not playing catch. He would be off to the side, kicking a soccer ball. Lindell would be crouched in the garden, with his knees bent against his ears, and poking sticks at earthworms and spiders. Owen would never interfere with Ford's time with their dad, and so far Lindell has little interest in baseball. Dustin never intended it to be this way. He invites Owen to play catch, and he sets up the tee for Lindell. But Lindell would rather play in the dirt, or chase birds, or bark at the neighbor's dog, and Owen will only play catch until Ford picks up his glove. It's as if he opens the show for his brother to warm up the crowd. Perhaps this is because Owen, like me, has also seen the way Ford and Dustin communicate across a baseball field, using only subtle nods and silent thumbs-up. Or maybe he is just the middle child.

The noodles on the stove bubbled to the surface of the water. I turned down the flame, and a breeze blew out the pilot light. The stove made a clicking sound until I turned it off. Gradually, the noodles settled to the bottom of the pot. I went to the door to call Dustin and the boys in for dinner.

Just before I slid open the screen, and against the background music of robins chirping from trees budding new leaves, I heard this:

"So will you be able to call us, Dad?"

"No, not on a telephone. But we should be able to talk through the computer. Depends on the connection."

The baseball *thumped* into a glove.

"Will we ever see you again?" Lindell said.

"Of course."

Thump. Thump.

"When?"

"After I do my job, which is going to feel like a long time."

A squirrel ran across the pickets of our chipped and peeling white fence. A neighbor in the distance started his lawn mower.

"How long is thirteen months?" Lindell asked.

Ford sighed as he drew back his arm and threw the ball to Dustin. "It's thirteen months, Lindell."

More silence. More sounds of the ball hitting the thick leather of a glove.

And then Owen said, "Will you be here when I try out for Little League next spring, Dad?"

"No, I'm going to miss that, Owen."

"Will you be here when I go to kindergarten?" Lindell asked.

"No, I'll miss that, too."

Ford, speaking in his deeper, authoritative voice—the voice of a firstborn son—said, "I'll help get you ready, buddy."

Ford was a baby the first time Dustin deployed. The second time, in 2002, Ford was two years old and Owen was six weeks old. Back then, the boys never understood—not in a concrete way—that their dad was missing. Back then, my young children primarily needed their mom—for nursing and kisses on scraped knees. Back then, there wasn't Little League or kindergarten or junior high school. There wasn't looming adolescence.

Owen saw me standing in the doorway and came to the screen. "When's dinner, Mom?" His shoulders looked like the edges of a coat hanger beneath his shirt. His legs had grown an inch or more in length over the winter, but they were still thin.

"It will be ready in just a minute," I said, turning to go back to the kitchen.

"But, Mom, we've been waiting for like an hour!" Owen slid open the screen door and followed behind me.

Owen survives on a diet of peanut butter and bread. Yet, he's always anxious for dinnertime. One day, after he had been pestering me for several minutes, I turned around and said, "Why do you care when dinner will be ready? You're not going to eat it anyway!"

Owen had looked up at me through his long, straight hair hanging too far past his eyebrows and said, "I just want to sit together at the table."

At a different time, I told Lindell that we were eating leftovers for dinner but that he could have cold cereal or a grilled cheese instead.

Lindell said, "I like the nights when we all sit down and eat the same food, Mom."

Apparently dinnertime is about more than just eating.

I went past Owen with a bowl of spaghetti sauce. Steam followed in a trail behind me.

I set the bowl on the table and said, "You can call your brothers and Dad in now." Soon, feet pounded on the wood deck. Ford threw his ball and glove on the ground. Dustin told him to put it where it belongs: "What if it rains tonight, Ford? You can't leave your glove out in the rain."

Lindell came into the kitchen and grabbed my legs. "What's for dinner, Momma?" His hands were covered in powdery, gray dirt.

"Everyone needs to go wash their hands," I called out over his head. "But hurry. The spaghetti will get cold."

Dustin took Lindell's hand and led him to the hall bathroom, where Ford and Owen already had the water running and were eagerly scrubbing their hands in between yelling about giving each other more room. I knew that dribbles of dirty water would be slung across the pedestal sink and the floor by the time all four of them had finished.

I took my place at the table and waited.

One by one, the boys and Dustin came to their seats, hands still dripping with water. Ford had a large, round wet spot on the front of his shirt, and he was dragging his left hand across his chest.

Our dinner table is a five-foot-long wooden farm table passed down from my parents. From the time I was a baby until I left to marry Dustin, I ate at the same table with my two older brothers, my mom, and my dad. We each had our own place. Dad sat at the head of the table, and I was on his left. Mom was across from me and next to my brother Van. My brother Will was beside me. No matter how many people we had to dinner—whether it was just us, or my grandparents, too, or a whole other family of five—Mom always squeezed everyone in at the table. There was no balancing plastic plates in your lap in Mom's house. The dinner table was the center of our house. I sat there to do puzzles or homework, Paint by Number, play Monopoly, or bake brownies in my Easy-Bake Oven. The wood was soft, and nothing got past it without leaving a mark. Where I sat, the top was marred with indents from my spelling words, letters to my friends, and the leftover swirls from the Spirograph I got one Christmas. When sunlight came through the bay window of the kitchen, every dent and every shadow of a math problem was highlighted in the grain.

When Dustin and I moved to Maine, my parents gave us the family dinner table. Dad spent hours sanding it down, erasing all the marks and words, and then he stained and varnished it. In the kitchen of our white, weathered cape, it looked like a brand-new table. Nearly forty years of raising a family had vanished from its top. Of course, my boys wasted no time putting new marks in the wood. When Lindell was still a baby, he liked to bang his fork, tine-side down, against the table. His place looks like it has chicken pox. Ford's place (next to me) is tattooed with lists ("Favorite *Star Wars* Characters," "Best Book Characters," etc.) and pie charts ("How I Spend My Day" and "The Smiley Family's Favorite Movies"). Owen's place has the shadow of cartoon drawings and the beginning of a letter he wrote to a friend: *Dear Caleb . . .*

In the beginning, I asked the boys to keep something under their paper. "You'll dent the wood if you don't," I told them. "And Pop just refinished this for us." But it was a losing battle. Letters and homework and drawings crept onto the wood, evidence of a table raising three new children.

Nothing was or is formal about our time spent at the dinner table. The kids reach across one another. Lindell leaves his seat and sits on the floor. Ford presses his knees against the edge of the table and rocks his seat backward. Spoons and forks clatter against chipped plates, and souvenir drinking glasses drip water into puddles that run toward the seams where the table's leaves fold down. Our napkins are folded paper towels.

Just as the five of us got settled around the table that night, a neighbor boy came to the front porch and asked to play. Ford said, "After dinner," and the boy left, our glass front door slamming closed behind him. The row of plates hanging on the wall beside our kitchen table vibrated on their springs. I dished out spaghetti and Dustin buttered Lindell's bread. Once everyone's plates and mouths were full, Dustin asked the usual question: "What did you learn at school today?"

Owen looked up at Ford, waiting for the answer.

Ford just shrugged. The tail of a noodle slipped between his lips.

"I don't go to school, Daddy," Lindell said, eager to be part of the conversation. He was holding a green plastic cup with both hands. His lips were ringed with red juice.

"But did you learn anything here with Mom today?" Dustin asked.

"Not really." Lindell set down his cup and picked at noodles with his fingers.

Dustin looked at Ford and Owen. "How about you guys?"

Owen looked up at Ford again.

"Dad, I don't learn anything at school," Ford said.

"Oh, you must have learned something."

Owen pushed pasta around his plate with a fork. He looked up again, first at Ford, and then at Dustin. Then he said, "Dad, when you go, where will you be?"

"I'll be on a base on the other side of the world," he said.

"Like in China?" Lindell asked.

"No, not China. Africa."

Lindell's dark brown eyes widened. He got on his knees and leaned toward Dustin's place at the table. "You mean like with lions and giraffes?"

Dustin laughed. "I might see some of those."

"What will you be doing there?" Ford asked. "Navy stuff?"

"Will you fly your helicopter?" Lindell asked.

"No, I won't be flying this time," Dustin said. "I'll be working with our navy and a lot of other navies from other countries, too."

There were a few minutes of quiet, except for forks and knives scraping plates.

Then Owen said, "It will be weird to not have you here at the table."

"But you've got Mom and Ford and Lindell, so I know you will be okay. And I'm going to miss you guys, too."

Dustin had made it sound better, but Owen was right: Dinnertime is usually the most difficult time for families separated by a military deployment. The service member's empty seat makes the absence that much more vivid. The rituals everyone has grown accustomed to—Dad asking, "How was school?" every night, for instance—are off balance. There are empty pauses—places where the service member might have spoken.

This loneliness is not military families' alone. It's shared by widows and widowers, divorcees, singles, and even people in unhappy marriages. Every night, thousands of people eat alone. I have always thought that if houses and apartments were like dollhouses, with one exterior wall removed, we'd see plenty of people eating alone, their faces highlighted by the blue-green glow of a television. I was one of those people during Dustin's first two deployments. That wouldn't be me again.

"We don't have to be lonely," I said, looking around at each of the boys. "We'll invite friends over for dinner. Shoot, we can invite someone every week if you want."

"Even our teachers?" Owen asked.

"I get to invite Mr. Bennett first!" Ford said. He was raising his hand, as if he were in school.

"I wanna invite my teacher, too," Lindell whined.

"You don't have a teacher," Owen said.

"But he will have one in the fall, when he goes to preschool," Dustin said.

Lindell was standing in his chair now, dancing with excitement. "Can we invite the president? Or the mayor?"

We all laughed. "I suppose," I said. "Why not?"

The neighbor boy appeared on the front porch again.

Ford hurried to eat the last of his pasta. "We'll be out in a minute," he yelled.

The room was quiet again as the older boys rushed to finish. Lindell was sitting in his chair again, but he wasn't eating. He was looking at Dustin.

"Daddy, will you die?" he said.

Dustin swallowed and cleared his throat. He took a sip of water and looked at me over the rim of his glass.

"It's not like in the movies," Ford said, rolling his eyes at Lindell.

"Well, sometimes—" Dustin began.

"Yeah, Dad will be fine," Owen said.

Dustin set the glass back down on the table and turned toward Lindell. "I'll do everything I can to come back home to you," he said.

Owen dropped his fork on the plate. "Done!" he said. "Can I please be excused?"

Ford, still chewing a mouthful of bread, got up from the table and said, "Let's go, Owen." He called over his shoulder, "See ya guys!"

Lindell slid out of his chair and went to the living room to finish a puzzle on the floor. The glass front door slammed closed behind Ford and Owen.

The kitchen was quiet again. I looked at Dustin. The muscles in his square jaw rippled under the skin as he chewed. He grinned at me and stared back.

"When you're gone," I said, "it will just be me sitting here finishing dinner by myself."

Dustin squeezed my hand beside my plate.

DUSTIN USUALLY CAME home from work at 5:00 or 5:30—the perks of living in a small town and thousands of miles away from the heartbeat of the navy: Norfolk, Virginia. He was stationed at a Navy Operational Support Center (or, NOSC) in Bangor, Maine, where he was commander of navy reservists in the state. During the three-year tour, we had been lulled into pseudocivilian life. Sometimes I could almost believe we weren't military at all.

In the absence of a major military base, I shopped at civilian grocery stores, not the commissary. Living on base was not an option in Bangor. And there wasn't a spouse group like I had grown accustomed to in San Diego and Pensacola, Florida. Most of my local friends had no military background, so few of them knew what IA (Individual Augmentation) meant when I told them that Dustin was being sent on a yearlong one. It would be the first time Dustin deployed from a mostly civilian community, and secretly I worried about what that meant for me.

Would we have support? Would people understand? Would we be forgotten?

Now that it was spring, it was still light outside when Dustin pulled our blue Ford Freestyle into the cracked and crumpling driveway. I could hear the car door slam shut through the kitchen window screen. Then I'd hear Dustin call out hello to our neighbor Gloria, who was eighty-seven and living alone. Dustin would come through the front door, drop his bags on the porch, and then, after giving me a quick hello, grab a water from the refrigerator and say, "The boys out back? I think I'll go play some catch with them" (meaning with Ford).

The night after our spaghetti dinner, however, Dustin was late. He had stayed at work to finish the usual predeployment paperwork: filling out his will, setting up my power of attorney, and making sure that his "wishes" are known.

Just in case.

Through the back screen door, I heard the familiar *thump* of the baseball hitting a glove. I looked out the window, past the budding screen of the maple tree, and saw Ford and Owen playing catch. In silence.

Thump. Thump. Thump.

Lindell pushed a toy truck through the garden. The sun, setting on the front side of the house, cast cool dark shadows across the lawn.

I heard Dustin's car door shut, and I ran to the front door.

Dustin stopped on the sidewalk to talk to Gloria. I knew she was probably asking about his upcoming deployment. Dustin smiled over her shoulder when he saw me standing in the doorway. Gloria patted Dustin—a thin, frail hand against his smooth, broad shoulder—and I heard their muffled good-byes through the glass door.

Dustin jogged up the brick walkway, opened the door, and dropped his bags on the floor. "Sorry I'm late," he said, leaning in to kiss my cheek. He moved past me and picked up his glove from the table where we keep our keys. "Are the boys out—"

"Wait," I said, interrupting. "Come look." I took his hand and led him to the back door. I motioned with my finger against my lips for him not to talk. We stood at the screen door and looked out across the deck, through the maple, at our three boys playing in the backyard. "Ford and Owen are playing catch," I whispered.

Dustin put his arm around my shoulder.

"Soon, they won't have you," I said. "Let them learn to play together."

Dustin squeezed me closer and whispered through my hair into my ear. "Does this mean it's just you and me here in the house right now?"

I acted disgusted and playfully shooed him away. He put his glove on the kitchen table and disappeared into the living room. When he turned on the television, the familiar, grating sound of sportscasters filled the space.

I watched the boys out the window for a few more minutes. Ford told Owen, "Don't be afraid of the ball. Come toward it. Let your glove be part of your hand."

I returned to the stove to finish dinner.

Lindell and Ford

CHAPTER TWO

The Good-bye

M ovies, books, and iconic photographs have given the general public an unrealistic view of military departures. You might expect that the boys and I did nothing but fall to our knees and sob as Dustin left on a cold morning in November, one day before Ford's eleventh birthday and the week of Thanksgiving and Owen's ninth birthday. But the reality is much more ordinary. Dustin was leaving from Bangor International Airport and headed to South Carolina for training before going overseas. He was flying commercial, so he was dressed in jeans, sneakers, and a collared shirt. It was Sunday.

Dustin held Lindell's hand on one side and his carry-on on the other as we rode up the escalator to the second floor of the terminal. Ford and Owen were behind him. They were excited that a Sunday morning send-off meant no church. I don't think they completely understood that it also meant their dad wasn't coming back for a full year. Time, it seems, is incomprehensible to children. As I watched from behind, I tried to memorize everything: the width of Dustin's shoulders, his tightly cropped hair, the way his shoes always look like they are about to come untied. I wanted to store it all. There are so many looming "lasts," so many things

to remember, when your spouse is about to deploy. The week before, I had punctuated every moment with the dreaded thought:
Dustin won't be here for _____ *next year.*

We were early to the airport, so we sat in the hard plastic chairs
and tried to be normal. No outsider would have known that
Dustin was about to say good-bye to us for a year. We looked like
any other family of five headed for a fun vacation. Maybe Disney.
Except none of us were smiling.

Lindell found a Lego table across from our row of seats, and he
got busy building an airplane. Ford and Owen asked for money to
buy donuts at the airport coffee shop. Dustin put his arm around
me, and I rested my head on his shoulder. I was tired because it was
early and I was unable to sleep the night before. I hadn't wanted to
waste those eight precious hours. Now I found myself wishing we
could just say good-bye. Just get it over with. Then I could go
back home to sleep.

But it didn't seem right to leave.

Could I really cheat all of us out of our last hour and a half together?

On the other hand, staying felt dreadfully ordinary. It wasn't
like I could curl up against Dustin or kiss him endlessly. He's not
one for public displays of affection anyway. But making small talk
about the weather or our upcoming schedules seemed to cheapen
the experience. So we sat in silence while Ford and Owen ate their
donuts and Lindell played with Legos. The silence was marked by
awkward attempts at normal conversation:

"So, is it a long flight?"

"Not too bad."

"I hope you didn't forget to pack anything."

"If I did, you can send it to me later."

We talked more about the dinner idea, which is what we were
calling it then. When I had mentioned it so many months earlier,
I didn't really know what I meant by "let's invite people to eat

dinner with us each week." I just thought it sounded good. But as Dustin's departure loomed near, the idea evolved and grew. Dustin talked about it the most of anyone.

"I hate to think of you guys being alone at dinner," he'd say. "I know it's hard to reach out sometimes, but, seriously, try to have people over. It will help you feel less alone."

Dustin knows my tendency to withdraw and hibernate. "Plus," he once said, "it's a great way to count down the time. I'll be gone about fifty-two weeks; you can have fifty-two dinners."

He was right about this. In the past, I had counted down the days of a deployment by making paper chains or filling a jar with M&M's and letting the kids eat one for each day that their dad was gone. The problem this time was that we didn't have room for a 365-link chain in our fifteen-hundred-square-foot home. And the M&M's posed problems, too. Military deployments are not well defined. Dustin's first deployment, for example, which was only supposed to be six months, unexpectedly turned into seven and a half months. Just when the M&M jar was looking empty, I had to buy more candy to fill it up again. Also, back then, when the kids went to sleep and I was feeling alone and anxious, I sometimes "drank" M&M's from the jar and had to replace them the next day. Counting dinners and being social seemed like a much more productive (not to mention healthy) alternative.

About thirty minutes before Dustin's plane's scheduled departure, he sighed and said, "You guys should probably get going. There's no sense dragging this out."

I sat up straighter. Suddenly I wasn't tired anymore. My heart was pounding. My throat felt uncomfortably tight. Dustin took my hand and pulled me to stand. He wrapped me in his arms, and I buried my face in his shoulder. "You guys are going to be fine," he whispered, petting my hair. "Remember, you can call Military Family Assistance anytime you need. There are people here to help. And I'll call you just as soon as I can."

The boys, sensing the change of mood and activity, gathered at our legs. Owen was crying, and Ford patted his back. One by one, Dustin took each of the boys aside, knelt down in front of them and told them good-bye. Owen pulled at his eyes and wiped away tears. I could see from the corner of my eye that Ford was biting on the inside of his cheek. He watched me closely.

We followed Dustin across the terminal, past other waiting passengers half-asleep in the hard chairs, to the line that was forming at the security checkpoint. Once Dustin got in that line, he would officially be separated from us.

With his free arm, Dustin pulled me into him and kissed the top of my head. The tears finally came, and I cried into his chest.

The boys wrapped themselves around my legs and waist.

"This part is never easy," Dustin said. "But I have to go."

"I know," I said into his shirt.

"I'll be thinking of you guys every day."

He kissed the top of my head before pulling away to hug each of the boys again. Then he turned around and got in line.

Now onlookers, who had already gone through security, knew this was no ordinary good-bye-see-you-in-a-week kind of thing. Some of them started crying, too. Others smiled sympathetically. There they were, strangers on the other side of the PASSENGERS ONLY sign with my husband. And there I was, across the DO NOT ENTER signs, suddenly feeling both heavy and empty at the same time.

Dustin gave me a thumbs-up once he was settled in line. I picked up Lindell and held him on my hip. Ford took my hand. Before I turned around, Dustin said, "Hey, do that weekly dinner thing, Sarah. It will be good for you guys."

I nodded.

The boys and I started toward the escalator.

I knew I couldn't look back. I had to keep walking.

As I paid the parking attendant, a tear rolled down my cheek. But crying isn't unusual at an airport. The man passed my receipt through the open car window and half-smiled, half-nodded. The long orange arm on the other side of the ticket booth rose. I drove away from the terminal.

OUR HOUSE ISN'T far from the airport. Maybe three miles. Still, I knew I couldn't go home. Not yet. It wasn't even noon, which meant we had a whole lonely day ahead of us. I could not bear the emptiness of the house. I did not want to see Dustin's toothbrush still wet from the morning, or his razor sitting in a puddle of water on the edge of his sink. There would be so many little reminders that he had just been there. And yet, the morning—his shower, his shaving and brushing teeth—already seemed like ages ago.

When I passed our street, I kept driving.

"Where are we going, Mom?" Ford said.

"I don't know. Somewhere. Maybe church."

"But we're not dressed for church."

I looked down at my lap. I was wearing sweatpants, an old wool sweater, and heavy L.L. Bean boots. The boys were dressed similarly. In fact, I thought I had probably just put a coat over Lindell's pajamas. And did he have on shoes or slippers? It didn't matter. I couldn't go home.

I drove toward downtown, just a few blocks down the hill that leads to the intersection of Main and State streets. Old brick buildings with large windowpanes were stacked like stairsteps along the side of the sloping street. I stopped at Exchange Street to allow a group of walkers to cross.

"That's the school secretary," Owen said, waving through the window at one of the women.

The secretary waved back and smiled.

When we passed by Giacomo's, a local deli and coffee shop, Gibran, who works at the children's bookstore on Central Street, lifted up a steaming Styrofoam cup in a makeshift wave.

I parallel parked in front of the barbershop, and we walked toward the 150-year-old stone building of our church. The copper steeple, turned green with age, pierced the gray morning sky.

"Mom, do you really think we should go in like this?" Ford said. He was pointing at his sweatpants with holes in the knees.

I didn't answer.

"Mom, seriously! We're late, even. Church started fifteen minutes ago."

I didn't answer.

When we were just outside the arched sanctuary door, below the circular stained-glass window with muted blues, greens, and purples, I whispered instructions to Ford and Owen: "Walk quietly. Find an empty pew toward the back if you can. I'll follow you."

Ford rolled his eyes and pulled open the heavy wooden door. It creaked throughout the sanctuary, the noise bouncing off the vaulted ceilings. Several heads turned our way.

There was our pediatrician, past schoolteachers, neighbors, shop owners, friends, and classmates.

And there we were, a mom and her boys dressed in sweatpants and winter boots.

Just then, I remembered that I hadn't even showered.

Sitting in the back was not going to be an option after all. It was too full. So Ford found an empty spot in the first row, right in front of the minister. As I followed him—squatting and ducking, trying not to make a scene—I was suddenly more aware of my clunky, wet boots that were surely leaving a trail of wet snow down the church aisles.

I didn't take off my winter coat when we sat down.

The congregation stood to sing. I searched the pew for a hymnal, because normalcy and routine were what I needed, even though

I wanted to stay seated. My eyes were filling with tears again, and I couldn't see the text on the thin pages as I flipped through them. I didn't even know which page to turn to.

The song was "It Is Well with My Soul."

I sat back down and cried into my hands.

Owen

CHAPTER THREE

The Holidays

By far, the most difficult winter holiday was Thanksgiving. Dustin had just left, and Ford and Owen were both celebrating birthdays. Renee from church invited us to spend Thanksgiving at her home with a group of other displaced or lonely church members: recent empty nesters and college students who couldn't get home for the holiday. As we sat around a makeshift table of two smaller kitchen tables joined together and covered with several tablecloths, I wondered, *What would have become of all of us without this invitation? How many of us would have stayed home alone? Would I have even cooked? The kids don't like turkey, after all. What would we have done?* But there we all were, a table full of misfit family members with no other place to go.

We spent Christmas with my parents, but by then I realized that Thanksgiving and Christmas, as difficult as they were, were not nearly as hard as, say, November 28 or December 5, the ordinary days when Dustin's seat was empty. Those were the days when the kids quickly ate and fled from the table, and I was left alone, in silence, with my food.

One area in which we were fortunate was the weather. The snowstorms sputtered and failed, and the sun and warmer temperatures kept returning to melt what ordinarily becomes a several-feet-high wall of snow in our front yard. It was as if Old Man Winter had a giant sneeze that just wouldn't come. And I was grateful, because that meant less shoveling.

I frequently and randomly remembered Dustin calling out to me at the airport, reminding me to invite people to dinner. I still liked the idea of inviting one guest each week, but I hadn't gotten around to organizing anything. I was too busy going through the motions of everyday activities, like working at the university, where I taught journalism, or writing my weekly newspaper column, which appears locally in Bangor, but also in newspapers across the country. The boys and I talked about who we'd like to invite—the mayor, schoolteachers, the principal, senators (why not?)—but I couldn't coordinate anything until I had my bearings as a "single" mom.

By mid-December, Dustin had already finished stateside training and was halfway across the world at Camp Lemonnier in Djibouti, Africa. He was eight time zones away from us, which made arranging meetings through Skype or e-mail difficult. Sometimes, though, despite the physical distance, it felt as if he had just been at home. There were so many reminders of his recent presence. I was still processing the dirty clothes he left behind, and his old tennis shoes hadn't yet been buried beneath our snow boots and the boys' basketball shoes. I knew from past deployments that those reminders would quickly fade as our new life and routine replaced what we had had before Dustin left. All his laundry would be clean, folded, and put away. His books and papers would be pushed to the back of the bookshelf. A whole winter would come and go without us getting out the wooden Radio Flyer sled Dustin liked to use on the hill at Thirteenth Street. His clothes would be sent to the back of the closet.

Dustin knew all this, too. It was just a matter of time before our family routines would be unfamiliar to him. The boys would have new friends, new teammates, and new interests. Eventually they'd have new teachers, too. I would have a new schedule, a new group of students at the University of Maine, and—let's be honest—I'd probably have several different hair colors and styles, too.

Life would be going on without Dustin.

So Dustin, more than anyone else, persisted about us inviting people to dinner. For him, having someone "fill" his seat at the dinner table meant his absence was more present, not just to us, but to everyone in the community. Also, he worried about us being lonely.

"Have you invited anyone to dinner yet?" he asked one day when we finally found a time to Skype.

I was a little annoyed. Didn't he realize I was doing well just to get everyone out of bed and out the door each morning?

"Let me get caught up," I said. "Then I can think more about that."

"It will be a good way to fill up the time," he said. "You don't want to be isolated like last time. Remember that? And it's a chance for the boys to meet new people, too. I'm looking forward to hearing about how it goes. Are you guys getting out at all? Seeing people?"

I was beginning to realize that the dinner idea was not just a project for the boys and me, but it was a lifeline for Dustin, too. For him, it would be one familiar thread of a routine he could share with us across the miles.

The boys came around the computer to say hi to Dustin. As usual, they were distracted by their own image in the small box in the corner of the screen, and they started making faces. Lindell resorted to his old standby: mooning the camera.

"Who are you going to invite to dinner if Mom does the weekly guest thing?" Dustin asked, eager for meaningful conversation instead of the circus unfolding in front of him.

"My teacher!" Lindell shouted, pulling up his pants and spinning around.

"I don't know," Owen said, adjusting the baseball cap on his head. "Maybe the mayor."

"Great idea," Dustin said. "I actually know Mayor Weston, so say hello for me. And don't forget Dr. Haddix from church. He is very smart and would have a lot of neat things to teach you about history. Oh, and Gloria next door, and Earle—or, "Mr. Earle" as you guys call him—on the other side. I bet they'd love to come over for dinner. And how about you, Ford?" Dustin said. "Who do you want to invite?"

Ford shrugged. "I don't know. Maybe Senator Collins, or something. We've been talking about government in class."

Dustin smiled. "Wow, that's an awesome idea," he said. "I hear she's very nice. And did you know she's a member of the Armed Services Committee? So it's kind of like she's one of my bosses."

Senator Collins is a familiar face in Bangor, Maine. She keeps a home on the east side of town and still has family in northern Maine. It's not unusual to see her shopping at the grocery store or enjoying a meal at a downtown restaurant. The boys know plenty of people who have worked for Senator Collins or who are related to her. Indeed, inviting her to dinner seemed more plausible to them than inviting Bangor's mayor.

After our Skype with Dustin, the boys and I began talking more frequently and seriously about planning dinners with someone in the community each week. Our guest wish list was growing. A few days later, Ford sat down to write a letter:

Hello, my name is Ford Smiley. I am eleven years old and in fifth grade. I have two younger brothers and of course my mom and dad. My dad is a U.S. Navy Pilot, and he's on deployment for thirteen months. He left the day before my eleventh birthday and the week of Thanksgiving.

My mom is letting us invite one person to dinner each week our dad is gone. We are wondering if you would like to come to dinner some time this year (which is stretching it quite a bit but my mom insisted that we be flexible).

We live in Bangor. Do you have any food preferences? Would you like to bring a guest?

Ford Smiley (as stated in first paragraph)

After a couple of weeks, I had mostly forgotten about Ford's invitation to Senator Collins. I never anticipated her being able to accept. But I was fully immersed in inviting guests now. I talked to Gloria and Earle and Dr. Haddix. I mentioned it to the boys' teachers. And I started thinking about other people—policemen, firemen, musicians, artists—who might serve as positive role models for the kids. I didn't want to call our guests replacements for Dustin, so I usually just said, "Would you come fill Dustin's seat at the dinner table?"

Then, one day in late December, I had just returned from walking the kids to school, and I was kicking off my snow boots on the front porch when I heard the phone ringing. I ran inside to find a handset, and I answered the phone just before it went to voice mail, but too late to see the caller ID.

"Is this Sarah Smiley?" a woman's voice said on the other end.

"Yes."

"Hi, I'm calling from Senator Susan Collins's office in Washington, DC. How are you today?"

"Oh! Um, I'm good. Thanks."

"We got your older son's—is it Ford?"

"Yes, Ford."

"We got his request for Senator Collins to fill your husband's seat at the dinner table, and I have to tell you, everyone here at the office nearly cried."

"Well, I haven't really decided how it will all work, but—"

"It's a wonderful idea, Sarah, and the senator would love to join you for dinner. How does January third look for you?"

I ran to the calendar hanging on the side of the cupboard in the kitchen. The entire month of January was completely—blindingly, even—white and void of any plans. "I think we could make that work," I said. "I'll pencil it in to the calendar right now."

After we said good-bye and I double-checked to make sure the phone was indeed turned off, I leaned against the kitchen counter and banged the phone against my head. *Why did I think this would be a good idea?* I don't cook. I'm not good at small talk. And now I was hosting a US senator?

I'd love to tell you that the news of Senator Collins's acceptance was met with the boys' raucous applause and cheers. But they seemed stunned instead. Perhaps because now everything became very real. Ford, in particular, had a strange reaction. Although he was delighted that his request had received a response, he was inconsistent with how he felt about the senator's reply. The early weeks and months of a deployment are difficult and emotional, especially for a preteen boy missing his dad. Emotions and tempers were running high. Ford was content one day and sullen the next. And as January 3 drew near, Ford and I fought daily. He went back and forth between being curious about the senator and regretting his invitation to her.

"I wish she wasn't coming," he said.

"So why did you invite her?" I said, stirring macaroni and cheese on the stove. Ford paced behind me, just like his dad when he is frustrated or anxious. His steps rattled the sliding pantry doors.

"I don't know, but I wish I hadn't. I want to take it back."

"We are *not* canceling the dinner!" My mind was reeling. I was still trying to get a handle on what was going on. "You can't just take back an invitation. And what happened to being excited about having dinner with the senator?"

"The only reason we're having dinner with a senator is because my dad is gone," Ford yelled. Then he stomped to his room and slammed his bedroom door so hard that all the decorative plates hanging on the wall in the kitchen bounced on their hooks.

I turned off the stove and stared at the steam from the pot collecting at the ceiling. I thought about how much easier it was when Dustin was deployed while the children were too young to understand. Back then, Ford had only needed me. He had clung to me, in fact. But now, as he entered his teen years, what he needed most was his dad, and I felt in the way. Finding a balance between the roles of both mom and dad was tiring.

I gave Ford some time alone, then I knocked lightly on the door and asked to come in. He mumbled, and I couldn't understand what he had said, but I opened the door anyway. I quickly slipped through so that Lindell, always at my heels, wouldn't follow me. Ford was propped up in his bed, half of his face illuminated by the book light on the table beside him. His knees were bent under the covers, and I knew he had a paperback book leaned against them. I sat down at the end of the bed and patted his foot under the comforter.

He pulled it away.

"I'm not going to be home for that dinner," Ford said in a flat tone.

"Where will you be?"

"I'll go to a friend's house, or I'll just sit upstairs, but I'm not going to be someone's pity dinner."

"Senator Collins doesn't pity us, honey."

"Then why did she say she would come to dinner with people she doesn't even know?" Ford put down his knees and threw the book to the ground.

"Because you wrote her a very nice letter and invited her."

"Whatever."

Above Ford's head was a bulletin board with awards, photographs, drawings from Lindell, and a paper envelope marked FORD'S MAILBOX hanging unevenly and precariously from pushpins. At the top of the board (prime real estate for collages) was an old pennant for the San Francisco 49ers. Ford has never been to San Francisco, or even to California, but the 49ers are his team. Not coincidentally, Dustin, who *has* lived in California, also says the 49ers are his team. Below the pennant was a certificate presented to Ford for being "drug free." It was signed, Lt. Cmdr. Dustin Smiley. Behind the certificate and sharing the same pushpin was an old, faded article about the 49ers that Dustin had torn out of a magazine when he was a kid.

I sighed and looked again at Ford, searching his face for answers. His expression was totally blank.

"Can I just be alone?" he said without looking at me.

I left the room and closed the door behind me.

Owen, desperate to restore balance to the usual family dynamics, met me in the hallway and pledged his alliance with Ford. If Ford wasn't going to the dinner, neither was Owen.

I didn't understand. One week the boys were excited; the next week they were angry. It didn't make sense. I reasoned that Ford had simply dug himself too far into this preteen funk, and he had dragged Owen with him. Now they didn't know how to get back out. But then I started paying more attention to conversations with neighbors and friends. I noticed things that the boys overheard, and my understanding changed.

"I can't believe you're making dinner for a US senator!" people said. "What will you serve? Will you use china? Do you even have china? What will you wear?"

What had begun as an idea to help the boys through the deployment was turning into something else—something formal and full of expectations. All the kids wanted was to be less lonely. They didn't care about menus and china. They didn't even really care that Susan Collins is a US senator. They just wanted to fill up what felt like a never-ending amount of time without their dad.

So I made a decision: If this idea was for the boys, it would stay on their terms. This wasn't about showing them off or teaching them manners. This wasn't a school project or an experiment. It was a gift to them from me. Gifts shouldn't have expectations. I decided the dinners wouldn't either.

One day, when I had Ford alone in our van, I said, "I think I understand your frustration about the dinner now. You invited Senator Collins, and suddenly it became this big *thing*—"

Ford interrupted me, suddenly excited that I understood. "Yeah, like everyone's saying, 'Oh, poor you, your dad is gone, and now a senator is coming because she thinks your family is lonely.' And everyone is talking about table manners and stuff. I just want it to be like when Dad is home."

"Then let's make it that way," I said.

"What do you mean? It can't ever be like when Dad is here."

"Well, what's your favorite part about having Dad at the dinner table?"

Ford stared out the window and shrugged. "I don't know, like maybe how he makes jokes and we talk about our day. And remember how we used to take family walks after dinner? I liked that, too."

"So it's casual?"

"Yeah, casual."

"Then our weekly dinners will be, too. No expectations. No pressure."

Ford turned to look at me. "You mean, like, we don't have to wear a coat and tie to the dinner with Senator Collins?"

I stopped at a red light and met his glance. "You're darn right 'no coat and ties'! I'll be doing well just to keep Lindell from pulling down his pants and mooning someone."

Ford laughed. "We probably do need to keep him from doing

that, Mom. Mooning the senator is a little *too* casual, don't you think?"

We both laughed and shared quick stories about Lindell. When we pulled into the driveway, I turned to look at Ford. "So you'll be there for dinner?" I said. "It wouldn't be the same without you."

"Alright," he said. "But if things get all fancy, I don't want to do dinners anymore."

"Deal!"

A few days later, on the night before the dinner, Ford and Owen officially agreed to participate. Perhaps this was because they now had actual proof that I was serious about the "no expectations or fancy stuff" promise: I hadn't bought any china. I still didn't know what I would make for dinner. And the house was in its usual state of disarray, with a mountain of laundry piled high on the living room couch and Lindell's nose- and fingerprints all over the glass front door.

There was, however, still one member of the family (besides Dustin) who, despite all my casualness, would not be at dinner, and not because he didn't want to be there, but because he was unequivocally not invited. Dustin and I had surprised the boys with Sparky—a liver-and-white brittany spaniel puppy—two weeks before Dustin left in November. And although Sparky was sweet and incredibly mild mannered for a six-month-old puppy, I didn't want to risk it at dinner.

"But you said 'no expectations,' Mom," Ford argued. "Why can't Sparky stay?"

I convinced Ford that Sparky would have more fun playing with his dog friend Coda at my friend Julie's house than he would being locked away in his crate during dinner. Ford didn't agree, but he quit arguing. He didn't want to push it.

The morning of January 3, Ford sat down to breakfast and said,

"Mom, don't you think we should get this place cleaned up before tonight?"

I glanced at the kitchen floor covered with muddy paw prints and chewed-up dog toys and bones.

"Meh," I said, shrugging my shoulders. "I'll get to it . . . maybe."

Sarah and Lindell

Chapter Four

January

Moments before Senator Collins was to arrive for dinner, Owen and Lindell sat in the living room watching *Sponge-Bob SquarePants*—in reverse. Every time Patrick Star inhaled a stream of soda—which in normal forward play would be Patrick Star spewing soda—they laughed and pounded their feet on the floor. It wouldn't be long before they set the DVR to another language just to hear SpongeBob speak Spanish.

On the other side of the wall, in the kitchen, I began to panic. There is a very fine line between "keeping it real" and "train wreck waiting to happen." I held the cordless phone between my shoulder and ear as my friend Morgan told me again how to make lasagna. "Use less ricotta cheese and more cottage cheese," she said.

"Cottage cheese in lasagna?"

"Trust me, the cottage cheese makes it creamier."

I stirred marinara sauce and ground turkey as she talked.

"Did you get bread?" Morgan asked. "What about a salad? And did you make dessert?"

"The senator is bringing brownies. Wait, do I call her Senator? Or Senator Collins? Ms. Collins?"

"Don't overthink it," she said. "Just be yourself and have fun." And then: "What are you going to wear?"

I hadn't thought about what to wear. I was busy all day getting ready to teach a new semester of journalism students at the university and editing my column for the week. I hadn't had time to think about clothes. I was lucky I had time to shower.

"I'll think about that after I get this lasagna made," I said.

Not long after I put the lasagna in the oven, however, headlights swept through the front window and shone against the hedge alongside our driveway. I still had on my old beige cardigan and black pants, the ones with the hem that fell out two months ago.

"She's here!" Lindell screamed.

"Aw, but she's not in a limo," Owen said.

He and Ford were on their knees on the sofa, peering over the back and out the front window.

Lindell jumped up and down on the opposite couch and clapped his hands. Suddenly I regretted not giving them a minicourse in table manners. Or any manners, for that matter. I wiped my hands on a kitchen towel and quickly called the boys to me. "No potty humor or whoopee cushions," I said with the most serious face I could manage. "And just forget about that pack of trick gum you have, Owen. You know, the one that slaps people's hands."

"Aw, what?"

"Maybe the senator likes whoopee cushions," Lindell said.

I glared at each of them. Then I licked my fingers and reached out my hand to smooth their hair. First, Ford batted me away, then Owen. Lindell squirmed and squealed, but I managed to pat down the sideways cowlicks above each of his temples.

That was the last moment I felt nervous all night. I mean we were hosting a senator, but although I was ever aware of the respect due Susan Collins, in many ways, once she was standing in our living room, I forgot about her being a United States senator.

Senator Susan Collins with the boys

She and companion Carol Woodcock, a representative from the senator's Bangor office, were like a pair of favorite aunts coming over for a meal. In fact, Senator Collins, with her characteristically warm speech filled with careful pauses, reminded me of my aunt Louise in Alabama. Her hair was perfectly coiffed, with wispy pieces elegantly feathered around her ears. She wore black pants and a blue silk top—basic, but professional and without a wrinkle or piece of lint.

All of this might have been intimidating if not for the senator's ability to make herself at home on the living room sofa. There, she pulled Lindell onto her lap. "I want you all to know that I am delighted to be here with you tonight," she said, looking at each boy in turn. "I'm honored to sit in your dad's chair for dinner."

Ford sat across from Senator Collins and Lindell on the opposite couch. He smiled awkwardly, without showing his teeth, and he sat on his hands. Owen leaned into Ford, despite room enough on the couch for four or five adults.

But Lindell—well, Lindell patted the Senator's smooth cheeks and rubbed her hair and snuggled against her arm. Senator Collins, while returning Lindell's pats, deftly divided her attention and conversation evenly among the three boys. So far, though, Ford was only giving her one-word answers:

"How is school?"

"Good."

"Do you like Bangor?"

"Yes."

I couldn't tell if he was nervous or unhappy.

Before dinner, Senator Collins knelt on the floor in front of Ford and Owen and presented them with a flag that was flown over the United States Capitol in their honor. Although the flag was meant for all three boys, Senator Collins directed most of her focus on Ford. Maybe she knew that he, as the oldest, was most likely to understand the significance. Maybe she sensed his aloofness and was trying to win his favor. Or maybe she instinctively knew that Ford wasn't going to get in her lap or pet her arm, like Lindell, but that he needed attention just the same.

The flag, perfectly folded into a tight triangle, brought a rush of emotions. It looked like the ones military widows are given at a funeral. But Ford didn't know that. His mouth hung open in awe.

(It would be another few days before I realized that when Senator Collins said, "flown over the Capitol," the boys thought she meant she had dragged the flag across the top of the building with an airplane.)

While I made a salad and checked on the lasagna, the boys showed Senator Collins their bedrooms. Her heeled shoes clicked across the creaking wood floors and I heard their conversations through the thin walls.

"These are our fish," Owen said. "We used to have five of them, one for each of us, but the big silver fish ate some of the little fish. We have a dog, too, named Sparky, but Mom made him go to a friend's house tonight."

Senator Collins asked the boys about the trophies and team pictures displayed on the shelves and walls in their rooms. She talked to them about the books they were reading. By the time I went to collect everyone for dinner, she was sitting on the foot of Ford's bed and asking about Dustin.

"You'd really like my dad," Ford said. "He knows a lot of stuff about the United States."

"I bet he does," Senator Collins said. "And I hope to meet him when he comes home."

Back in the kitchen, the boys rushed to their seats, and, rudely, grabbed bread from the plate in the middle of the table. Senator Collins and Carol stood in the doorway, their hands loosely clasped in front of their waists. Carol asked where they should sit.

This is the part where I consistently fail: I don't know how to entertain. Quite frankly, I was starved and wanted to grab bread from the table, too. I realized I had yet to even offer our guests drinks.

"You sit in my dad's chair over there," Owen said to Senator Collins. He pointed at Dustin's empty seat at the head of the table.

Behind it, Lindell's preschool artwork—a drawing of Sparky, a picture made with finger paints, a self-portrait—was taped to the glass panes of the French door. Senator Collins took her seat. I winced as she unfolded the paper-towel napkin and put it in her lap.

Dinner was served family-style. I didn't know any other way to do it in my small kitchen, so everything—the steaming lasagna, the salad, the bread—was crowded on the table, and there were a busy few minutes when everyone was passing around bowls and plates. Ford complained about the lasagna dish being hot, and because he doesn't eat salad, he kept that bowl beside his plate without passing it for too long.

"If you aren't eating salad, please pass the bowl to Mrs. Woodcock," I whispered to him.

Ford clumsily passed the bowl of salad to his left. The spoon fell out and took several pieces of lettuce with it.

As Carol replaced the spoon and filled her plate, she caught my eye and winked.

Senator Collins asked the boys to tell her what it's like to be part of a military family. She wanted to know how they managed missing their dad. As usual, Owen and Lindell waited for Ford to answer. And now Ford was in his element: the center of attention, a table full of people waiting for him to pontificate about his experiences.

"Dad being gone has been tough," he said. He was up on his knees and reaching across the table for the butter. He cut open another roll while he talked. He didn't make eye contact with anyone. "I always thought I couldn't live without him, but I guess it's been okay. I've had Owen, at least."

I looked at Lindell and hoped he hadn't heard that last part. He was busy pulling crust off his bread.

"You and your brothers are really close, aren't you?" Senator Collins said.

"If I can't have Dad here, then I'm glad I have my brothers. I know I couldn't live without them."

"And your mom," Senator Collins said. "I bet it would be much harder if you didn't have her."

Ford wiped his hands on his shirt and said, "Nah, I think I could live without Mom."

My cheeks turned cold. I stared down at my plate to blink away the sudden tightness I felt in my eyes. *He could live without me?*

"I mean, no offense to Mom," Ford said. "But I think I could probably manage with just Dad. I mean, like, if she was gone and he was here, that would probably be easier."

I wanted to cry. I wanted to tell Ford to take it back. I wanted to ask him why. I wanted to remind him of all the miles I carried him on my hip or sat with him when he couldn't fall asleep. I wanted to yell at him and tell him he had hurt me. Instead, I looked up, smiled, and asked Owen to please pass the salad.

The rest of the dinner was a blur. I was trapped in my own head, thinking about what Ford had said. I could so easily remember when, during Dustin's first deployment more than a decade ago, it was just Ford and me. His gummy smile was the first thing I saw in the morning, and his long lashes resting on his plump, rosy cheeks were the last thing I saw at night. When he woke from a bad dream, he called for me. He patted my hair and face, much the same way Lindell had done to Senator Collins.

Now he thinks he could live without me?

Of course, I knew that in another ten years, he would, in fact, live without me. But I wasn't ready for that yet. It had been years since I was able to pick up Ford and physically carry him. Yet I carried him with me—in my mind, in my heart—all day long, when I was at the university or the grocery store or out with friends. There never is a moment when I'm not Ford's mom. Now I could see that Ford was starting to separate himself from me. He didn't want to only be Sarah's son.

In this way, parenting is one long experience in grief. Ford was not the same baby I held eleven years ago. He never would be that person again. Sure, I see glimmers here and there—in his wide, open-mouth smile and the way his hair still seems to grow from one circle on the top of his head. But the baby I remember is gone forever. As children grow and change, they leave their former selves so far behind that even they don't know who that toddler is in the orange-tinted photograph smiling back at them.

And so each year, I feel as if I'm mourning the child my boys were the year before. I miss their toddler voices and smells, the way they said "yea-yow" instead of "yellow," and how bits of drool fell off their chin when they laughed. I miss the way Ford would stare out the bus window and wave to me on his way to kindergarten. I miss the way he ran across the front yard, throwing off his backpack and jumping into my arms when he came home. Back then, I never could have imagined that Ford would say he could live without me. I couldn't have imagined any of my children changing as fast as Ford seemed to be changing now.

I wondered if I could ever recover from Ford's comment.

After dinner, Senator Collins offered each of the boys chocolate brownies she had baked that afternoon and brought in a metal tin.

"I hope no one is allergic to nuts," she said. "I should have asked before, but those brownies do have walnuts in them."

The boys' eager smiles quickly faded. They aren't allergic, but they hate nuts.

I spoke to them in that silent, wordless way mothers do—with my eyes and clenched jaw that spoke volumes: *You will eat the brownies and be grateful.*

While the boys considered the nut-filled brownies in front of them, I went into the living room and brought back my laptop. Dustin was eight hours ahead of us, so it was about 3:00 in the morning for him. I had asked him ahead of time to Skype with Senator Collins after dinner. This meant Dustin had to set his alarm for the middle of the night, leave his CLU (Containerized Living Unit), go to the facilities to shower and shave, and then get dressed in his uniform. After all, Senator Collins is in his chain of command. His hair was still wet, but neatly combed, when Senator Collins took a seat in front of the computer at the end of the table.

"Well, hello, Dustin," she said. "It was quite an honor to eat with your wonderful family tonight."

Dustin nodded. "Yes, ma'am. I'm glad you could be there. It is an honor for them," he said.

Senator Collins asked Dustin about everything from his living conditions to the food and his assignment. Dustin eagerly answered her questions and heavily peppered each response with "Ma'am." The boys crowded around the senator.

"Hi, Dad! We had brownies!" Lindell screamed.

"Hey, Dad," Ford said, waving from behind Senator Collins. "Oh, the brownies had nuts in them." He was still waving.

"Dad, Senator Collins brought us a flag," Owen said.

"That's really cool," Dustin said. He was still sitting with stiff posture, but a reflexive smile spread across his face when he saw the boys.

Lindell climbed into Senator Collins's lap.

Dustin fidgeted. "Oh, hey, Lindell," he said. "Maybe you should ask Senator Collins if you can sit in her lap first. She might not want you to."

"Oh, no, we are old friends now," Senator Collins said as she hugged Lindell and pressed her cheek to his.

Dustin alternated between the easy expressions of a father and the guarded look of a soldier. After about ten minutes, we said good-bye, urging him to go back to sleep.

When I closed the laptop, I gasped at what I saw on the other side: three piles of nuts mixed with chocolate brownie crumbs. The boys had picked every last nut out of their brownies and left them on the table.

Before she left, Senator Collins offered to help me with the dishes. Informality was the order of the day, but I knew I couldn't allow a US senator to load my dishwasher. I refused—multiple times—and we said our good-byes at the front door. The next day, while I packed the boys' school lunches with leftover brownies, I told them that they probably would be the only kids at school with desserts made especially for them by a US senator. The boys didn't

Senator Susan Collins, Sarah, and the boys

think it was that unusual. To them, Senator Collins was just another nice lady. When the boys got home that afternoon and I unpacked their lunch boxes, I smiled at what I found: three baggies filled with discarded walnuts and brownie crumbs.

A few days later, I sat in my fourth-floor office at the university, where I was working on my master's thesis. Snow drifted like feathers from the sky and disappeared into the wet, muddy grass of the quad below. Afternoon light came sideways through the old wooden panes that rattled when the wind blew.

The now-familiar bubbly sound of an incoming Skype call disrupted my thoughts. I saw Dustin's screen name flash, and I accepted the call. His face was grainy and pale on the computer. Everything from his shirt to the walls and lockers behind him were a drab beige. But he was smiling when we were both finally able to see each other.

I hadn't talked to anyone yet about Ford's comment at dinner with Senator Collins. I knew that as soon as I did, I would cry aloud. I wasn't even sure I wanted to tell Dustin either. It's always hard to know how much to tell him. Should I worry him with things back home? Or does not sharing make him feel more distant?

"I can see the snow," Dustin said excitedly. "Have you guys had a lot this winter?"

I swiveled my chair to look out the window. "No, not really." I turned back around and rested my chin on my hand. "I bet it's hot there, huh?"

"Yeah," Dustin said. "You look sad."

I lied. "Me? What? No."

"You don't seem yourself."

"No, I'm okay, just busy—" I tried to look cheery, but just then, tears spilled down my cheeks. I wiped them away with the heel of my hand.

"Sarah, talk to me," Dustin said. "Are the kids okay?"

I nodded.

"Are you feeling overwhelmed?"

I shrugged.

"Is it Ford?"

I nodded and wiped away more tears. I believe parents always have one child who keeps them in a state of suspended, uncertain emotion. Ford is that child for us. He is an excellent kid. He's smart and capable. He never gets into trouble at school, and he always has good grades. But Ford tests us more than Lindell and Owen, and as the oldest on the brink of puberty, he was leading us through unchartered territory.

I told Dustin about what Ford had said at dinner.

"He doesn't mean it," Dustin said, his voice soft and steady. He leaned closer to the camera on the frame of his laptop, and his face filled my screen. "Kids say stuff like that. I bet you said mean things to your parents, too. He's growing up. That's a good thing. And I'm not there, so he's trying not to be dependent on you."

"But he's so prickly lately," I cried. "He's angry one day, and then like a child again the next. I never know what to expect. And I feel like I'm doing it all wrong."

"Doing what wrong?"

"Parenting."

We stared at each other through the computers in silence while I cried. I smeared tears on my cheeks and Dustin frowned.

"I feel helpless," he said. "I wish I was there."

"I know. I wish you were here, too."

"The beginning of a deployment is always rough," he said. "You know that. We're all adjusting. But you'll get into a routine soon. Things will get easier. They always do."

I nodded and sniffled.

"Just remember that Ford is a kid," Dustin said. "He's the oldest, but he's still just a kid. Let him have his feelings without him feeling guilty for yours."

That last part stayed with me for days. *Let him have his feelings without him feeling guilty for yours.* Sometimes, when I reached out to touch Ford's hair or rub his shoulders, he recoiled. He fell asleep at night with his door shut. If I was late getting him from school, or if I burned the pizza, he rolled his eyes and puffed out his cheeks. He said things like, "Dad does this better," and "Dad would never do that," and "I wish Dad was here." But I kept my eyes forward and never let on that I was hurt.

Lindell's fifth birthday was a week after our dinner with Senator Collins. When I asked him how he wanted to celebrate, he said, "Can I have my teacher over for Dinner with the Smileys?"

I liked the sound of that: Dinner with the Smileys.

The next day at school, Lindell's preschool teacher was absent, but her assistant, Mrs. O'Connor, was there. I gave Mrs. O'Connor an invitation to Dinner with the Smileys. Her smoky eyes twinkled and she grinned through long strands of dark, wavy hair that framed her face. "But I'm nothing important like a senator," she said.

"To Lindell," I said, "you are more important than a senator."

It was true. To then-four-year-old Lindell, Mrs. O'Connor and Senator Collins were the same. As in, they are both nice people. But Mrs. O'Connor was one of Lindell's teachers. She spent more time with him in a week than anyone—including me. So having her to dinner was on a whole different level. Lindell counted down the days until Mrs. O'Connor's Dinner with the Smileys.

And that night, before Mrs. O'Connor arrived, Lindell ran through the house with nervous excitement. He wasn't screaming about his birthday or the presents he would open later. He was yelling, "My teacher is coming! My teacher is coming!"

Ford, lying on the couch with a book, sighed.

Dinner included all of Lindell's favorites—chicken, noodles, rolls—plus dog-bone-shaped chocolate chip cookies that Mrs. O'Connor had made. It was the first Dinner with the Smileys that included Sparky. He sat on his haunches beside Lindell's chair and made his best sad-dog face. Lindell desperately wanted to share a cookie with him.

"No! Chocolate isn't good for dogs," Owen told him.

"But look at him," Lindell said.

Sparky's brown, floppy ears perked up. He tilted his head.

"No, Lindell. Sparky can't have a cookie," Owen said.

Mrs. O'Connor distracted Lindell with questions, and Lindell, forgetting about Sparky's begging, basked in her attention. Ford, on the opposite side of the table, sulked and occasionally sighed.

Later, Lindell wanted to show Mrs. O'Connor his whoopee cushion and his favorite dance—the silly tap one that makes everyone laugh and usually ends with him running to the bathroom, crouched over in a fit of giggles. Lindell asked Mrs. O'Connor to toss a tennis ball, and then he fetched it on his hands and knees and brought it back in his mouth like a dog. Sparky romped behind him, his entire backside wriggling from his beating tail.

At preschool the next day, Mrs. O'Connor said, "I've never seen Lindell like that. He was so talkative and funny."

"He's not that way here at school?" I asked.

"Never. He's very serious and focused," she said. "I mean he likes to say he's Scooby-Doo, which is why I brought the cookies, but mostly he's quiet. It was interesting to see a different side of him."

I watched Lindell slip off his backpack and walk calmly past Mrs. O'Connor and into his classroom.

It seemed as though, with Mrs. O'Connor's insights, maybe I was seeing a new side of him, too.

Ford and I continued to argue in the days that followed.

He was resistant to everything from my offers to help him with his homework to my neutral, casual questions like, "Whatcha reading there?" I felt like he was slipping further and further away from me. He, more than his brothers, seemed to be taking his dad's absence exceptionally hard. I just wasn't enough for him.

Our next dinner was with Dr. Haddix, the minister of our church, and his wife Fay-Ellen. The year before, Ford had asked to meet with Dr. Haddix. He wanted to know why church teaches us to be humble, but then parents tell us to put on a nice shirt and tie for Sunday morning.

Dr. Haddix had leaned back in the upholstered chair of his office and rubbed at the full white beard framing his face. "I don't think anyone has ever asked me that, Ford," Dr. Haddix said. "It's an interesting question."

I couldn't stay to hear their full conversation, because Lindell, then just a toddler, was running through the church halls.

But when I came back to get Ford, he was standing in front of Dr. Haddix, shaking hands like a proper young man.

The Haddixes were no strangers to my boys' many behaviors (from Ford's deep questions and occasional moodiness to Lindell's potty humor), so I was less worried about their behavior at dinner than I would normally be with any other visiting minister and his wife. I did, however, feel that it was necessary to apologize for the scene my family had made at the Christmas Eve service the month before.

Dustin had just left and I was learning how to manage all three children without an extra set of hands. The church asked us to light the advent candle at the Christmas Eve service, and I said yes. All we had to do was go in front of the congregation, with our backs to the two-story stained-glass window, and look out across the dark wood beams and hundreds of families dressed in red-and-green festive clothes. Ford and Owen would light the candle, and I would stand at the lectern and read a prayer. Easy.

What I hadn't planned was what to do with Lindell. And once we were in front of the congregation, I was more concerned with the older boys waving the lit candle lighter too close to my hair, which was, of course, sprayed with flammable hair spray.

I began to read the prayer. Ford and Owen elbowed each other and argued behind me. I pictured my hair going up in flames. Ford hissed at Owen, and Owen said under his breath, "It's my turn, Ford." I didn't even know what I was reading anymore. I had this horrible vision of the boys knocking over the candles and lighting my hair on fire.

Then I heard the congregation laugh.

At first it was just a few scattered giggles erupting from the pews. Then it was roaring laughter. I looked up. Everyone was looking to my right, at Lindell, who was in front of a spotlight that cast his long, exaggerated shadow across the sanctuary. And he was dancing. He moved his hips and his arms, doing the wave and a semi-moonwalk, and delighting in his gigantic shadow doing the same.

I tried not to laugh, but nerves caused me to lose control. I

Ford and Owen with Fay-Ellen Haddix, wife of
Dr. Haddix, minister of All Souls

chortled my way through the end of the prayer, and when we walked back to our pew, I felt humiliated and ashamed.

It was certainly time to apologize for that.

As we sat around the family dining table, however, Fay-Ellen, with her turtleneck and cross hanging from a long gold chain, just chuckled about the Christmas Eve incident. "Don't forget that we raised six children," she said. "We know what it's like. Plus, many people in the congregation seemed to think that it was delightful."

We ate spaghetti, salad, and Fay-Ellen's homemade bread.

There was the usual chatter and noise at the dinner table as the boys got what they needed.

"It's my turn with the butter."

"Hey! Pass me the butter!"

"You took my knife. Give me back my knife."

Sparky's nails clicked on the wood floors as he moved from seat to seat hoping for a crumb.

Ford was quiet. He did not engage in conversation with Dr. Haddix or Fay-Ellen. But when we gathered around the computer afterward to Skype with Dustin, Ford's face came alive.

"Hi, Dad," he said. "What's the weather like there?"

Dr. Haddix stood behind Ford as he talked to Dustin. Occasionally he put a hand on Ford's shoulder. At some point, one of the boys brought out a light saber. I whispered, "No weapons at the table." But Dr. Haddix had already seen the red plastic sword.

"I remember these," he said, reaching for the toy.

And just then, at that very moment when he picked up the light saber, we all saw it: Dr. Haddix, with his white hair and full beard, looks like Obi-Wan Kenobi from the original *Star Wars* movie.

"Oh my gosh," Ford said.

"Wow, he really looks like—" Owen said.

"Like Ben. Ben Kenobi. From *Episode IV*," Ford finished.

The boys ran to their rooms to put on their *Star Wars* costumes and get out more light sabers. Owen came out in a cloak. So did Ford. And what I didn't realize until many months later was that this was the last time Ford would put on a costume. Already, the old Halloween costume fell three or four inches above his ankles. The sleeves looked like three-quarter sleeves. He seemed awkward and uncomfortable, like suddenly he realized that he was too big to run around the house like a Jedi.

Maybe that uneasiness is what caused Ford to tackle Owen from behind and slam him on the couch. Maybe it is what caused him to say "make me" when I told him to go to his room. Maybe it is why he pushed Owen to the floor again, causing Dr. Haddix to reflexively say, in his deep, booming voice, "Hey, knock it off in there, boys." And maybe it is why Ford slammed his door and told me to leave him alone.

"I don't know what's gotten into him," I said as I hugged Fay-Ellen and Dr. Haddix good-bye. But I didn't need to explain anything to the Haddixes. If anyone else had seen the changes in Ford, it was certainly the people at church. In the two months since Dustin had left, Ford had stomped out of Sunday morning services, punched his brother in the vestry, and sat by himself, with his arms folded, while the rest of us greeted neighbors and friends at the weekly church dinner. He shook the usher's hand with an arm that was as limp as a dead fish. He stared at the ground and complained.

Many Sunday mornings, after the kids left the sanctuary for Sunday school, I sat alone in the pew and blinked back tears.

I started to wonder if these dinners were still a good idea. *Was it too much? Could I handle the embarrassment? Had I asked for more than my children were capable of handling?*

As I was cleaning dishes from the Haddixes' dinner, I started to cry.

At first, it was a small cry. But soon, there was so much water in my eyes I couldn't see the dishes in front of me. I was thinking again about what Ford had said during our first dinner, and I was thinking about all the ways he had hurt me in the last two months. I remembered Dustin's advice: *Let him have his feelings without feeling guilty about yours.* I thought about going up to my room and crying alone. But when I passed by Ford's closed door, I changed my mind. Maybe, I thought, Ford needs to see that I have feelings, too. I swung open his door and stood at the foot of his bed with a red, wet face.

Ford sat up in his bed and looked alarmed. "Mom, what's going—"

I was hiccupping and crying. "You need to know that you have hurt me. You hurt me when you said it would be easier if Dad was here and I was gone. You hurt me when you scream and slam your door, and when you turn me away when I'm trying to help. Sometimes, my heart feels broken. I miss Dad, too, you know." Then I turned around and walked out.

Fifteen minutes later, Ford shuffled out into the living room, where I was under a blanket on the couch. He squinted at the bright light and scratched at his hair. "I love you, Mom," he said. "And I'm sorry."

"I know. I'm sorry, too. I'm just emotional and overtired, that's all."

Ford started to go back to his room. Then he stopped and turned around again. "Well, um, Mom," he said, "the next time I hurt your feelings, could you maybe like tell me right then instead of three weeks later?"

I laughed and nodded.

"What?" he said. "What's so funny?"

"You remind me so much of your dad," I said, and I got up to hug him.

The next day, a well-meaning acquaintance asked me if I needed "help" with Ford. Of course, this person wasn't offering help. No, they were speaking in code, where questions are really suggestions and offers are actually slights. I looked down the sidewalk at Ford, who was too far away to hear. He was kicking the toe of his boot into a snowbank. The frozen-over snow crackled like glass with each kick. He had his arms crossed, and when he finally stopped kicking, I noticed that he still stood with his toes turned slightly inward, just like when he was a baby. He bit his lip and admired the hole he had made in the snowbank.

He's just a kid, I thought. *He's a kid who misses his dad.*

I thanked the person for their concern, but as I walked away, my heart raced with anger: Other people would just have to understand what we're going through and cut us some slack.

I had been doing a lot of apologizing for my children, but I wouldn't do it anymore. Dustin was gone and we were trying to cope. To young boys, thirteen months probably seems like forever.

I was teaching at the university during the day and working on my master's at night. I felt like I was just barely keeping my head above water. I had stopped putting away clean laundry, and we were taking our day's clothes directly out of the basket.

At night, I lay in my bed and felt like my tired bones would sink right through to the mattress springs. So, no, I wouldn't apologize anymore. Instead, I'd ask for the community's patience and help.

What I clung to was this: Our family was separated, but it wasn't broken.

With this in mind, I knew that our fourth dinner, the final one in January, would become a turning point. It would send us down a path that, at the time, I could not fully visualize or understand, but that would transform Dinner with the Smileys from a project to a mission.

That dinner was with Bangor's mayor, Cary Weston. Cary is young, tall, and handsome. He has children of his own, and, before the dinner, he told me he couldn't imagine being without them for a year.

Cary wanted to do something fun for my boys. He wanted to give them an experience of a lifetime to distract them from missing their dad. I gave Cary the okay to plan whatever he wanted. So after a dinner around our table with Morgan's homemade turkey lasagna—the one with cottage cheese—and salad, Cary wiped the corners of his mouth and said, "I have a surprise for you guys."

"A surprise?" Ford asked.

"Is it a present?"

"Is it a new toy?"

"Well, your mom told me that guests usually bring dessert," Cary said. "And I forgot to do that. Or, actually, I couldn't bring the dessert to you. It's too big. So I'm taking you to the dessert."

The boys looked back and forth at each other, and then up at Cary.

"Let's go outside," Cary said.

He put his arm around Ford and led him to the front door.

The boys stuffed their bare feet into their snow boots and raced out onto the freshly shoveled front sidewalk. A stretch limousine purred next to the curb, and a red carpet made a bridge across the snowbank.

"What?" the boys screamed. "Is this for us?"

"It is," Cary said. "But hop inside. There's more."

The limo driver, a tall man with salt-and-pepper curly hair wearing a black suit, helped each of the boys into the limo. The inside was decorated with neon lights and a carpeted ceiling that had multicolored swirls on it.

The boys had never been inside a limo before. They opened all the compartments and gasped at each new finding: "They have glasses in here, Mom! And peanuts!"

"Let's turn up the music," Owen said, twisting a dial on the wall.

The driver took us to Dysart's truck stop on the edge of town, where Cary arranged to have an 18 Wheeler—Dysart's famous eighteen-scoops-of-ice-cream dessert shaped like a tractor trailer—waiting for us. The boys—even Ford—were giddy with excitement. Lindell waved to the crowd of onlookers as he walked through the diner.

"It's like we're famous," Lindell said.

"They're laughing and waving because of your hat," Ford said, referring to the red Mario hat from last year's Halloween costume that Lindell was wearing.

After dessert, the restaurant let all of the kids pick out a T-shirt, and Cary gave the boys City of Bangor pins and stickers. On the way home, Owen proclaimed it to be the "best dinner ever."

For Lindell, so far, nothing could top having Mrs. O'Connor to dinner.

Ford shrugged and tried to hide a smile. "Yeah, I guess this is pretty cool," he said.

Later that night, after I was done cleaning the kitchen and the boys were already in bed, Ford called me into his room. He was lying on his back, the covers pulled up to his chin. An open book rested on his chest. "Mom, why is everyone so nice to us?" he asked. "Why do they want to do all that stuff for us?"

"Because they want to help, and because they want to see you happy. It makes people feel good to make other people happy."

Ford flipped the pages of his book and chewed the corner of his lip. "I guess so," he said. And then: "Mom?"

"Yes?"

"Is it bad that sometimes I feel guilty for getting so much stuff?"

"No. I mean it's good to be grateful, but it's also important to remember that a lot of people have worse circumstances than us."

"Yeah, that's what I mean. It's like, you know, living without Dad is hard and everything, but at least I still *have* a dad."

I nodded. "And you have a family that loves you, and you're healthy," I said. "There are lots of things to be thankful for. Mayor Weston is grateful that he gets to be home with his kids each night, so he wanted to do something for you that maybe Dad might have done if he was here."

"And it was totally awesome, wasn't it? Did you see that limo? It even had glasses and music in it."

I laughed.

"Tonight, for once, while we were riding in that limo," Ford said, "I was able to forget how angry I feel about Dad being gone."

I smiled at him, but he turned away and looked at the edges of his book again.

"Dad said that some kids in Djibouti don't have shoes," Ford said. "He told me that they sometimes play soccer barefoot in the street with a ball that's falling apart."

"Kind of makes sitting in school for six hours seem like less of a hassle, doesn't it?"

Ford rolled his eyes.

But then he said, "Mom, for our next dinner, can we do something for someone else? Can it not be about us?"

I reached over and put my hand on his soft cheek. "Of course," I said. "I think that is an excellent idea."

Before I went to bed, I sent a message to Jenifer Lloyd, a cancer survivor whom I only partially knew through mutual friends.

"I need your help. Our next Dinner with the Smileys needs to show the boys how lucky they are."

In the morning, I had a reply from Jenifer: "I know just what to do!"

Ford's fifth-grade teacher, Joe Bennett

CHAPTER FIVE

February

I saw Jenifer's long, slender figure walking toward us, backlit by the sideways winter light coming from the open end of the parking garage. The sound of her heels echoed throughout the nearly empty space. Lindell pulled on the arm of my overcoat and fussed about his socks being bunched up inside his snow boots. Ford and Owen yelled "Hey! Hey!" to hear the sound bouncing off the walls. I was carrying two oversize, shiny gift bags, one purple and the other silver.

"Well, hello Smileys," Jenifer said as she came closer, her arms outstretched to me for a hug. She wore a long, tan wool coat with the collar turned fashionably up. "I'm really excited about today," she said. And then, turning to the boys: "Has your mom talked to you about what we might see when we go inside the hospital?"

"She said we'll see sick people," Lindell said. Wind blew through the parking garage and lifted his wispy bangs.

"Yes, there will be a lot of sick people," Jenifer said. "Most of them are children, just like you."

"Mom said you were sick," Lindell said. "But you look okay."

"I used to be sick," Jenifer said. She kneeled down to be closer to Lindell. "That was seven years ago, and I'm better now. Would you like to ask me more questions about my sickness when we go to dinner tonight?"

Lindell nodded.

Owen pulled out a pair of Groucho Marx glasses, the kind with the attached nose and mustache, from the Velcro pocket of his jacket. "Can I wear these inside?" he asked.

Jenifer looked surprised. "Of course," she said. "I think the children will love it."

She turned to look at Ford. He was standing on the sides of his feet, so that his snow boots bent and slouched at his ankles. "And you must be Ford." She held out her hand to shake.

Ford took her hand, then pointed at Owen's glasses and said out of the corner of his mouth, "I don't know why he wants to wear those."

"We brought toys," Lindell yelled, jumping up and down for Jenifer's attention. "Mommy has them in the bags."

"Your mom told me," Jenifer said. "And I know the children will be really glad to meet you and see the toys you brought for them."

The day before, I had talked to the boys about what our next dinner would involve: visiting sick children in the pediatric wing of Eastern Maine Medical Center. Together we decided it would be nice to bring gifts for the patients.

"Our dinner guests usually bring something for us," Ford said. "So we should bring the kids in the hospital a surprise, too."

"Can we buy a toy for us?" Lindell asked.

"That's not really the point," Ford said. "It's not about us."

I had given the boys fifty dollars and took them to the Dollar Store. On the way, we talked about what we should buy. Owen, in particular, was very deliberate—almost methodical—in his choices.

"If I was the age that I am now, and in the hospital, I'd proba-bly want books," he said. "But younger boys who can't read—kids like Lindell—might like Matchbox cars or something."

"And puzzles!" Lindell screamed from his car seat. "Little boys can do puzzles!"

None of the boys knew what a girl in the hospital would enjoy.

"What kind of things did you like when you were little?" Owen asked.

"Oh, I liked Barbies, and paints, and coloring books," I said.

"And probably stuffed animals," Lindell yelled again.

"Yes, stuffed animals, too."

"I'd want a stuffed animal if I was in the hospital," Lindell said. He hugged his arms against his chest.

We left the Dollar Store with two large bags filled with toys: coloring books, plastic horses, dolls, stuffed animals, activity books, crossword puzzles, Matchbox cars, and sticker albums. When we got home, the boys sorted the toys by age appropriateness and gender.

I listened to them from the kitchen:

"I think this coloring book would be good for a younger boy," Ford said.

"And this horse looks kind of girly," Owen said. "Let's put it in the girl pile."

"I really want to keep this stuffed animal," Lindell said.

"No, Lindell. We aren't keeping any of this," Ford said.

At dinner, I tried to prepare the boys for what they might see, even though I had never been to the pediatric wing of the hospital either. In my mind, I imagined fluorescent lights down long corridors of dark, quiet patient rooms with the doors pulled closed. I thought we would visit the children in their rooms and by their bedside, next to beeping machines and yards of plastic tubing.

Owen wiped upward at his nose with the palm of his hand, a clear sign that he was nervous, as they asked me questions:

"Will we have to wear gloves?"

"Will we catch what the children have?"

"What if I get sick?"

"What if I feel like I'm going to throw up?"

"Remember when we went to see Mr. Earle in the hospital?" I said, reminding them of our ninety-two-year-old neighbor who was hospitalized for pneumonia the year before. "We're going to the same hospital, but we'll be on a different floor, a floor just for children."

"So we'll get to ride the elevator?" Lindell said.

"Yes, we will ride the elevator."

"And we can keep a stuffed animal?"

"No, Lindell," Ford and Owen said together.

"It seems like this dinner will be kind of sad and scary at the same time," Owen said.

Ford put his hand on Owen's shoulder. "Not exactly *scary*," he said. "But definitely sad."

Now, in the parking garage, Jenifer's dark, flawless bob blew in the wind. She offered to carry one of the gift bags filled with toys. "Let's get out of the cold," she said. "Then we'll talk a little bit more about our day."

We rode an elevator to the eighth floor, and Jenifer told the boys what she had planned: First we'd check in at the nurses' station, and then we'd go to the staff room and make Valentine's Day cards for the patients. We'd visit with the patients, and then we'd leave the hospital and go to the Black Bear Inn, in neighboring Orono, Maine, for dinner and a little debriefing.

When the elevator doors opened, the first thing I saw was a sign that read SHHHHHH! and had a photograph of a little girl, dressed as a nurse, holding a finger to her lips. I had forgotten to talk to the boys about being quiet. Now I was panicking. *What else did I forget to tell them?* Then we turned the corner and entered the lobby of the eighth floor.

In the center of the room was a child-size lighthouse suitable for climbing and exploring. Lindell threw off his coat and ran straight for the arched doorway of the lighthouse. A button on the side activated a spinning light that shone on the floor-to-ceiling mural of fish on the wall.

Ford climbed through the window of the lighthouse. "Here, Lindell, look in here," he said excitedly.

"Come look at this side," Owen yelled.

Suddenly, the space was filled with noise.

The boys' voices—and in particular, Ford's—bounced off the raised ceiling. I knew I couldn't expect Lindell to come out of the lighthouse, but I was counting on Ford, at least, to set a better example and not get his brother excited.

"Ford, get out of there," I hissed. "You're too old for that!"

"Mom, I was just trying to—"

"I don't care what you were doing. Get out of there."

"He's fine," Jenifer said, touching my shoulder.

Ford glared at me as he backed out of the lighthouse.

"Geez, I was just trying to help with Lindell," he said. He slouched down on one of the padded benches under the fish, and Owen soon joined him. Ford looked at the ground while Jenifer and I waited for a nurse to let us inside the double doors that led to the patient rooms.

Each of my children has varying degrees of what I call recovery time—the amount of time it takes for them to bounce back from a scolding or bad mood. At one end of the spectrum is Lindell, who, of course, has a short attention span and can be easily distracted so that he forgets a negative experience. On the other end of the spectrum is Owen: amiable and agreeable for impressive lengths of time, but once he has hit his wall, there is no turning back. It takes a meal and a good night's sleep to change Owen's mood. Ford is somewhere in the middle, but also less predictable. I can usually tell at first which way things will go by looking at his face. If he's animated and making eye contact, I can get him out of a mood. But when the muscles in his face go flat—when he holds his full lips in a perfectly straight line and won't meet my eyes— well, it's all downhill from there.

As Ford sat on the bench with Owen, his face was expression-less, his eyes cast downward.

Oh, damn, I thought. I needed Ford. I needed him to be the example for his younger brothers. But now he was light-years away, in his own head, and totally unwilling to cooperate.

I shouldn't have snapped.

We walked through a long hallway, past the nurses' station and into what the nurses called the Courtyard. It had tall, vaulted ceil-ings with sun lights that allowed bright sunshine to spill into the room. There was a painting of clouds on the wall and tables with umbrellas in each of the four corners. The Courtyard had a toy kitchen, a foosball table, a toy piano, boxes of toys, and a rocking dinosaur. It took a second look to actually see any evidence (a roll-ing blood pressure machine, hand sanitizer stations, and sharps containers on the wall) that this was actually a hospital. Just be-yond the Courtyard was the Play Room, a space filled entirely with toys and padded mats for gymnastics. Ford and Owen ran to the foosball table; Lindell went to the Play Room and climbed up the foam blocks.

I worried again about the noise.

"Should we go into the Family Room and make the Valen-tine's cards now?" Jenifer said.

"Aw, just one more minute," Owen said.

"Not yet," Lindell yelled.

I wasn't sure the kids even realized we were in a hospital any-more. This was not what I had prepared them for. It wasn't gloomy, or scary, or even really sad.

The Family Room, which was the size and decor of a nice hotel suite, had a kitchenette and a colorful mural of a hearth next to the dining table. Jenifer unpacked a bag filled with construction paper, markers, and glue while I coaxed the boys away from the Courtyard and Play Room.

"I don't even like making cards," Ford said, throwing himself down into a padded chair.

Lindell rummaged through Jenifer's materials. "Look at all the markers," he said. "And glue!"

Owen put on his Groucho Marx glasses and asked Lindell to pass him a sheet of red paper. "So we're making Valentine's Day cards, right?" he said, his voice muffled by the mustache and large, plastic nose. "But do I have to put hearts and stuff on it?"

"You can make the cards any way you'd like," Jenifer said. She turned to Ford. "Ford, would you like to make a card?"

He shrugged. "If I have to." He came to the table and folded a sheet of orange construction paper in half. The edges were lopsided and uneven. Owen watched through the dark circles of his glasses.

"Do you want me to fold that for you?" he asked.

"It's fine, Owen! Geez!" Ford said.

When the boys were halfway done with their first card, a patient came into the room. He was probably eight or nine years old, but he was the weight and stature of someone much younger. His face was pale, his eyes sunken with dark circles beneath them. He pushed a colostomy bag on a pole with wheels, and with his free hand, he held closed the back of his hospital gown.

"Would you like to do some crafts with us?" Jenifer asked. "We have plenty of paper and markers. There's glue and glitter." She pushed around the materials and held up random pom-poms and pipe cleaners.

The boy sat at the head of the table and adjusted the line leading to his colostomy bag. If he answered Jenifer, his voice was too quiet for any of us to hear.

Owen looked at the patient, then at me, and back at the patient again. He pushed the glasses farther up onto his nose.

The room was awkwardly silent.

It was too late to explain the colostomy bag.

Owen looked at the pile of crafts on the table and found a foam cutout of a bear. "You could use this and make something," he said, pushing the bear across the table to the boy.

The patient took the bear and searched the materials for glue. Owen gave him his. They sat close together. Owen helped with the orange tip of the glue bottle that was stuck, and suggested googly eyes to complete the bear. Lindell ran back and forth from the Family Room to the Play Room. When he was in the Family Room, he scribbled on cards. When he was in the Play Room, he jumped on the foam mats. Ford had finished his one card, and he was done. He paced behind the table and chewed on his thumbnail.

"Ford, sit down," I said multiple times.

He would sit for a minute, then he was up again and pacing. Sometimes he grumbled and sighed. "Can we go now, Mom?" he whispered. "Please!"

I stared up at him with fierce, angry eyes. "Sit down and make a card," I said through clenched teeth.

"I don't want to make another card," he said. He ran both hands through his hair. "I'm actually kind of bored." He paced more and chewed his thumb until I thought his nail bed might bleed.

I motioned for him to follow me into the next room. When he didn't come, I grabbed him by the arm and dragged him there. I positioned my face within inches of his. "You are being rude and inconsiderate," I said.

Ford stared at the ground.

"Look at my face when I'm talking to you!"

Ford looked up at me with lazy, watery eyes.

"You go back in that room and show some respect—to Jenifer, to the patient, to me, and to yourself."

"No, I'm not going back in there," Ford said, pulling away from my grip.

I grabbed his arm again. "You are the one who is supposed to set the example for your younger brothers."

"I don't want to be their example."

"Well, you sure as heck aren't being a good example right now. Look at your younger brother in there, and don't tell me you're too young for this. Owen is doing exactly what he should be doing."

"Lindell's not. He's running back and forth to the Play Room."

"Lindell's five, Ford. You're eleven. Start acting like it."

"Mom, I'm bored," he said, pulling away again. "I hate this."

"We've been here less than an hour. How could you possibly be bored?"

Ford spun away from me.

"You're embarrassing me, and you're embarrassing yourself," I said as he walked away, back into the Family Room.

I found him slouched in a chair again, staring at the salt stains on his snow boots.

Owen and the patient were finishing another Valentine's Day card. The boy asked Owen where he got his glasses, and that reminded Owen: "Oh, Mom, can we pass out the toys now?" Owen asked.

"Yes, actually," I said. "Ford, why don't you go get the gift bags and bring them in here?"

Ford dragged his feet and walked with shoulders hunched into the hallway to get the bags. He came back and dropped them next to Owen at the table.

"Can I pick out something?" the boy asked Ford.

"Um, sure," Ford said. He started to walk away. But then he turned around. He shrugged. "There's lots of cool stuff in there," he said. "You'll probably like what's in the silver bag though, because the purple bag has girl stuff in it. Here, look." Ford opened the silver bag and let the boy peer inside.

The patient selected Matchbox cars. Then he asked, "Can I help you guys pass out the rest?"

"I guess so," Ford said. "You probably know this place better than we do."

"Yeah, I probably do."

Ford still wouldn't make eye contact with me, but he held the bags while the patient pushed his pole and held his gown closed.

Owen dug through the gift bags and handed toys to other patients we saw in the Play Room and Courtyard.

Afterward, at the Black Bear Inn, hours of pent-up energy was released as Lindell ran circles around the mostly empty, family-friendly restaurant.

Cancer survivor Jenifer Lloyd

Jenifer shared her breast cancer story and showed the boys pictures on her phone.

Ford laughed into his hand when he saw a picture of Jenifer's bald head.

"Ford!" I snapped.

"No, it's okay," Jenifer said. "I looked very different, didn't I? Oh, and look at this picture." She flipped to a photograph of her naturally bald husband wearing a wig that was meant for her. Jenifer was standing beside him, her head as shiny as a bowling ball.

"Now that is funny," Ford said.

"I know, isn't it?" Jenifer said. "It's weird because I was so very sick, but I was still just me. I laughed and cried, and I had good days and bad days."

"It's weird to think that was you," Ford said. He leaned across the table to get a better look at Jenifer's phone.

"And these are my daughters," Jenifer said, flipping to a new picture.

Lindell climbed into my lap and rested his head on my shoulder. "Momma, will you pat me?" he asked. I stroked his back with one hand and reached across my chair to put my other arm around Owen.

LARGE DROPS OF frozen rain pelted the windshield, like nails being thrown at glass. Ford tied his basketball shoes in the passenger seat. Owen and Lindell were at friends' houses. The minivan was silent, except for the squeak and thump of the windshield wipers.

"I want to talk to you about the dinner last night," I said.

"What about it?" Ford asked. His foot was propped up on the seat. He rested his chin on his knee as he worked on his shoelaces.

"Do you think you behaved appropriately?"

Ford didn't answer.

"Well, do you?"

Ford shrugged.

My jaw grew tight. "You don't have anything to say?"

"Not really."

"So you think it was perfectly fine to say 'I'm bored' in front of a boy who is sick and might die?"

"He wasn't dying."

"How do you know? He's been in the hospital for a long time. If anyone had the right to say they were bored, it was him."

Ford stared out the window.

Slush spilled from the wipers and slid down the windshield. I was frantic now, unsure how to get through to him. Self-doubt always clouds my mind when Dustin is away and I have no one to bounce ideas off of, but especially in moments like this, I asked myself, *Am I doing this right? Am I a good enough parent? Am I totally messing up my kids?*

The hardest part about parenting alone is that you have no relief pitcher. There is no one to step in and say, "Let me handle this one." Dustin had always been more effective with Ford. He understood him in a way I could not. And now, at this critical period in Ford's development, Dustin was halfway across the world.

My chest hurt at the thought.

I stopped at a traffic light and turned to look at the back of Ford's head. "How dare you say you're bored in front of that boy yesterday!"

Ford continued to stare out the window.

"Do you not even feel bad for the way you acted?"

Ford slowly turned around. His big brown eyes were full of tears. Drops spilled out over his lower lid and made a trail down his cheeks. "I'm sorry," he said. "I didn't know what to do, Mom. And I don't like making cards."

The light turned green. Cars behind me honked.

We drove the rest of the way in silence.

When we arrived at the gymnasium, I turned off the engine and looked at the side of Ford's face. "Ford, I'm trying. I'm really trying," I said as tears came to my eyes. "This is hard on all of us."

"I hate the navy!" he screamed. "I hate that Dad is gone. And I hate being here with just you."

He kicked the floor of the car and pushed the door handle to get out. When it slammed behind him, I watched in the rearview mirror as he ran, his basketball shorts nearly invisible beneath his winter coat, into the gymnasium. Without the windshield wipers, and without Ford's quiet sniffling, the car was suddenly, devastatingly quiet. I listened to my own rapid breaths until I felt panicky.

I called Morgan, whose husband had been deployed the year before. Her kids are younger so they weren't in the tween stage yet. And while Morgan had dealt with her share of emotions and stress, she hadn't been through this exact experience.

"I don't know what to say," Morgan said. "But I'm sure this is all very normal. Should you take a break from Dinner with the Smileys? Is it too much for him? Too much for you?"

"I thought it would help them—help me," I said. "But now . . . I don't know."

"You'll get through this," Morgan said. "It's still early. You're all adjusting."

I sighed deeply.

"We are always here for you guys," Morgan said.

Inside the gym, I sat alone on the bleachers and cried. Streams of tears ran down my face, but I was beyond being embarrassed or trying to hide it. Everyone knew, and they politely looked away. My eyes were red and hot with emotion. I had no idea which team had the ball or if Ford's team was winning. I tried to send Dustin an e-mail from my phone, but I couldn't even see the letters on the screen through my tears. And, anyway, an e-mail wouldn't help; I needed to hear my husband's voice. I needed to talk to him in real time, in that back and forth way that doesn't involve waiting twelve hours for a reply that doesn't answer all the questions or say the things I needed it to say.

I stared across the shiny wood floor at Ford, who was sitting on the sidelines. His winter coat was on the floor behind the bench. His arms and legs looked bright white against his orange-and-black uniform. Two teammates sat about six feet away to Ford's left on the bench. They were laughing and talking to one another, but Ford sat alone and quiet. His back was rounded, and he rested his elbows on his knees. I could see that his eyes, although dry now, were also red. One of his shoelaces was untied again.

I remembered what Dustin had said: *He's just a kid. Yes, he's our oldest, but he's still just a kid.* Floods of tears came again, and I choked on my breath.

I left the bleachers and went outside.

After the game, Ford found me sitting on the school floor, my back against the tiled wall. "The game's over," he said. He was carrying his coat in his hand. The bottom of it dragged on the floor. "Ummmm." He looked over each of his shoulders. "Uh, so, do you want me to help you up?" He held out his hand.

We walked out of the building in silence.

Once we were back in the car, Ford said, "I'm sorry, Mom. I'm sorry about yesterday and about today."

I reached over and touched his bare knee. "I'm sorry, too."

"I didn't mean those things," Ford said, his voice trailing off.

"I know. In fact, I've been thinking a lot about yesterday. I don't know if I could have handled that when I was your age either. I mean I'm an adult, and even I felt kind of uncomfortable."

"Yeah, like, what was that thing the boy had on the pole?" Ford asked. "I was kind of afraid to look."

Just then, I realized how horribly unprepared I had left my children for what they had experienced. How had the hospital affected them? What questions did they have? Were they scared? I had expected the boys—and especially Ford—to respond like adults.

But even adults have a hard time in situations like that. I explained the colostomy bag, and we talked for a while about what it would be like to stay in a hospital for so long—no basketball games, no friends, no snowball fights.

"I feel bad that I said I was bored," Ford said.

"I know."

"I didn't mean it. And I know that Owen acted better than I did. But Owen's kind of gifted with people, don't you think, Mom?"

I was stunned that Ford could recognize that, and even more stunned that he would admit to it. "You're right," I said. "Owen is gifted with people. That is his strength. But you have strengths, too. You are incredibly smart and capable."

"Oh, here we go with the whole 'smart and capable' thing." Ford blew his breath up so that it rippled the hairs hanging in front of his eyes.

"No, really," I said. "It's not a bad thing. You're a lot like Dad, actually, because you think things through with your head."

"You really think I'm like Dad?"

"I do. And, you know, Dad isn't the best in social situations either."

Ford laughed. "Yeah. Remember that time when he was going to treat someone to lunch, but when the bill came, he had forgotten his wallet?"

"Yes, that was Mother's Day. He was going to buy lunch for his mom, but he forgot his wallet."

"Oh, man, that's bad," Ford said.

"Luckily, it was just his mom, right?"

"Well, but even doing that to your mom is bad," Ford said.

The van was quiet again.

"I'm sorry," Ford said. "I really am. But I don't know how to make it better."

"I know you're sorry. The Ford at the hospital wasn't the Ford I know and love."

We were both quiet.

Then I said, "Now that you realize Owen is gifted with people, use him as your example."

"Um, okay," Ford said in that long, drawn-out, skeptical way. "What do you mean?"

"What I mean is if you're ever in doubt about how to act in a certain situation, look at Owen and follow his lead."

"Like copy him?"

"If you need to. Use him as your guide. Your teacher."

Ford thought about that for a long time. Then he said, "Okay, Mom. I think I can do that." He looked at me and smiled. His smile lit up his eyes—just the way it always had done when he was a baby.

NEAR VALENTINE'S DAY, Dustin surprised me with a gift. We don't usually make a big deal out of February 14—Dustin says we should love each other all year, not just one day—but I suppose he knew the day, with all of its advance retail displays and sales, would be difficult to spend alone. So he e-mailed Laura, the owner of Fiddlehead, a restaurant downtown, and arranged for me and Morgan and my other friends, Shelley and Ally, to have dinner there. He even messaged our go-to family of babysitters—the Cowans—and set that up, too. It wouldn't be an official Dinner with the Smileys because the boys would be at home, but I was excited about a night of conversation and food with my friends.

Fiddlehead is a small restaurant—about the size of a studio apartment, actually—with less than a dozen tables. Local artists' work hangs from exposed brick walls, and the scuffed wooden floors creak beneath the waitress's feet. The large storefront windows look out onto the sloping city street and the brick courthouse on the opposite side. From the sidewalk in the winter, behind snow-drifts packed against the building's side, flickering candles inside

Fiddlehead make the restaurant seem like something out of a Dickens novel.

Laura met us at the hostess stand. She wore a black V-neck sweater, blue jeans, and brown cowboy boots that clicked against the floors as she walked us to our table. "Happy Valentine's Day, ladies," she said, pouring our drinks. "Dustin has some great things planned for you guys." She came around to my seat and leaned in close. "Your husband—well, he had all of the staff here in tears. That he would think to set this up for you—" Laura shook her head and put a hand to her chest.

I smiled at Morgan on my left and nudged her with my elbow. Because the truth was that Dustin had only copied Morgan's husband's idea from the year before. When Lincoln was deployed during Valentine's Day, he arranged for us to go to dinner at another downtown restaurant.

When Laura walked away, Ally, whose husband is not in the military, said, "Okay, I really love this tradition of celebrating Valentine's Day with you guys, but if it means that it's my husband's turn to go away next year—well, then, I'm out."

We all laughed.

At some point during our meal, Laura came back to check on us. "Have you taken a guess at tonight's trivia question?" she asked.

Far above Fiddlehead's bar, nestled between trailing plants and vintage glasses, is a small, square chalkboard. Each night, there is a Maine-related trivia question on it. Supposedly diners who guess correctly get a free drink, but I've never gotten the trivia right, so I can't know for sure.

I looked up at the board and read: "What is Dustin and Sarah Smiley's wedding song?"

"Awwwww," Morgan, Ally, and Shelley said in unison.

Laura smiled warmly. "Dustin asked us to put that question up tonight," she said.

Shelley reached over and rubbed my arm.

"So? Do you know the answer?" Morgan teased.

" 'The Long and Winding Road,' by the Beatles," I said.

Laura came back with a tall glass of my favorite drink, Dr Pepper. Fiddlehead doesn't actually sell Dr Pepper, but Morgan had arranged for Laura to have it on hand when I got the trivia question right.

By now, our dinners were well known because readers of my weekly column were following my posts about them on Facebook. Diners nearby at Fiddlehead teased, "Is this a Dinner with the Smileys?" On a daily basis, people around town suggested dinner guests and sent invitations for us to come to dinner with them. I realized the project had become larger than our family. It wasn't about us anymore. It was about community, loneliness, and returning to the family dinner table. I received letters from widows, divorcées, and other military spouses who said that our dinners had reminded them to sit down together as a family or to invite someone new to their table.

I talked to readers and friends about how our generation says "let's do dinner" all the time, but we seldom follow up. It's like saying "how are you?" when we pass someone in the hall; we don't really expect an honest answer. And yet, so many of us are alone as we eat our meals. There were countless people in my community who were just as lonely as the boys and I were. There were countless people in my community who could be a support system for us, and vice versa.

Nonetheless, Morgan was right. The boys and I needed a break. Our fifth dinner at the hospital was heavier than any of us had expected. The sixth dinner, I thought, should give the kids time to process and exhale. So we invited Morgan and her family to see the 3-D version of *Star Wars: Episode I—The Phantom Menace* with us, and then come back to our place for fajitas. Not only would the dinner be easy and familiar, but also Lincoln's presence would remind the boys that service members go away, but most of them come back. And soon after, things get back to normal.

A few days before the dinner, Morgan sent a special letter to Ford in the mail. In it, she told him that he is a wonderful role model for her younger son and that if he ever needed anything—to get away from his mom, to talk to another grown-up, to go to the batting cages—he could count on her. She included her phone number and e-mail address.

After the movie, while the kids walked with Lincoln to the car in the parking lot, Morgan pulled me aside and said, "Let this be a supercasual dinner. Just let the boys be themselves, and don't worry about us."

And it was a very casual dinner, indeed. We all pulled up extra chairs to the farm table, and we reached over and across one another as we built our fajitas. Owen and Morgan's son put on *Star*

Morgan Mazzei, fellow military wife, clearing the table

University of Maine men's hockey head coach Tim Whitehead

Wars costumes and had a sword fight in the living room. Lindell chased Sparky and Morgan's daughter up the stairs and down again. Ford stayed in the kitchen with the adults and talked to Lincoln about baseball.

One week later, our seventh dinner was with the University of Maine's men's hockey coach, Tim Whitehead, his son Zach, and two of the players, Nick and Kyle, one of whom had been my journalism student the semester before. We had to bring in an extra table from the front porch to make room for everyone. The dinner table was quickly filled with the broad shoulders and large feet of two college athletes. And by the end of the night, there was not even a morsel of leftover lasagna.

Ford's behavior changed dramatically around Nick and Kyle, who weren't old enough to "not understand" like his parents, but also weren't young enough to be his peers. They were somewhere in the middle, kind of like uncles or cousins. Ford's prickly edges, so evident in previous weeks, softened. He chewed on his bread and smiled when Nick asked him about Little League. And, taking a cue from Kyle, Ford asked, instead of grabbed, for someone to pass him the cheese or butter.

As a kid who *is* the older brother and has none for himself, for one night, Ford took his lead from Nick and Kyle. And he had the chance to be a little boy again.

At the end of the night, I asked my boys if they had any questions about college for either Kyle or Nick.

"I do. I do," Lindell said, throwing down his spoon against a bowl of melted ice cream.

"Sure, buddy. What's your question?" Kyle said.

"Um, is it scary to live at college without your mom?"

Nick laughed. "Yes, Lindell. Actually, it is."

By LATE FEBRUARY, the boys and I were finally in a routine. Our weekdays were packed with school and basketball, and I went back to the university at night to take classes for my master's program. Time seemed to be moving quickly. Instead of measuring the deployment in months, we had our minds set on the next week's dinner.

"Who comes to dinner this week?" Ford often asked. He liked to keep track of the numbers and names: "So, our first guest was Senator Collins, and then Mrs. O'Connor. Who was third? Oh, yeah, Dr. and Mrs. Haddix. Then we went in the limo with the mayor. And then we met Jenifer Lloyd—" His voice usually trailed off when he remembered that day.

In his room, he kept a calendar of the dinners, and he rated each one on a separate sheet of paper he tore from one of my notebooks. He never said one dinner was better than another—just different. They either scored high for what he had learned, what we ate, or whom we met. There was something meaningful in each of them. Regarding our dinner at the hospital, Ford just said, "Well, at least Mrs. Lloyd was really nice."

Owen and Lindell looked forward to the dinners, too. For Lindell, each one meant a new audience and the chance that someone might bring him a treat or surprise. He was affectionate and open, often climbing in people's laps or snuggling against their arms, and he fought anyone who tried to take his spot near the head of the table, to the right of the guest.

That is, until Ron Gastia, Bangor's police chief, came to the eighth dinner.

Chief Gastia had just been to a news briefing about a bomb threat in a building downtown. So he was wearing his uniform, and a pistol hung from his thick, black leather belt.

"Is that a real gun?" Owen asked, a safe distance away on the living room couch.

"Yes, it is," Ron said, his pale blue eyes soft and friendly beneath an expanse of forehead framed by gray, receding hair. He patted the gun at his side.

"Like, it could shoot someone?" Lindell asked.

"Well—" Ron looked at me, as if for guidance. "Technically, yes," he said.

"Then I'm not sitting next to you at dinner." Lindell hugged himself.

"Okay," Ron said. "How about we talk to one another across the table. Would that make you feel better?"

Lindell nodded.

In the kitchen, Owen sat in Lindell's spot at the table. Technically Lindell took Owen's seat in return, but mostly he climbed in and out of my lap. He never actually ate the steaming bowl of chili and cornbread waiting next to his glass of chocolate milk. Owen asked Ron questions in between rubbing his nose and coughing into his hand. Ron thoughtfully answered each one, usually pausing first and looking at the ceiling to gather his thoughts. Like me, Ron realized that the boys were all at different stages of understanding things like crime and violence.

"I'm afraid I won't know all the laws by the time I'm a grown-up, and I'll accidentally break a rule," Owen said.

"That's what your mom and dad are here for," Ron said. "They are teaching you right from wrong so that you will make good choices by the time you're an adult."

"But what if I do something accidentally?" Owen rubbed his nose with the heel of his hand. His urgency to be protected made me wonder, *Did my children feel safe without their dad at home? Was I doing enough for them?*

Ron thought about his answer before speaking aloud. In the

Bangor police chief Ron Gastia and Lindell

meantime, while we waited, Lindell crept closer to Ron's seat. First he watched Ron from a distance, his index finger in his mouth. Then he shuffled closer. Eventually, he peeked around Ron's back and smiled up at him. Ron looked down at his side and tousled Lindell's hair.

After dinner, Ron took the older boys for a ride in the police car.

Although Lindell had warmed to and accepted the idea of Ron's gun, he drew the line at getting in a police car.

"No, I will not get in that car."

Ron laughed. "And let's keep it that way," he said. "I never want to hear about any of the Smiley boys being in the back of a police car."

Our community was enjoying news of the weekly dinners, especially the ones that involved public citizens like the police chief. Everywhere we went—the bank, the gas station, the bagel shop downtown—people asked, "Who's next, Smileys?" George at the post office guessed and made suggestions for guests. He especially liked our dinner with Lindell's preschool teacher.

Readers did, too.

"I never thought about inviting my son's teacher to dinner," a reader said. Another one asked, "*Can* we invite teachers to dinner? Like, is that even allowed?"

This struck me as sad, and yet so typical of the culture we live in. All the pieces of our world are compartmentalized. We have work friends and school friends and Friday night friends, and often, these people don't overlap. We even divide groups of friends into lists on Facebook. Teachers can't hug children anymore—because it might be misconstrued as something else—and it's considered questionable to invite to dinner the person who spends six hours, Monday through Friday, September to June, with your child.

"Isn't that favoritism?" someone asked. "It's like the teacher is saying they like your child best."

"Maybe no one else has invited the teacher to dinner," I said.

My boys' teachers hold keys to their growth and development that I can never access. I don't often see them with a large group of peers. I don't see the way they interact in a lunchroom full of friends, or how they respond when they answer incorrectly in class or trip over their shoelaces. Why would I *not* share a meal with the person who knows my child in a completely different environment from the one I know them in at home?

Mrs. O'Connor had brought many insights when she came to dinner in January: Lindell—my loud, wonderful youngest child who moons us from across the dinner table—is studious and quiet at school.

As far as the kids were concerned, the idea of having their teachers to dinner ranked right up there with the university hockey players and Senator Collins. So we decided that for the rest of the school year, we would invite one teacher to dinner each month. On Leap Day, the week after our dinner with the police chief, Ford's fifth-grade teacher, Joe Bennett, came to fill Dustin's seat.

Joe is the kind of teacher most boys hope they'll have. He's the umpire for Little League games. He has a shrine to the Red Sox in the back of his classroom. He wears red tennis shoes. He plays in a band. He comes to all of his students' athletic events—even during spring break and winter vacation. But most of all, Joe is funny. He even does gigs here and there as a comedian.

Joe arrived for dinner in a long, black wool coat and a scarf with the Boston Red Sox emblem on it. The rims of his round glasses perfectly matched his rust-colored hair and mustache. He was carrying a guitar case.

"I hope you don't mind," he said in a thick Boston accent. "But I brought my old guitah heah to play a few tunes."

"Like in school?" Ford said. "Like, the explorer one?"

Joe writes his own jingles to help the kids remember science and social studies facts. Then he plays them on his guitar at school. Everyone who's had Mr. Bennett knows about early America thanks

Ford at dinner with his fifth-grade teacher

---

to his song about Christopher Columbus. And each morning, Mr. Bennett's class sings the national anthem.

"We can do the explorer one," Joe said. "And I've got wicked fun new ones, too. How about after dinner?"

Ford showed Joe to Dustin's seat at the head of the family table, and when Ford sat down across from him, the little-boy face returned: His eyes twinkled when he smiled; his voice was soft, not angry; his posture was straight and proud.

Joe asked Ford what he likes best about fifth grade.

"Managing the school store," Ford said. "And that our class decides what to do with the money we've raised."

"What's a school store?" Lindell asked.

"It's where we sell pencils and erasers and other things, bub," Joe said.

"Everyone in Mr. Bennett's class works at the store," Ford told Lindell. "And then we donate the money to charity." Ford turned to Joe again. "Next time," he said, "I'd like to donate the money to the kids my dad sees playing soccer in Africa. Maybe we could send them new soccer balls."

Joe sat back in Dustin's chair and smiled at Ford. "What an excellent idea," he said.

"My dad says they are really poor over there," Ford said. "And the kids' soccer balls are falling apart and stuff."

Joe nodded as he listened. Then, over Red Sox–flavored ice cream and cake, he and Ford came up with a plan.

Several months later, Joe and Ford sent a box full of soccer balls to Dustin in Djibouti. Dustin took the balls to children in an

Ford's fifth-grade teacher, Joe Bennett

orphanage near the military base, and he sent back pictures for Joe to share with Ford's class and school.

After dessert, Joe got out his guitar, and we spent the rest of the evening listening to his quirky songs. Lindell danced and yelled out answers when Joe left dramatic pauses:

"And this type of animal must be a—"

"Bird!" Lindell screamed.

"No," Ford said, laughing. "It's a mammal. Mammal rhymes with animal. Get it?"

"Mammal!" Lindell screamed during all the next pauses.

"No," Ford said again. "It's different every time, Lindell. You have to listen for the rhyme."

Ford's face was flushed with red from smiling and laughing. He even sang along with Joe. I knew we were on an upswing again. Ford was happy. He was his old self again.

Unfortunately I couldn't yet see how badly I would mess it all up with dinner number ten.

Sarah and the boys looking at photographs on Jenifer Lloyd's phone

Lindell and Sparky

CHAPTER SIX

March

It was 11:15 A.M. I remember that because I had only fifteen minutes before it was time to pick up Lindell at preschool. I was watching the clock. Also, I was cleaning my wedding band. Who does that? Not me. Not very often, at least. But on that day, at precisely 11:15 A.M., I stood at the bathroom sink, a small, wiry brush in my hand, and cleaned my rings.

This, of course, made me think of Dustin. I felt intimately attached to him as I thought about our wedding day: a warm, blue-sky Virginia day in July thirteen years ago. The rings on my finger—those cold, circular objects—were a tangible reminder of our love and our vows, even though for the past four months Dustin had been entirely intangible to me.

But the ring on Dustin's finger now wasn't the one I gave him in 1999. He lost the original twelve years after our wedding, and just a few months before he left to go overseas. We had taken the kids hiking at Mount Katahdin in northern Maine, and before heading home, we stopped at one of our favorite swimming spots at the base of the mountain. Abol Falls, as it's unofficially known, is a small offshoot of the Penobscot River. From the rushing rapids, where rafters bounce across the foam, a stream of water splits to the side and around an island of land. The effect is that of a funnel. As the water squeezes past and cuts through the small space, it bubbles and churns and creates a strong undercurrent. A rope swing hangs from the canopy of trees there, and hanging on to it, with the rapids pushing through the water beneath, is like being dragged behind a speedboat. About a hundred feet away from the rope swing there is a calm, clear pool of water with a pebble floor. That's where Lindell and I stayed while Dustin helped Ford and Owen onto the rope swing.

Every few minutes, a raft full of screaming thrill-seekers bounced in the distance as it came off the bumpiest rapids to our right. I sat with Lindell at the water's edge and ran my hands through the sand full of pebbles. Although Dustin, Ford, and Owen were just a hundred feet away from us, I couldn't hear them because of the rushing water. But I watched closely as Dustin put Owen on his back and hung from the rope swing.

At one point, after Dustin let go of the rope and he and Owen were pushed by the current through the water, Dustin came up for air and his face looked worried. He dove down into the water and came back up again, peering into the foam like he was looking into the bright sun. He swam each of the boys through the rapids and onto a safe rock. Then he went back near the rope swing and dove down again.

"Dad must have lost something," I said to Lindell. "Wonder what it could have been?"

Lindell threw pebbles into the water and laughed at the sound. *Kerplunk!* I kept my eyes on Ford and Owen on the rock and Dustin nearby diving in and out of the water.

About ten minutes later, Dustin swam to the shore. As he waded through the calmer edges of the water lapping at the pebbly beach, he stared directly at me and frowned. When he reached the spot where Lindell and I were sitting, Dustin took my hand and pulled me up to stand.

"I lost it," he said.

"Lost what? I saw you looking—"

Dustin held out his left hand. It was white and shaking from the cold. At first I didn't understand. I thought he had a leech on his finger, or, maybe, he had cut his hand. And then I saw the indentation where his wedding band used to be. I looked at Dustin's face.

He blinked and breathed in deeply. "I'm so sorry," he said. "It was stupid to wear it out here."

I took his shivering hand in mine and felt along his ring finger. In twelve years, his body had actually morphed around the white-gold metal. His finger was dented and disfigured. There was a band of white where the skin below his ring had never seen the sun.

Dustin pulled my head to his shoulder, and I cried.

"We'll get me a new one before I leave for deployment," Dustin said. "I promise."

"But it won't be that one," I cried. "It won't be the one I gave you."

"I know."

The month before, a jeweler at the mall had stopped Dustin in the hallway and offered to buff and clean his ring. "I can get those scratches right out of there," the man said. "Your ring will be like new again."

"I don't want it to be 'like new,'" Dustin said. And then later, in the car, Dustin told me that he loved the dents and scratches on his wedding ring. They represented our history together—not perfect, and definitely flawed, but ours. He told me that he loved me more now than he did on our wedding day, and a like-new ring would not reflect all that we had been through.

As we stood on the pebbly beach and I cried into Dustin's shoulder, he mentioned that day at the mall. "I loved every scratch on my ring," he said, running his fingers through my hair.

I hiccupped from my crying.

Dustin pulled me back so he could see my face.

"I'm sad, too," he said. "You know I am. But, Sarah, I wear my ring here." He pointed at his heart and smiled goofily.

I laughed through tears at the corniness.

Dustin's face looked hopeful. "Imagine all the bumps and scratches it's getting now at the bottom of the river?"

I wiped at my wet cheeks.

Dustin hugged me close again. "If I had to lose my ring anywhere," he whispered into my ear, "I'm glad it was here. It's like I left a piece of me—a piece of us—here at home before I have to go."

I looked up at the large, puffy white clouds in the sky, marked by the tips of lush pine trees. I heard the rushing water and felt the pebbles under my feet.

"This will forever be our place now," Dustin said, and he kissed me on the cheek.

A few weeks before Dustin left to go overseas, and while the kids were away at school, he and I held hands and walked into a blue-carpeted jewelry store to buy a new wedding band. We stood at the glass counter and giggled like a newly engaged couple. But when the employee handed Dustin a shiny new ring in a velvet-covered box, I felt sad.

It wasn't scratched. It had no history.

I put the ring on Dustin's finger. He smiled and said, "Well, I better get started banging this one up."

I laughed thinking back on all of this while I scrubbed my rings with the wiry brush in our bathroom. I wondered how Dustin's new ring was holding up. I knew I wouldn't be sad if he lost it. Not that one. The real one was already gone.

When I finished cleaning my ring, I got ready to pick up Lindell. It would have been 6:15 P.M. in Africa.

Five hours later, I Skyped with Dustin while I made dinner for the boys.

"There's something I need to tell you," he said. "And don't get mad, because the ending is good."

"Okay." I moved between the sink and stove, stopping occasionally in front of the laptop on the counter.

"I lost my wedding ring today," Dustin said.

I stopped midstep. "What?" I moved closer to the computer screen. "Your new one?"

"Yes. I was playing softball on the base. I lost it in the turf field, but I found it after the game. See?" He held up his left hand to show me the ring.

I looked down at my freshly cleaned rings.

"Dustin, what time would that have been?" I asked. "What time did you find your ring again?"

"I don't know. Why?"

"Just tell me. What time?"

"Well, let's see, it was right before I went to dinner at six thirty, so, um, I guess I found the ring at like six fifteen my time."

Goosebumps started on my shins and rose up my chest and to my cheeks. I didn't know if Dustin would believe me about cleaning my rings and thinking of him at 11:15 that morning, but I told him anyway.

"There are no coincidences," he said.

We stared at each other and smiled for a long time through the computer.

OUR TENTH DINNER was doomed before it even began, and it was entirely my fault. Keeping with the theme of giving back and "it's not all about us," I had decided in February to plan one of the dinners each month around a charitable event or business. For March, I talked to my friend Melissa Huston, a representative for the Good Shepherd Food Bank in Brewer, Maine, just across the water from Bangor, and asked if she could arrange a tour.

I had known Melissa for about a year, ever since I heard her voice from across the vestry in the church basement during a coffee hour, and I was drawn to her like a kid to the ice-cream truck.

"This is going to sound completely crazy," I said. "But are you by any chance from Alabama?"

Melissa's round, soft face brightened, her cheeks like perfect, blushed apples. "In fact, I am," she said, and her voice was full of the rich Southern accent I remember from my youth.

My grandparents, Doris and Big Jack, were from Birmingham, Alabama, and I lived with them while I was going to school at Samford University. I can recognize an Alabama accent—distinct, softer, and fuller than any other southern accent—anywhere.

Soon, Melissa became a mentor to me. She is an accessible, nurturing, and totally nonthreatening mother of two. I often felt like she was the patient kindergarten teacher holding my hand through the obstacles of being a parent. And, as it turns out, these traits—patience, tolerance, acceptance—were excellent ones for our tenth dinner guest to have.

I planned to pick up the boys after lunch, when Lindell was dismissed from preschool. We weren't meeting Melissa until a few hours later, but it didn't make sense to make multiple trips to the school.

"You mean we'll miss half a school day for this dinner?" Ford said.

"Only because the food bank closes early," I said. "And also it makes sense to get you and Owen when I pick up Lindell."

"I'm liking the food bank already."

"What about me? Don't you like me?" Lindell asked Ford.

Ford smiled and tousled Lindell's hair. "Yeah, it's pretty cool that your short day means we get out of school early, too."

I sent a note in Ford's and Owen's backpacks telling their teachers that I'd pick them up at 11:30 A.M. for a "special opportunity." That morning, the boys leaped out of the car as I dropped them off at school. Owen called over his shoulder, "See you in a few hours, Mom!"

I drove to the University of Maine, twenty miles north of Bangor, to teach a class that was scheduled to end at 10:50 A.M. At 11:00, however, a student was still at my desk asking for help with his writing assignment. At 11:15 the adviser for my master's thesis stopped me in the hallway and asked if I had a moment.

"Uh, only one," I said, eyeing the time on my phone.

I fidgeted in my seat on the other side of the adviser's large metal desk littered with papers and books with worn, soft edges. Balancing my roles as "mother" and "student" had always been difficult, but never more so than in that moment.

At 11:30, I finally said, "I'm so sorry, but I have to go get my kids. I'm already late."

I ran through the hallway, down four flights of stairs, and across the parking lot with scattered piles of brown, melting snow on the sides. When I got to my van and turned the key, a light in the dashboard came on: low gas. I banged my head against the steering wheel. My chest felt tight from the anxiety and stress. These were the moments when I wished I could call Dustin and say, "I need a little help."

I took a deep breath and called Alyssa, one of Lindell's babysitters and a college graduate who worked as a nanny for Ford's best friend, Noah. I asked her to pick Lindell up from preschool. Then I called Ford's and Owen's schools and told the secretary to tell the boys that I would be late—in fact, maybe even a couple hours late. Now that Lindell was with the babysitter, what was the rush? Maybe, I thought, I could even have a few moments to myself.

At home and all alone, I fell asleep. It was a deep sleep, the kind where you hear yourself snoring, and you don't care. My body sunk into the mattress; the cool side of the pillow soothed my tense jaw. Since Dustin left, I had taken to sleeping on his side of the bed. It made me feel closer to him. I used his alarm clock and bedside table, and at night, when I couldn't sleep, I stared at my empty side of the bed and listened to the creaks of the house settling.

The babysitter brought Lindell home at 2:00, and Melissa arrived at 2:30. I was disoriented and heavy after my nap. I rushed to comb my hair, straighten my clothes, and put on lip gloss. Downstairs, I heard Melissa talking to Lindell about preschool.

When we piled into her van at 3:00, we were already late to pick up Ford and Owen. I had said I would get them at 11:30 A.M.; now I was going to be even later than the regular school bell.

Ford and Owen glared at me as they got into Melissa's van and threw their backpacks onto the floor.

"You said you'd pick us up at eleven thirty," Ford said.

"And then it was 'a couple of hours'!" Owen folded his arms across his chest.

I motioned with my eyes toward Melissa, as if to tell the boys, "Say hello to our dinner guest, Mrs. Huston."

They sunk farther into their seats and scowled at me.

"Look, I'm really sorry about the mix-up," I said. "But can you please say hello to Mrs. Huston?"

Silence.

"Boys! Say hello to Mrs. Huston?"

"It's okay," Melissa whispered to me. She looked in the rearview mirror at Ford and Owen as she pulled out of the elementary school parking lot. "I'm really excited to show you where I work," she said. "Have you ever been to a food bank?"

No response.

"I hope you had a good day at school today," Melissa said.

Ford stared out the back window. Tears went down Owen's cheeks.

"You said you'd be there," Owen screamed, and he kicked the back of my seat.

"Owen!" I said.

"I still got out early," Lindell said. "So she didn't do everything wrong."

"Be quiet," Ford yelled at him.

"You got to go home at eleven thirty," Owen screamed at Lindell.

I sighed and looked at my lap.

Melissa whispered, "Reminds me of raising my kids."

When I glanced up at her, she winked.

As we drove across the bridge into Brewer, Ford complained that he was hungry. That's when I remembered: I hadn't packed any after-school snacks. We couldn't stop to get anything, either, or we'd be late for the food bank.

Ford and Owen moaned in the backseat as if someone was driving a nail into their back. "I'm so hungry," they whined.

"I had peanut butter crackers after school," Lindell said cheerfully.

Melissa chuckled softly. "You know, this is actually a really great example of why food banks are necessary," she said. The boys weren't listening, so she talked to me. "One in four children in Maine are hungry. Did you know that? It's hard to pay attention and learn when you're hungry. People get cranky—as we're witnessing now—and they misbehave. A lot of childhood behavior problems are actually due to hunger."

Ironic, I thought.

"Imagine going to work hungry," Melissa said. "Imagine going to a job interview hungry. A lot of social problems begin and end with food."

The wheels of the van crunched gravel as we pulled into the parking lot beside the warehouse of the food bank.

"I'm not going in," Ford said when the van stopped.

"You *are* going in." I unfastened my seat belt and turned to look at him.

"You picked us up late. You didn't bring snacks. And now,

when I'm starving, you want me to go into a warehouse full of food that I can't eat," Ford said.

"Don't say 'starving,'" I snapped. "You don't know what 'starving' is."

Ford stared at me without blinking. "I'm not going inside," he said.

I looked at Melissa, who was getting out of the van and seemed entirely accepting—or, maybe even oblivious to—the deteriorating behavior in the backseat.

She smiled warmly at me as a March breeze blew her brown hair.

I decided to take her lead.

Ford and Owen could be unhappy, angry, and obstinate, but they wouldn't ruin the day for the group.

Eventually Owen did come inside, but he complained and dragged his feet the whole way. Ford, unable to stay in the car alone, waited just outside the warehouse, in the lobby. Lindell skipped beside Melissa, occasionally holding her hand, and asked questions about the boxes of food stacked floor to ceiling:

"Is that a gigantic box of rice? Do you have juice boxes? What about cookies?" He loved the big walk-in freezer and the industrial-size scale he could step on.

I checked on Ford in the lobby. He paced back and forth with his hands shoved in his pants pockets.

Back at our house, around the wooden kitchen table, Melissa planned to make dinner for us using items someone might find at a food bank: macaroni and cheese, apple sauce, oven-baked chicken nuggets. Ford and Owen fought in the living room, and the house shook as their knees pounded the floor and their bodies landed on the living room sofa. At some point, Ford hit Owen in the back, and what once was boys being boys and letting off steam turned into world war three.

I sent them both to their rooms. Ford slammed his door.

Lindell cutting apples with help from Melissa Huston

Then the house was quiet again, except for Sparky going from room to room and Melissa and Lindell chopping carrots on the kitchen table.

After fifteen minutes, I went into Ford's room and sat on the edge of his bed. "Remember how you felt after the dinner with Mrs. Lloyd? Remember how you felt bad about the way you had acted?"

Ford didn't answer, but he didn't tell me to go away either, so I continued.

"Remember that feeling of being ashamed? Use it as a lesson for tonight's dinner. You don't want to feel that same way tomorrow. And there's still time to turn this around."

"Mom, you were supposed to be at the school at eleven thirty!"

"I know, Ford. I screwed up. And I'm sorry. But apologizing is all I can do. I can't go back and change anything."

Ford looked at me. His face was flat.

"Can we move forward now?" I asked.

Ford didn't answer.

"Please, come out in the kitchen and help Mrs. Huston cook," I said. "You'll feel better about it in the morning if you do."

In Owen's room, I was met with the same cold stares and resistance. I told Owen that it was his choice about whether or not to come out of his room. Then I returned to the kitchen to help Melissa. Soon after, Ford shuffled across the wood floor in his sock feet. "Can I help?" he mumbled.

Ford and Lindell helping Melissa Huston cut apples

"You sure can," Melissa said, her face lighting up. "Do you want to help me peel apples?"

Ford shrugged. "Sure, I guess so."

Owen never came out of his room. His loyalties were split. First, like Ford, he was angry at me for not picking him up on time. Then he was angry at Ford for hitting him in the back. Like a typical middle child, he had been bounced from one alliance to another, and now he was making a stand—by opting out.

A week later, early in the morning, before most of the boys' friends had turned on morning cartoons, we had our first Breakfast with the Smileys. It was a weekday, but local schools were not in session due to a teacher in-service workday. Still, the boys felt like they were bucking the system—and the routine—when we drove through Bangor in the dark on our way to help host Kiss 94.5's popular *Mike and Mike* morning radio show. We would be, according to our guests Mike Dow and Mike Elliot, live on air, broadcasting without a safety net.

"Really, you don't have an eight-second delay?" I asked, my throat suddenly turning dry.

We were already in the studio with padded walls. It was too late to back out. Lindell had made himself at home on one of the tall stools that gave him access to microphones hanging from the ceiling. He was singing what the boys call "Time Love" but is actually "Change of Time," by Josh Ritter.

"We're on a commercial break right now," Mike Dow said. "No one can hear him."

Lindell put his hands on either side of the microphone and crooned into it.

"But what about when you come back from break?" I asked. "I mean, this could go anywhere." I pointed at Lindell and wondered if potty humor was against FCC regulations.

Mike put up his hand to stop me. He was looking at the digital clock with bright red numbers behind me. He and the other Mike

Owen and Ford on air with Mike and Mike

quickly put their headphones over their ears again. Pieces of Mike Dow's feathery hair stood up beneath the headband.

"Kiss 94.5, today's best variety," Mike Elliot said in a deep, radio voice. "It's Mike and Mike, and it's seven forty-one. We've got a studio full of Smileys."

"Yeah, we have Sarah Smiley and her three boys," Mike Dow said. "We have Lindell, Owen, and Ford, and it's a real treat for us to have the family here because we've been following all of the Dinner with the Smileys events since early January."

Ford and Owen, each with headphones on their ears, watched with big eyes as the two Mikes clicked buttons and flipped switches on the board in front of them.

Mike Elliot said anticipation of our breakfast had moved him to song. He smiled mischievously and rolled his seat closer to the control panel with blinking lights. He flipped a switch, and the other Mike motioned for me to put on a pair of headphones that were looped around the arm of a microphone. Through the padding of the ears came a familiar tune, the smooth notes of Hall and Oates's "Sara Smile." Only it was Mike Elliot, not Daryl Hall singing, and the words weren't "Sara Smile," but "Sarah Smiley."

I gasped and laughed at the same time.

"They played this at my wedding," I said. I remembered dancing with Dustin, dressed in his navy dress whites, on the top floor of the Chamberlin Hotel in Virginia. I had laughed back then, too, thinking of my new last name. Dustin twirled me around

Sarah on air with Mike and Mike

so that my long, silk organza dress spun out in all directions. When he pulled me back close to him, he sang into my ear, "Sarah Smiley."

In the studio, Lindell screamed, "Mom, Mom, Mommy!"

"Um, are we still on air?" Ford asked.

Mike Elliot's version of "Sara Smile" faded out. Without thinking, I touched my wedding band with my right hand.

Mike and Mike gave the boys "total editorial control" over the program—even after I asked them, "Do you have any idea what might happen if you do that?"—and the rest of the morning program consisted of playing the *Star Wars* theme song multiple times and Owen, according to Mike Elliot, "putting the smack down" on any Justin Bieber news.

Juggling the three boys and their needs became a heavier task as the months went by. It weighed on me constantly, and I usually felt like I wasn't doing enough. To friends, I joked that I was playing Whac-A-Mole: as soon as one boy was settled and happy, another one popped up. But privately, I knew I was coming up short. The boys needed their dad.

Ford and Lindell drew attention naturally. Lindell had emerged as the clown of the family, Ford as the steady, logical older brother. When the kids played Nerf guns outside, Ford always had the biggest weapon, and if Lindell wasn't getting his way, he'd do something shocking, like pee on my hydrangeas or turn his eyes crossways. Owen, however, was the mediator, always giving up his gun for Lindell, or putting away dirty socks that weren't his so Ford wouldn't get into trouble.

Back in November, before Dustin left, he and I had anticipated that the deployment would be hardest on Ford and most confusing to Lindell. "But Owen," Dustin joked, "might need a few weeks to even realize that I'm gone." When Owen was a baby, we said that even if he were starving and Dustin had a cheeseburger in his lap, Owen would still choose to sit with me. Owen had never been overly affectionate with Dustin. So it just made sense that Dustin's absence might affect Owen least of all.

We were wrong.

One day, when we were driving in the car, Lindell said he would count to "one billion and one hundred."

"You've never successfully counted to fifteen," Ford said.

The two of them fought. Lindell cried.

Owen stared out the window.

Lindell said he wanted to marry me when he was "one billion and one hundred years old."

"You can't marry Mom because she's already married to Dad," Ford said. "Also, because she's your mom."

"But I love her in my soul," Lindell said.

I looked at him in the rearview mirror and smiled.

"Doesn't matter," Ford said. "That's gross."

Owen didn't say anything. He still stared out the window and held his hand against his mouth.

We went into the post office to mail Dustin a care package.

George, who had mailed many other packages to Dustin for me, asked, "How many more months?"

I couldn't stand to think about how much was left. It was easier to think of how much time had already past.

"We've finished four months. That's all I know," I said.

George smiled through his salt-and-pepper mustache. He smoothed an adhesive clear pocket onto the package and put the customs form I had filled out inside it.

"Hey, you should come to dinner with us," I said.

"Really?"

"Really! I think you should come to dinner."

"Well, maybe," he said. "I don't know. Let me think about it."

When the boys and I turned back around, a crowd of customers stared at us with their mouths open.

"Mom, did you just invite the postman to dinner?" Ford asked.

"What if the people behind us don't know about Dinner with the Smileys?"

He had a point.

We were driving again when Owen suddenly said, "It makes me feel kind of angry when I see other boys with their dads."

I wanted to slam on the brakes. I wanted to jump out of my seat and hug Owen. How could we have overlooked his suffering? How could we have thought he'd be the least affected?

Instead, I looked in the rearview mirror and asked, "Would you like to Skype with him alone in your room next time he calls?"

Owen looked out the window and shrugged. "Sure," he said. "I guess." Then he glanced sideways at his brothers.

That week, our twelfth guest was Josh Alves, a local graphic artist whose comic *Tastes Like Chicken* often appeared in the *Bangor*

Owen and graphic illustrator Josh Alves

Daily News. Since Dustin left, Owen had developed an interest in drawing. His doodles—of *Star Wars* characters, Sparky, and his brothers—were everywhere. He drew self-portraits, too, which always included fine details, like the brown, flat mole to the left of his nose. Cartoons seemed to be his favorite, however, and recently he was reading Garfield comic books in his bed at night.

We were outside on the back porch playing Pictionary with Josh, his wife, Amy, and their daughter, Lily, when Owen said, "Do you want to see my cartoons, Mr. Alves?"

"I'd love to," Josh said, his square glasses glistening in the afternoon sun.

Owen went inside and came back out with his DSi, a handheld game system. He used the stylus to flip through several pages and options on the screen. Then he pushed Play on a video. It was a black-and-white drawing of Dustin. Owen had set the drawing to animation, so that the mouth moved open and closed in a jerky, repetitive sort of way.

"Hello, I'm Cartoon Dad," the recording said. It was Owen speaking with a British accent. "I'm Owen's father and he turned me into a cartoon. Isn't that cool?"

"This is amazing," Josh said. "Did you do this all by yourself?"

"Um, yeah," Owen said. "Want to see Cartoon Owen?"

He flipped through several screens and options again.

Then there was a black-and-white drawing of a boy, also set to rudimentary animation and speaking in a British accent: "Hello, I'm Cartoon Owen. I'm Cartoon Dad's son. I've got this really nice dog, Sparky. He's my new dog. I got him on Halloween. My mum surprised me with him."

Josh and Owen talked about the details of the animation and how Owen had recorded the voices. The next morning, Owen organized all of his drawings into a folder. He asked me to upload

Cartoon Dad and Cartoon Owen on YouTube. And he spent the rest of the day perfecting his technique. He couldn't wait to show Josh his next set of drawings.

OUR LAST DINNER in March was with Owen's third-grade teacher, Lindsay Savage. Lindsay had been Ford's teacher as well two years before, so I kept getting confused: Was Lindsay here because of Ford or Owen? It was difficult for me to think of Lindsay as Owen's teacher, even though she had been, at this point, for six months already. Out of habit, I still thought of Lindsay as Ford's. It was the same habit that made me refer to Owen's shirts as "the one Ford used to wear" or his baseball glove as "Ford's old one."

Owen at dinner with his third-grade teacher, Lindsay Savage

Owen had had Ford's second-grade teacher, too. Every September it was the same question: Are you Ford Smiley's brother? And although this made me feel sorry for Owen, months later I would find out that it was Ford, not Owen, who wished he could trade places.

"No one ever asks me, 'Are you so-and-so's brother?'" Ford said one day in the car. "Owen's so lucky. Everyone already knows him."

I thought about that for a long time. For all of his largeness, Ford at times seemed to crave attachments most of all. There he was in center stage, when all he really wanted was for someone to connect him to someone else: "You're Owen's brother, aren't you?"

I liked to call Ford the "human weed whacker." He was in front of the siblings, catching with his face every wayward limb and weed that life threw in his path, and his younger brothers—or Owen especially—merely drafted off him. There weren't any weeds in Owen's face. Ford had already cleared the way for him.

And when I thought about it this way, I understood why Owen stayed so quiet. It was strategy: watch, listen, and observe.

Lindell's personality had also evolved since Dustin left, reminding me again of one of the most difficult things about having your spouse on deployment: Kids—especially little ones—change quickly. I knew Lindell wouldn't be the same when Dustin came home thirteen months later. His legs were getting longer. His knobby knees touched in the middle. And his shoes looked like giant weights on the bottom of stilts. His shoulders were getting thinner, his collarbone showing more definition and less baby fat. He didn't wear diapers to bed anymore, and he was beginning to read words like "up" and "open." Dustin left him as a baby (our last baby), but he would come home to a little boy.

As the baby, Lindell had learned that the best way to get attention and to be included was to do something outlandish and funny.

In my role as mother, I often had to discipline him for things like pulling his pants down. But later, when I described these situations to Dustin in an e-mail, I'd laugh to myself.

Others laughed, too.

When Jeff, the handyman who never sent me a bill while Dustin was deployed, came to fix a leaking window one day, he asked Lindell, "So where is your dad, bub?"

Lindell turned around and pointed at his butt.

Jeff looked at me and tried not to laugh. "What? Did he just—?"

"Dustin's in Djibouti," I said. "Get it?"

Dustin being in Africa made no sense to Lindell, even though we pointed it out on the map and looked at pictures of Djibouti online. But the idea of time difference is too much for a five-year-old. So (apparently) were camels, which Dustin told us outnumbered people in parts of Djibouti.

One night at dinner, Lindell said, "Mom, I believe in God, and I believe in the Easter Bunny, but I *do not* believe in camels."

I put down my fork and covered my mouth to keep the food from flying out. "Excuse me? Camels?"

"Yep. I don't believe in them."

"Why not?"

"Because I've never seen anything they've done."

I thought about that. Then Ford said, "But you've seen them at the zoo."

"I've never been to a zoo," Lindell said. Then looking at me: "Have I?"

My heart broke a little.

It was true. Lindell had never been to a zoo. We had been so deliberate about exposing Ford and Owen to as many things as possible—live shows, museums, zoos—but life had gotten busy by the time Lindell was born.

The summer before, we had taken the boys to the Harvard Museum of Natural History in Boston. On our way out, Ford said, "That was cool, but seeing all those stuffed animals isn't the same as seeing live ones at a zoo."

Lindell stopped in his tracks on the sidewalk. "Wait a minute," he said. "You mean there's a place where we can go see animals that aren't dead?"

And still, even after that, we hadn't gotten him to a zoo.

That night at dinner, I knew: We'd have a Dinner with the Smileys with a zookeeper. I just needed to find one.

Reading at an assisted living facility
as part of dinner number seventeen

CHAPTER SEVEN

April

One day in late March, Jenifer Lloyd, our guest from dinner number five, called and invited me to a "relaxing girls' night" at her home. A night away with grown-up women was exactly what I needed. Except I couldn't arrange a babysitter on such quick notice. I told Jenifer I'd have to decline but for her to please include me in the next gathering.

A couple of hours later, Jenifer called again. "I have a babysitter for you," she said. "And if it's okay with you, he'll be there at five thirty."

"Oh, you don't have to do that," I said. Then I stopped. "Wait, *he* will be here?"

"You need this, Sarah," Jenifer said. "His name is Buddy, and he will be there at five thirty."

Buddy was Jenifer's new son-in-law. He arrived promptly at 5:30 wearing a collared shirt, jeans, and old-school high-top sneakers. His hair was neatly cut but stylishly gelled and tousled in the front. I thought he couldn't be older than twenty-five.

"So guys, what are we going to do tonight?" Buddy asked, his deep-set blue eyes sparkling.

"Nerf guns!" the boys screamed.

"Perfect," Buddy said, smiling at me as I slipped out the door.

When I came home that night, after three wonderful hours of grown-up conversation, dozens of Nerf bullets littered the walkway. Guns were strewn across the front porch. A pizza box was still on the kitchen table. Each of the boys, still dressed in their clothes, was passed out, mouth open and drooling, on their bed.

Buddy became a regular sight at our house in April. He loved Nerf guns and had energy to play with the boys when I did not. This might have had something to do with Buddy waiting to begin graduate school at the University of Maine and me being about to finish. I spent most of my free time (when I wasn't teaching, going to class, or taking care of the boys) working on my master's thesis. Things like sleep, food, and exercise had, unfortunately, become low priorities. Ironically, my master's thesis topic centered on portrayals of motherhood in first-person narratives in national magazines and newspapers. It was as if I were writing myself into my own research project. The more my studies revealed to me what a fallacy the concept of "the perfect mother" is, the more I was living that reality.

But when Buddy was there, the kids, at least, were happy.

It was during this time that people often asked, "How are you doing it all?" and "Have you ever thought about stopping Dinner with the Smileys?"

I hated the first question, because, really, what is the alternative to doing it all? Keeping busy felt right.

I had not considered the second question. Not since February, at least. We had to eat dinner, so why not have a guest with us when we did it? Looking forward to the next Dinner with the Smileys was easier and more manageable than looking forward to Dustin coming home—in about a year. Also, I knew that people who asked me this question assumed Dinner with the Smileys was more formal than it actually was. They didn't realize I was giving our guests a paper towel to use for a napkin, and that some nights

I had nothing more than water to offer them to drink. It truly was dinner as it would have been if Dustin were home eating with us and there wasn't a guest in his seat. Dustin had never worried about napkins, matching dishes, or other formalities of a typical dinner party, so I never let myself believe that our guests would either. I didn't have the time to believe it.

Buddy, in fact, reminded me a lot of Dustin when we were young and newly married. Maybe it was Buddy's easygoing nature, his quick smile, or his ability to be all things to all people. But more likely it was his khakis-and-button-down-shirt style that masked a geeky, grown-up boy who can jerry-rig a Nerf gun. Buddy was calm and he kept perspective. Just like Dustin.

But there was something else that was special about Buddy, something that could not be discounted or overlooked: Like Dustin, he connected with Ford in a way I could not. Buddy understood when Ford made a pie chart of how he spends his day, and, as a budding engineer, Buddy suggested ways for Ford to make his graph more to scale. When Ford grew embarrassed that his brothers told half the neighborhood that his real name is Henry, Buddy helped him shake it off.

He asked, "How would you feel about being called Buddy?"

Ford smiled. "Buddy isn't a bad name."

"Ever seen Buddy the elf?"

"Hey, that's a great movie!"

"And Henry is a great name."

Buddy effortlessly moved between saving the world's problems with Ford, sticking up for Lindell on the Nerf-gun battlefield, and posing for Owen to draw his portrait. He stayed at the house even after I had paid him, sometimes just to continue hanging out with the boys, other times to help me bring in groceries. Lindell and Owen needed a playmate. Ford needed an advocate. And I needed help. Buddy checked every box.

I attribute most of April's easy beginning to Buddy. Also, I

The boys sitting at the WLBZ2 news desk

figured, it was the calm before the storm of May, when I would complete my master's thesis and finally graduate. Dinners fourteen through sixteen were relaxed and enjoyable. All of the children seemed to be getting into a routine. Buddy's leveling influence helped, and there were no major meltdowns or protests.

Dinner number fourteen was with Steve McKay, a local weatherman, and his co-worker Chris Facchini, the anchor of WLBZ2 news in Bangor. We joined Steve and Chris at the studio, where they gave the boys a tour and let them sit in on an actual newscast. I had to take Lindell out of the studio multiple times, because five-year-olds don't know how to whisper, but Ford and Owen watched the entire newscast and had many questions afterward over dinner at Pizzeria Uno:

"What if you can't read the cue cards?"

"What if you laugh on air?"

"How do you predict the weather?"

Ford was quiet and attentive during Steve's minilesson about weather, and he seemed intrigued by the idea that these two men made a living essentially out of talking.

Dinner number fifteen was with Lindell's other preschool teacher, Mrs. Bragdon, and just like during dinner number two with Mrs. O'Connor, Lindell was in love. He stared adoringly at Mrs. Bragdon and held her hand as he showed her around the front and side yards.

Before dinner, Mrs. Bragdon asked Lindell to sit with her on the couch. She had a cloth sack at her feet. "I have something very

Lindell with his preschool teacher, Mrs. Kristin Bragdon

important to show you," she said, and when she pulled a stuffed turtle out of the bag, Lindell gasped with delight.

"This is our class pet, Tommy the Turtle," Mrs. Bragdon said to the rest of us. She looked again at Lindell. "Monday is a holiday, and we don't have school. I was worried about Tommy being alone for three full days. Will you maybe let him stay the weekend with you?"

Lindell nodded enthusiastically. He reached out to grab Tommy, but Mrs. Bragdon pulled the turtle back and held him to her ear. "Wait, just a minute," she said, her eyes growing big and round. "Tommy has a secret for me." She pretended to listen to the turtle. "Uh . . . yep . . . okay . . ."

Lindell clapped his hands in excitement and jumped up and down on the living room couch.

"Tommy says that he is superexcited about his sleepover with you," Mrs. Bragdon said. "He wants to know if he can ride in your backpack to school Tuesday morning."

Lindell grabbed the turtle and hugged him to his chest. "I will even make sure his head sticks out of the backpack so he can breathe," Lindell said.

Ford whispered out of the corner of his mouth to Owen, "This is so weird."

Owen rolled his eyes and also pretended to be bored. It wasn't long, however, before both Ford and Owen wanted to get a closer look at Tommy.

The next week, when school was back in session, I had a regularly scheduled conference with Ford's teacher (and previous dinner guest), Mr. Bennett. I arrived early, so I waited in the hallway. Long sheets of paper made to look like the front page of a newspaper hung from a thin strip of corkboard on the wall running parallel to Mr. Bennett's room. They were part of an "All about Me" assignment in which the students made a front page about themselves. On the left-hand side was a box that read "Meet

My Hero," and beneath that: "Write a mini-article about a person who inspires you." Most of the students wrote about famous athletes or their mom or dad. I started at the beginning of the row of papers, scanning each one, looking for Ford's name.

I guessed that he had probably written about Dustin.

When I finally found his "newspaper," written with thick green marker, I was stunned. It read: "Owen, my brother, is my hero because he can make friends with anyone. I really admire that quality." Next to that, Ford had drawn a picture of Owen, with straight, long bangs hanging down into his eyes, and wearing his favorite color: green.

Dustin, I knew, might take issue with Ford's interpretation of the word "hero." To Dustin, heroes are soldiers who jump on a grenade to save their comrades, or firemen who rush into a burning building to save a family. Dustin bristles when people use the term too loosely and without consideration. But the dictionary actually gives a much more general definition of the word: a mythological figure, an admirable person, the object of one's devotion. In Ford's relatively small world, chances are, he isn't likely to face a grenade or tragedy (God willing). But he can still have heroes. The fact that his is Owen gave me chills.

After my parent-teacher conference with Mr. Bennett in his Red Sox shrine—floor-to-ceiling memorabilia, posters, figurines, books, old programs, and baseballs—our conversation naturally turned to baseball.

"Is Owen trying out for Little League this yeah?" Joe asked in his thick accent.

"Of course," I said. "I just hope he makes it."

"Ford's on the Lions, right? They had a pretty good run last season, eh?"

"Yes, so if Owen makes the team, he'll be on the Lions, too. But without Dustin here to help him get ready . . ." My voice trailed off.

I couldn't even imagine the possibility of Owen not making the team. What would I do? Would he ever get over it?

"Well, there's always next year," Joe said. He smiled sympathetically and the crow's-feet around his eyes radiated from behind his round glasses. "Quite the tribute Ford wrote to Owen outside there, eh?" Joe nodded toward the hallway where the newspapers hung.

I could only smile back. Speaking would make tears come.

I had been taking the boys to a Little League batting clinic at Bangor High School every Sunday, and so far, Owen wasn't hitting very well. He looked like a toothpick beneath the wobbly batter's helmet, and the heavy metal bat seemed to actually move him through the air instead of the other way around. I took videos on my iPhone and shared them with Dustin through e-mail.

He wrote back: "Owen needs a lighter bat," and, "tell him to get his feet farther apart."

When I took the boys to the local sports equipment store to get Owen a different bat, I felt like I had stepped into a foreign land. I had no idea that baseball bats have different weights and are measured using a term called "drop."

"This is the bat Owen needs," Ford said, pointing to a sixty-dollar blue-and-black metal bat.

"Are you sure? I mean how do we know?" I scratched my head.

"I'm telling you this is the bat," Ford said.

"I don't know. I wish Dad were here."

Lindell came around the corner with a bag of M&M's. "Can I get these, Mom?"

"Not today, Lindell—"

"Mom," Ford said.

"But they are getting things," Lindell whined.

"Just a minute, Lindell." I took the bag of M&M's from his hand and gave him my iPhone to play with.

"Mom," Ford said again. He was tugging on my sleeve.

"Ford, how do we know? What if we get the wrong thing?"

"Mom! Dad taught me all about this," he said, more exasperated now. "Why won't you just listen to me? This is the bat Owen needs."

"But what does it mean by 'drop'?"

Ford rolled his eyes. "Get him this bat, Mom."

I sighed and added the bat to our shopping cart.

"Now he needs a cup," Ford said.

I looked at Owen.

He smiled and shrugged.

We turned down another aisle where rows upon rows of athletic supporters hung from metal hooks. They were sized "peewee" to "extra large." I wasn't sure how much identity the boys had rolled up in their, um, parts yet, but I figured I'd be safe rather than sorry. In the female world, it's always best to assume someone is size medium. So I said, "You probably need, like, a medium, or something?" I picked up a plastic cup that was about the size of a cantaloupe.

"Are you kidding me?" Ford laughed. "You think he can wear that thing?"

"I don't know. What—"

Owen pointed to the far end of the aisle. "I'm probably more like a peewee, Mom."

"Owen has a peewee. Owen has a peewee," Lindell sang.

As I paid for our items, Ford and Owen plotted behind me. "It's going to be so cool to have you on the team," Ford said.

"But what if I don't make it?" Owen asked.

"Dude, you're totally going to make it." Ford draped his arm over Owen's bony shoulders and gave him a thumbs-up with the other hand.

Fittingly, our sixteenth Dinner with the Smileys was with my university colleague and baseball historian Dr. Scott Peterson. We met at a University of Maine baseball game to eat hot dogs and drink soda. The weather was getting warmer—although there still was a cool spring breeze—and the boys were sporting last year's summer clothes, which were too small and short.

Little League tryouts were the day before.

"How'd Owen do?" Dustin had asked me over Skype the previous night.

"It's hard for me to say," I told him. "I don't know how to judge, but he didn't make contact with the ball, and a lot of the kids were throwing harder and faster than he was."

"Is Ford practicing with him in the backyard?"

"Every day. And I've been taking them to the Little League clinic, too."

Dustin nodded. "If he doesn't make it this year, tell him I'll be there next year to help him get ready."

Owen and Ford practicing baseball in the backyard

Ford and Owen with Dr. Scott Peterson, a baseball historian,
at University of Maine baseball game

At the University of Maine game, I chased Lindell up and down the bleachers and to and from the concession stand while Owen and Ford huddled around Dr. Peterson. During the seventh inning, they followed him to the media box, where they were able to announce hitters on deck. Dr. Peterson taught Ford how to keep score and gave him his own score-sheet pad and pencil. Ford never turns down a hot dog or root beer, but on that day, with the sun making his cheeks pink and the breeze blowing through his thick hair, he took one bite of his lunch and spent the rest of the afternoon chewing on the end of the pencil while he watched the game and kept score.

Between innings, Dr. Peterson played catch with all three boys in a patch of grass behind the bleachers. The thump of the baseball hitting their gloves brought back warm memories of Dustin being home.

"Your mom says you play for the Lions in Little League," Dr. Peterson said to Ford.

Ford caught the ball in his glove and threw it back. "Yep, and Owen tried out for the team yesterday."

"How'd you do?" Dr. Peterson threw the ball to Owen.

"Not too good," Owen said. "I don't think I'll make it. Maybe next year when my dad is here to help me." He threw the ball back.

"What position do you play, Ford?" Dr. Peterson said, throwing the ball again.

"Mostly second," Ford said. "But this year I hope they'll let me pitch."

Dr. Peterson rolled a grounder to Lindell, who pretended to be unsteady on his feet as he said, "Whoa! Whoa! Whoa!" and dove into the grass. The ball went past him. "Oh, man!" Lindell said, banging his fist on the ground.

When we got home that night, the light was blinking on the answering machine. I pushed Play and listened: "Owen, give me a call when you get a chance tonight. This is Coach Boyce from the Lions."

My heart sank.

Did his voice sound positive or negative? Did it seem like he was calling with good news or bad news? Should I erase the message? Let Owen hear it?

I called Ford into the kitchen, and we listened to the message together while Owen was in the shower.

Ford grimaced. "It sounds like bad news. I mean, if Owen had made the team, wouldn't Coach have told him that on the message?"

We played it back again.

With each replaying, the coach's voice seemed more and more full of bad news. When Owen got out of the shower and was dressed in his pajamas, I told him that Coach Boyce had called.

"What did he say?" Owen asked. His face was freshly cleaned but pale. Drips of water ran down his cheeks from his sideburns.

"Just that he wants you to call him back," I said.

I handed Owen the phone.

Ford slapped Owen on the back. "Remember, buddy, if you don't make it this year, you'll try again next year."

Ford and I sat next to each other on the couch while Owen paced back and forth, waiting for Coach Boyce to answer. Ford chewed on his thumbnail. We listened to Owen's side of the conversation, and I watched his face for clues: "Yes, this is Owen . . . My mom said you left a message . . . I'm doing good. We just got back from a University of Maine baseball game . . . Yeah . . . uh-huh . . . Okay . . . Yes, I do . . . Uh-huh . . . I really want to play baseball . . . So, did I make it? Or—"

Owen turned around to look at us. His eyes brightened as a smile spread across his face. I put my arm around Ford's shoulder and looked up at the ceiling.

"So I made it?" Owen said on the phone. "I really made it? I'm on the Lions?"

Ford jumped up and hugged Owen. "You made it!" he yelled.

I could hear Coach Boyce's voice coming through the receiver now. He was laughing as he talked. "Okay, I'll see you guys next Thursday for practice. Have a good night."

Before Owen went to bed, he asked to use my computer to e-mail Dustin. He could hardly wait for his dad to hear the news.

By 10:00 P.M., Owen still lay awake in his bed, unable to sleep. I was across the hall in the living room.

"Did Dad write back yet?" Owen called out to me.

"Not yet, honey. It's really early in the morning over there."

"Okay."

A half hour later: "Did he write back now?"

"Not yet, Owen. Get some sleep. It's a school day tomorrow."

"Will you wake me up if he writes me during the night?"

"Yes."

Dustin's pride and excitement was evident in his e-mail reply the next day. "Being on a team together will be a bonding experience," he wrote. "Get lots of pictures for me."

That Thursday night, I dropped Ford and Owen off at baseball practice, and then Lindell and I took Sparky for a walk. When we came back to the fields two hours later, the rest of the team, including Owen, was practicing in the batting cages with the assistant coach, but Ford and Coach Boyce were on the diamond, Coach Boyce at home plate, Ford on the pitcher's mound.

"Oh my gosh," I said to myself. "He's going to pitch."

I thought back to the days when Ford was the one who looked like a toothpick beneath the batter's helmet, and the time not too long ago when I dropped Ford off for his first Lion's practice and he ran back to the car and said, "I don't think that's my team. Look at how big those kids are." Now he was the big kid.

My big kid.

On the pitcher's mound.

A few weeks later, after Mr. Bennett had sung the national anthem and announced the starting lineups over the loudspeaker, Ford jogged out to the pitcher's mound. Mr. Bennett's voice echoed through the fields: "Pitching for the Lions is Foooooord Smiley."

It was 2:00 A.M. in Djibouti, but Dustin had set his alarm to wake him up anyway. I stood next to the chain-link fence and held my iPhone so that the camera lens was pointed directly through one of the holes of the metal. I turned on Skype.

Before the first pitch, Ford looked over at me. I gave him a thumbs-up. Through the iPhone, Dustin called out to him, "I'm here. I can see you, Ford."

Ford threw the ball.

. . .

IN LATE APRIL I had planned a Dinner with the Smileys with our next-door neighbor Gloria. Gloria was one of the first people I met when we moved to Maine. She was outside on her front stoop the day I came with a Realtor to look at what would eventually be our new home. Her white hair, perfectly styled in gentle waves, shone in the June sunlight. Her arms were folded across her small, slender frame.

She called out across the yard, "It's a lovely house. Sad to see it vacant."

I walked down the sidewalk and up her short lawn.

"Hi, I'm Sarah Smiley," I said, holding out my hand.

Gloria's hand was moist and cool. I could feel the bones of her fingers in mine.

"I'm Gloria," she said, fiddling now with the top button of her collared shirt. She sort of danced in place, moving her weight from one foot to the other, making her appear younger than the wrinkles around her eyes revealed. "Do you have kids?" she asked, smiling.

I told her that I have three young boys, ages seven, five, and eighteen months. "Are you ready for some rowdy boys on the street?" I teased.

Over time, Gloria became something of a substitute grandmother for the boys. With their actual grandparents living in Washington State and Virginia, Ford, Owen, and Lindell were in need of the gentleness and patience of a grandmother.

Gloria, then in her mideighties and a longtime widow, always sent the boys birthday cards—through the mail. She put the stamped cards in her mailbox, no more than fifty feet from our front door, and the next day they would show up in the silver box hanging from our front porch. Each year, Gloria closed up her house and left for Halloween, but not without bringing the boys a sack of candy first. And when Ford was sad that he didn't have extended family to attend his second-grade performance as Thomas Edison, Gloria and our other elderly widower neighbor, Earle, then ninety-two, came and sat in the front row.

Over the years, Gloria grew used to my boys and their friends shooting dart guns through her hanging laundry, running across her grass and arriving at her back door with a plate full of cookies. She always waved out the window to us as we walked past on our way to school.

On warm summer days, Lindell sat with Gloria on her front porch, or he watched her plant flowers in the yard. Gloria had seen Lindell grow from a baby just learning to walk to a preschooler who pedaled a Big Wheel down the sidewalk with a football helmet on his head. Her small cape with the light-blue front door was always "Gloria's house" to Ford, Owen, and Lindell.

Gloria went to an assisted-living facility shortly after Dustin left for his deployment. I told the boys we'd go to visit her soon. In fact, the facility's events coordinator had asked me to do a reading for the other residents who read my column in the local newspaper. I decided to combine the reading with a Dinner with the Smileys with Gloria. The coordinator said I could read for about thirty minutes in the community room, and then the boys and I would join Gloria for dinner.

We planned for late January or February. But I had to reschedule—twice. Things—school, basketball, dog obedience class—kept getting in the way. Other dinners seemed more pressing, as those guests had limited nights available, and, well, Gloria wasn't going anywhere.

Finally, we settled on April 22 for the reading and dinner. It would be our seventeenth Dinner with the Smileys. The week before, I called to confirm our visit with the events coordinator. She told me that the residents were excited about the "author visit" and that word had just gone out in the community newsletter.

Then she said, "You're supposed to have dinner with your neighbor Gloria afterward, correct?"

"Yes," I said. "Is that still okay?"

There was a long pause on the other end.

Then finally the woman said, "You know that Gloria is no longer with us, right?"

"She's back home? I haven't seen—"

"No, I'm sorry. She passed away several weeks ago."

I breathed in deeply.

I wasn't sure how much the boys would understand about Gloria's passing. When I first told them, they were silent. Then they went back outside to play, and this confused me even more. *Did they not care? Didn't they have questions?* None of them talked about it again the rest of the evening, and I was awkward and unsure about bringing it up. *Was it too much to understand?*

I didn't know what to do about the scheduled Dinner with the Smileys, which was one week away at this point. It didn't seem right to replace our seventeenth dinner guest with someone else. Plus, I was scheduled to read in the community room. *Could I just read and leave? Should the boys go with me? Should I go alone?*

This was the boys' first personal, memorable experience with death. I knew my response was critical to their understanding and acceptance. Their great-grandmother and great-grandfather had died a few years before, but the boys had been too far away from them to truly understand. They had only visited their great-grandparents a handful of times. Gloria was someone who was very much a part of their recent daily lives. Even Lindell had vivid memories of her.

I struggled with how to help them.

Then, the day after I told the boys that Gloria had died, we were driving in the car past a cemetery. From the backseat, Ford said, "Do you think we could go see Gloria's grave on Sunday, since we won't be having dinner with her?"

"And take flowers?" Owen added.

I looked at them in the rearview mirror. "I think that is an excellent idea," I said.

Rows of graves dotted the hilly cemetery outside the car window like the ripples of a sheet blowing in the wind. The boys' questions came all at once as we passed by:

"Mom, will we see Gloria again?"

"What will happen to her house?"

"Did she die because she was sick, or because she was old?"

"Should we have done dinner with her sooner?"

Now that the conversation was open, the boys and I, together, came up with a plan to honor and remember Gloria as our seventeenth dinner guest. We decided that on Sunday we would visit Earle ("Because you never know when he might die, too," Owen said), now ninety-four and living across town with his daughter, then find Gloria's grave and do the reading at the assisted living facility as planned.

We decided not to stay for dinner.

We hadn't seen Earle since he left his home nine months earlier. His face was rounder than I remembered, but his daughter, Jane, told me it was a side effect from his medication for pneumonia. The fullness almost made him seem younger, but when he stood up from his chair, he was bent over like a question mark. He shuffled his feet to walk, and he was dependent on a cane. Considering that Earle was still manning a sailboat when he was ninety years old, I thought he was doing relatively well.

The boys became instinctively gentler next to Earle. Lindell pretended to pour tea for him using a tea set that belonged to Jane's granddaughter. Earle sipped the imaginary drink from a pink plastic cup that shook in his trembling hands. He asked Ford and Owen about Little League.

Earle's son-in-law, Dan, showed us a slide show of Earle's life, beginning with grainy, black-and-white photos from 1918. It was hard to imagine that the plump toddler with a pageboy haircut in the photographs was our elderly neighbor who has been mostly bald since we first met him. Then there was a picture of a teenage Earle standing on a dock, one foot propped up on a sailboat. His young face showed a glimmer—almost like a shadow—of his face as we now knew it. The narrow eyes and thin nose were recognizable, but in the photograph, his skin was tight, his shoulders broad and muscular.

"That actually looks like you," Owen said. "I can see you in that one."

One by one, images from a life flipped past us. A baby boy first grew tall and muscular, then shrunk down again and lost his hair. I wondered what Earle's mom was like. She had surely loved her little boy as much as I love my boys. She was also just as surely dead for many years—if not decades—by now. What would she think of this man, her son, and his long life? I imagined there was a time when she was like me, consumed by the details of daily life: lunches, baths, bedtime stories, laundry. She had probably asked herself, "When will it end?" Maybe she was tired like me. Did she cry when Earle left home? Could she ever have imagined how long he'd live?

I looked across the room at my boys sitting next to Earle on Dan and Jane's leather sofa. The boys' cheeks still had various amounts of baby fat in them. Their skin was pink and virtually without blemish. Ford and Owen's mouths were full of half-grown permanent teeth and loose baby teeth. Wisps of Lindell's baby-fine hair were blowing in the soft breeze of the overhead fan. All of them had their mouths open as they watched the slideshow. Suddenly, the fleetingness of it all overwhelmed me, and I swallowed back emotion in my throat.

It was cold and pouring rain when we said good-bye to Earle. We headed back through town, across the Kenduskeag Stream, which was rushing with water and melted snow, to the cemetery

Dinner with Earle Pierce, ninety-four-year-old neighbor

to find Gloria's grave. From the gravel parking lot, I looked out across the hundreds of graves scattered over the hillside. They looked like they were riding a wave. My hair was soaked and strands stuck to the sides of my face. Rain pelted my wool sweater, making it even heavier.

"So, let's go find it," Ford said loudly. He was hunched over to protect himself from the driving rain.

I sighed and looked out over the hillside again. Then I looked at the cemetery office and the CLOSED sign hanging in the window. That's when I realized I didn't know where Gloria's grave was.

"Boys, I hate to say this," I said, "but I don't think there's any way to find Gloria's grave today. We'll have to come back when—"

"Mom, we have to find it!" Owen said.

"You just have to look," Lindell said.

The boys were soaked, too. Their clothes clung to their bodies. Lindell ran to the muddy, wet grass and began searching tombstones. "Maybe it's one of these," he yelled back at us.

Owen ran over to read the names engraved on the stone.

Now that I had Ford alone, I spoke with urgency, "Really, honey, I don't think we can find it today. It would take hours. Let's come back when the office is open."

Ford looked resigned and nodded. He jogged over to his brothers, talked to them for a minute, and then all three came back to get into the van. Owen scowled at me as he passed.

The assisted-living residents were already gathered in front of the piano in the community room when the boys and I came in with our wet shoes and matted hair. I brought my second book, *I'm Just Saying . . .* , which is a collection of columns I wrote during the years that Ford and Owen were babies and then toddlers. Each of the boys, except Lindell, who couldn't read yet, picked a favorite column to read aloud to the residents. Many of the residents fell asleep in the chairs, their chins tucked into their chests.

Owen had chosen to read a column titled "Owen Drew a Masterpiece . . . on his Etch A Sketch," which is about younger brothers and how they are oftentimes overshadowed by their older siblings.

Owen read aloud:

Owen rarely gets his own clothes, just a drawer full of hand-me-downs. And as soon as Owen can rightly brag about accomplishing some feat (learning his "left" and "right," coloring in the lines, putting on his own pants), Ford has learned something seemingly "better" (reading the phone book and naming the 16th president) . . .

Owen stumbled over some of the words and nervously wiped his nose with the palm of his hand.

Owen was a late walker and talker, something that my husband,
Dustin, and I worried about. But the doctors said that Owen
had just one problem and his name begins with "F." Owen
didn't need to walk or talk; Ford did it for him.

Ford smiled at the audience. Then he quickly came to Owen's
aid when Owen stopped and pointed at one of the next few
words.

"Coaxed," Ford told him, looking over Owen's shoulder. "It
means to talk someone into something."

Owen continued reading:

Later, I was going through old photographs and noticed that
Owen's third birthday party was almost entirely overshadowed
by Ford and his friends. There was only one picture of Owen
alone, and no pictures of him standing next to his cake. Just a
picture of Ford standing next to Owen's cake.

A woman with white hair pulled into a bun winked at me and
smiled. The woman to her left snored into her chest.

When Owen was nearly to the end of the column, he looked
over at me with watery eyes and said quietly, "This kind of makes
me feel like I will cry."

Inside, I *was* crying.

We had not planned to stay for dinner, but as we were walking out of the lobby, a man, named Frank, with a rounded back
and thin gray hair stopped me. He held on to my arm and whispered, "Will you have dinner with us? There is room at my
table."

I looked at the boys. I had already asked a lot of them, and they
had been exceptionally patient and considerate all day. Was I on
borrowed time? I couldn't imagine anything worse than three

tired children melting down in the middle of the assisted-living dining room.

Frank's wife, Anita, stood beside him and held on to his arm for support. She smiled at me and said, "We could do some sorting. Would you like that? We can sort together."

Owen was standing beside me with his hands in the pockets of his khaki pants. He looked at Anita and Frank, shrugged his shoulders, and said, "Sure, what's for dinner?"

Frank turned and motioned for us to follow him. At first, Anita followed, too. Then she went in the other direction. While Frank pulled out my chair for me, Anita fluttered from table to table, circled back to the bathroom, opened the door, closed it without going inside, visited more tables, and started to go up the large staircase in the center of the room.

"Excuse me," Frank said. He shuffled over to Anita, where he looked even more bent next to her tall, straight body and head full of dyed-black hair. When Frank took Anita's arm, she looked surprised. Then she started singing loud enough for everyone in the room to hear.

Before Frank came back to the table, I quickly whispered to the boys, "Anita appears to have memory problems. She will say and do things that seem strange. Just go along with it and don't take anything personally."

The boys nodded with stunned, slightly worried, faces.

Frank led Anita to our table and held out her chair so she could sit down.

"Anita, this is the Smiley family," Frank said in a quiet, shaking voice. "They are going to have dinner with us tonight."

"Do you like to sing?" Anita asked Owen, who was sitting on her right.

"Um, I guess so. Well, not really," he said. "Sometimes."

Anita hummed a song and twirled her hands in the air. She

started to get out of her seat again, but Frank gently put an arm across her lap to keep her still.

"We'll be married sixty years next month," Frank said, "but she doesn't remember a thing. Nothing."

"I need to sort and file some things," Anita said. "Would you like to sort with me? We could do it tomorrow."

She was looking at Frank.

He just smiled at her and said, "Sure, we'll do that tomorrow."

The waitstaff pushed rolling carts full of dinners in covered dishes through the room. Nothing looked especially warm. At least no steam trailed behind the carts. I hoped the boys wouldn't complain about the selection: pasta with alfredo sauce, garden salad, and chocolate pudding. Our waitress offered to make grilled cheeses if the boys needed them. I was surprised when they didn't. Anita mashed her pasta between her hands and painted the table with her fingers covered in sauce.

Owen watched her out of the corner of his eye. He didn't touch his dinner. Every now and then, he pulled the copy of *I'm Just Saying . . .* out of my purse and read quietly to himself.

While we ate pudding, Anita continued to play with her pasta. She held out her gooey fingers to Owen and tried to touch his cheek. "Would you like a bite, dear?" she said. For a full minute, I didn't breathe. Owen had never been around anyone with Alzheimer's.

Owen looked at Anita's fingers, but not at her. He wiped at his nose with the palm of his hand. Then he said, "I'm okay, but thank you."

When Anita said, "Alright then, dear, you just let me know," Owen looked at her face and smiled.

I asked Frank what, if anything, Anita remembers.

"The only thing she knows is that I'm her best friend," Frank said.

Frank and Anita used to live in the same room at the facility, but within the last few months, as Anita's disease progressed, she was moved to a hall at the other end of the building. Twice a day, Frank goes down to visit with her.

"Sometimes she's glad to see me," he said. "Sometimes not." He smiled and shrugged his shoulders.

Anita asked us if we wanted to see her home. Frank wondered aloud which "home" she was talking about. "She gets confused," he said.

"I'll go see her home," Owen said to Frank.

So we pushed our padded dining room chairs away from the table and followed Anita down a long, carpeted corridor.

At one point, Anita turned around, put her hands on her head and said, "I'm here, but I need to get to there."

"Yes," Frank said, guiding her with her elbow. "Let's go, dear."

"But I'm here. Where is there?" Anita asked. Her forehead was suddenly wrinkled, her brow furrowed.

"Follow me," Frank said.

"We're going to your home, remember?" Owen said softly to Anita. "You invited me there."

We arrived at a door with a combination lock and alarm. "You'll have to get through the door fast," Frank said, "or the alarm will go off. Let's 'em know when someone gets lost."

The alarm beeped steadily as we all shuffled through the doorway. Anita's room was toward the end of the hall and on the right. It was a lot like a hotel room. She had a nice view of the courtyard and a cluster of bird feeders there. Pictures from Frank and Anita's wedding, plus their five children, lined the wall. It was as if Anita's entire life had been condensed and consolidated into a single room. She had a bed, a television, and a desk. And a wall of photographs that meant nothing to her now.

We said our good-byes to Anita in the hallway outside her room. When she realized all of us were leaving, she looked at Frank, her extraordinarily round blue eyes searching his face, and said, "You'll come back for me? To take me home?"

Frank said, "Yes. Tomorrow."

Then to me he whispered, "She won't remember by then."

I could tell by the way Frank walked us all the way out into the parking lot and held on to my elbow as we said good-bye that he didn't want us to leave. Maybe he didn't want to go back to his empty room, just like I didn't want to go back to our empty house that day after Dustin left. Sure, Frank could go to Anita's room and be in her company, but the essence of her wasn't there. My husband, on the other hand, was physically gone, unable to sit with me at dinner, but we had a life and family together that we both still remember. Didn't that make him less far away?

Over the years, I've found that my children are more open to conversations in the car than they are anywhere else. Maybe it's because we are all looking forward, not at each other. Maybe they forget I'm there. In any case, as we drove away from the assisted-living facility, the boys' questions came one after another:

"So Anita totally doesn't remember being married to Frank?" Owen asked.

"Apparently not," I said. "It's sweet though how she thinks he's her best friend, isn't it?"

"Why was she talking like a kid?" Ford said.

"Maybe she feels like a kid."

"Does she think she is a little girl again?" Lindell asked.

"Maybe. I don't know that much about Alzheimer's."

The car was quiet for a minute.

I felt horribly unprepared and uneducated to answer the boys' questions.

Ford stared out the back window. "When we went to Anita's room, she kind of talked to us like she was our mom," he said. "Do you think she was thinking about her own kids when they were little?"

Again, I didn't have answers.

I told Ford that mothers probably always carry their mothering instincts, even through disease and old age. "Mother" becomes part of our identity.

"It's interesting, isn't it," I said. "Anita's identity as a mother is still with her even after she's forgotten that she's a wife."

"Will you ever get Alzheimer's, Mom?" Owen asked. "I'd be sad if you didn't remember me."

"If I get Alzheimer's, it will be many, many years from now," I said. "You'll be grown men with families of your own."

They were all staring out windows now.

I looked back at Owen's profile and smiled. "Will you visit me when I'm in a nursing home, Owen?"

"Yeah, but what if you don't remember me?"

"Then just sit down at the table and tell me you're there for Dinner with the Smileys. Tell me that you're dinner guest number seventeen—my favorite number."

"Um, Mom, that's not really funny," Owen said.

That night, after the kids went to bed, I sat down to write a message to Dustin. I wrote about random things: our wedding song, our trip across country when I was pregnant, how we almost didn't make it to the hospital when I was in labor with Lindell, that time in Las Vegas when I lost my purse, the day he got promoted, our first date, our first kiss.

He happened to be online and wrote back: "Yes, I remember everything. And I love you."

And when I went to bed that night, somehow, he didn't feel quite so far away.

IN JANUARY, ONCE I knew that Dinner with the Smileys had become a *thing* and that we would actually go through with fifty-two dinners, I made myself a note: Invite R2-D2 and the conductor of *Star Wars Live*, the symphony. The boys wanted to invite George Lucas, too, but so far, I hadn't figured out a way to do that. R2-D2 and someone from the symphony would have to suffice.

Ford's knowledge of *Star Wars* surpasses that of even most adult fanatics. He's read every book about histories of the characters before *Episode I* and after *Episode VI*. One time, Dustin's friend challenged Ford to a game of *Star Wars* trivia. "Careful," Dustin said. "Ford even knows things they don't show you in the movies."

For the past two years, our lives had nearly revolved (not an exaggeration) around *Star Wars*. Ford was either talking about the movies at the dinner table or humming the theme song while he played catch in the backyard. Light sabers of various colors and styles were strewn across our front yard. We had a life-size, talking Darth Vader in our basement and a plastic tub full of *Star Wars* costumes from previous Halloweens. Indeed, Ford and Owen had not been anything but *Star Wars* characters for the past seven Halloweens. Even I had a wool cap with Princess Leia's buns.

In 2008, the touring symphony experience called *Star Wars Live*, which included not only music from the movies, but an extensive exhibit of memorabilia and costumes, came to Boston and played with the Boston Pops. We took the boys and sat behind an audience member dressed like Jabba the Hutt. It was the boys' first experience at a symphony, and what an experience it was! There was a laser show, pictures from the movie, and the original score playing so loud, it vibrated in our bones. The evening was even emceed by Anthony Daniels, the actor who played C-3PO.

When I found out that Lucas Richman, the conductor of the Bangor Symphony Orchestra, had also conducted *Star Wars Live* in various locations around the country, I knew he had to be our guest for Dinner with the Smileys. So for dinner number eighteen, we met Lucas at the red-carpeted and velvet-draped Collins

Center for the Arts at the University of Maine to watch an orches-tra rehearsal. Dressed in black and sweating under the hot lights of the stage, Lucas stood on a wooden box and led the musicians through their latest piece. The boys and I sat in the thick, padded seats of the empty concert hall, and, to our surprise, once we were settled, we spotted the mother of a boy on Ford and Owen's base-ball team. She was playing the cello.

"It's Mrs. Solomon!" Owen whispered to me. "She's playing the . . . the . . . What is that?"

"The cello," I whispered back.

The arms and elbows of the orchestra members were like a well-choreographed dance. Together they rose and fell with the notes of the music. Marisa winked at us as her long fingers moved up and down her instrument.

When rehearsal was finished, Lucas invited us onstage to meet some of the musicians. Marisa helped Lindell play "Twinkle, Twin-kle Little Star" on her cello. Ford stood on Lucas's box and moved his hands in the air like he was conducting. In a separate room off the side of the stage, Lucas banged out the *Star Wars* theme song on the black-and-white keys of a piano while the boys hummed along.

A few of the musicians and Lucas joined us for dinner at a nearby local restaurant and icon called Pat's Pizza. Marisa's eleven-year-old son, whose name is coincidentally also Lucas, met us there. He and Ford and Owen sat at the end of the long table and talked about baseball while they ate, long strands of mozzarella cheese making bridges between the pizza and their mouths.

Lucas (the boy, not the conductor) came for a sleepover that night, and in the days and weeks and months that followed, a wonderful friendship between Lucas and Ford unfolded.

Two days after our dinner with Lucas Richman, I was driving home from the University of Maine on a sunny, blue-sky day and thinking about how relatively easy things had been for us, despite how it felt earlier. Ford seemed more settled and was making new

Grammy Award–winning composer Lucas Richman
playing piano for Lindell

---

friends. We had a growing support network and we rarely lacked for something to do. I couldn't remember the last time we were lonely at dinner. We were blessed indeed.

Then I walked in the front door, and the whole day changed.

My thesis writing and teaching often kept me at the university past Lindell's 11:30 dismissal time at preschool. So three days a week, Alyssa brought Lindell home from school and stayed with him until I got back at 2:00. Lindell called it his "Alyssa time."

When I came into the house that day, Lindell was sitting on the couch with a book. Alyssa was next to him, her long, slender legs bent sideways and tucked into the cushions. She had her arm around Lindell.

"Hello! What a beautiful day," I said, throwing down my bags.

Alyssa has large round cheekbones, and her dark brown hair falls perfectly from the small widow's peak on her forehead and down around her face. She tried to smile, but it was the kind of smile that seems forced. She stood up and walked toward me with her bare feet. "You have some water in your basement," she said.

"Water?"

"Actually, quite a bit of it. Do you want me to stay for a bit while you go look?"

I still didn't understand. Or maybe I didn't want to understand. In any case, I knew Alyssa had to go pick up Noah's brother. She couldn't stay. Not really.

"No, that's fine," I said. "I'll go check it out in a little bit. Right now I just want to snuggle with this little guy." I kicked off my shoes, went to the couch and tickled Lindell.

Alyssa took her keys from the black chest next to the front door. "Okay, well, just call me if you need anything," she said. "And you might want to look at the basement sooner rather than later."

When Alyssa closed the door behind her, everything started to sink in.

Water. In the basement.

"I'm going to go take a peek at the basement," I told Lindell. "You just stay right here."

"Okay, Momma," Lindell said, still looking at his book.

The basement door creaked as I opened it. The familiar smell of oil and damp cardboard boxes filled my nose. I pulled a chain hanging from the exposed light fixture and bent down to see past the sides of the stairwell. An empty laundry basket floated past. A bedroom slipper, soaked with water, was flipped upside down and partially sunk. Only the heel was visible above the water. The laundry basket hit a wall and floated the other direction.

I slammed the door closed and put my back against it. *Can't I just pretend we don't have a basement?*

I turned around and creaked open the door again. The water seemed to be rising. I tiptoed down the stairs for a closer look. Several inches of water covered the basement floor. It surrounded the walnut-stained legs of the chairs to my grandmother Doris's dining room table. It buried piles of books stacked in the corner. It weakened and bent the sides of cardboard boxes so that they dipped in the middle or tipped to one side.

"What is all that?" Lindell said from the top of the stairs.

"Go back upstairs and stay on the couch," I told him. My heart was beating in my ears. I ran back up the stairs and got my laptop out of my messenger bag. Dustin was online.

As soon as I saw his face on Skype, I cried. My eyes were burning and hot. "It's flooding, Dustin. The whole basement is flooding. Everything is covered in water."

"Flooding? What? Where is the water coming from?" Dustin asked.

"I don't know. I can't see. It's just everywhere. And I don't know what to do."

"Okay, listen to me, Sarah. This is very important," he said. "Do not walk in the water. As soon as the water level hits electrical outlets, you could be electrocuted. Where's Lindell?"

"I'm on the couch, Daddy," Lindell yelled from the other room. "I'm reading my book."

"I just don't know what to do," I cried. "There's so much. And it's rising. How do I get it out? How do I make it stop?"

"Stay right where you are," Dustin said. "I'm going to sign off and see what I can do from here. Don't go in the basement."

I didn't understand. What could he do from there? But before I could ask, the screen went blank. He had already hung up. I stared at my lap for a long time, feeling heavy and overwhelmed to the point of being frozen. When I finally closed the Skype window, my Facebook account came onto the computer screen. I wiped at tears on my cheek and wrote this bitter, snarky status: "If you're wondering why my basement is flooding, it's because my husband is gone."

I opened the basement door periodically to see if the water had risen. It had.

I cried some more and paced the kitchen floor. I didn't understand what Dustin thought he could do from Africa, and I felt angry that he wasn't home to help. I was afraid to go in the basement after what he said about being electrocuted. But how would I ever get the water out?

The doorbell rang. I opened the front door and saw a petite woman with a narrow face and wavy black hair. "You don't really know me, but we're Facebook friends," she said. "I'm Marion, and I've got a husband and a sump pump on the way."

"A sump pump?"

"Yes, a sump pump." Marion scooted me to the side and came into the house. She was carrying a large cloth bag. "You need a sump pump to get the water out, Pookie."

Pookie?

"We have to get the water out, and then you'll be all nice and cozy again," Marion said.

I stood in the doorway and watched her, trying to remember where we had met before. Maybe a woman's group? Or church?

Marion reached into her bag and pulled out a long dark-brown loaf of bread. "I don't do sump pumps myself," she said. "That's what I have my husband, Mort, for. But I bake." She pointed the bread at me. "It's chocolate bread. I thought your three young men would like chocolate."

Mort came up the sidewalk and through the front door carrying an armload of equipment.

"Now, don't scare the children, Mort," Marion said. She wiggled onto the couch next to Lindell. "You look scary and you talk scary, hon, so just go into the basement and make things cozy."

Mort shook my hand and introduced himself. Then he disappeared down the basement stairs.

Next, Misty, a chief from Dustin's former command, came to the door. She was carrying a bucket and a fan. "The Skipper sent us a message and said your basement is flooding."

"The Skipper" was Dustin. That is what the people at the Navy Operational Support Center had called him. I realized then that Dustin had signed off Skype to get a message to the NOSC. He had asked them how he could get in touch with Maine National Guard Family Assistance. But Dustin, when he was still stateside, had always been the first to help when someone in the NOSC needed support. So along with putting him in touch with Family Assistance, the staff at the NOSC decided they wanted to help as well.

A crew of people followed Misty into the basement. Through the wood floors, I heard all the introductions, and then I heard Mort say this: "The bad news is that this isn't just water. It's coming from the sewer. It's sewage."

I swallowed hard and rubbed my forehead. *Sewage?*

Dave Smith arrived next. I had met Dave many times before at various military events, and I knew he worked for Military Family Assistance, a crisis center for military service members and their families. Dave paced in our living room while he talked on his cell phone to local plumbers. "Yes, I'm helping a military family whose basement is filling with water from the sewer," I heard him say softly but deliberately into the phone. "Uh-huh . . . right . . . Yes, I'd say there is a good four inches of water, and it's rising . . . okay . . . Could you come out today?"

I listened from the kitchen table, where I sat with my head in my hands.

Misty and Mort and the crew from the NOSC were in the basement. Dave paced and made phone calls in the living room. All of them were taking care of things for me because I felt frozen with despair. And it occurred to me all at once that this is what it would be like if Dustin died. Someone from the military would come to the door and take over while I fell apart. They'd make phone calls while I cried. They'd arrange to have my children picked up. They'd make plans for the funeral. They'd keep track of where Dustin's body was en route home. And I would sit there and cry.

But my husband wasn't dead. Dave and Misty weren't there to help with a funeral. They were there to help me in a crisis. How could I be frozen with despair when my husband was alive and I had the support of the military community?

I went to the front porch to put on my rain boots so that I could go into the basement and help. I saw my friend Shelley's car pull into the driveway and park crookedly so that one wheel was on the grass. Shelley ran up the sidewalk and onto the porch. "What can I do?" she said breathlessly. "How can I help?"

I looked at the time on my phone. Ford and Owen were getting out of school soon, and poor Lindell was still sitting on the living room couch, now watching cartoons.

Shelley took Lindell, Ford, and Owen to her house and kept them there until 8:00 P.M. that night. Misty, Mort, Marion, and Dave stayed well into the evening draining the basement. The next day they came back to help me bleach the floors and to meet the plumber who would remove a tree root that was plugging our pipes underground.

By the end of those two days, I felt like a shell of a person. I had a constant, throbbing headache. My body was so tired it felt like exercise to lift my arms. I was too exhausted to cry anymore.

It was April 30. I was supposed to finish my master's and graduate by the end of the week.

Lindell on the shoulders of Congressman Michael Michaud

CHAPTER EIGHT

May

M ay 4 is like a holiday at our house—a *Star Wars* holiday. It's
May the Fourth (Be with You) Day. Usually, I surprise the
boys with some kind of *Star Wars*–themed dinner or special treat.
From the beginning of Dinner with the Smileys, however, I knew
we'd celebrate this year's May the Fourth (Be with You) with Paul
Bussiere and his homemade, life-size replica of R2-D2. Except, as
it turned out, my graduation from the University of Maine would
be on May 4, so we had our nineteenth dinner with Paul and R2-
D2 the night before, on May 3.

Paul maneuvered the silver-and-blue metal robot down the
sidewalk and up the brick walkway. The boys ran outside to greet
them. My in-laws, Robin and Phil, who were visiting from Seattle
for my graduation, watched from the living room window. R2-
D2 was larger than Lindell, and nearly as big as Owen. His dome-
shaped silver head spun 360 degrees as he beeped and whistled.

Paul stood on the curb, a boxy, black remote control in his
hand, and positioned R2-D2 to greet the boys.

"R2!" Ford yelled as he ran out the front yard.

"R2-D2, it's me, Lindell!" Lindell screamed, his arms outstretched.

The boys greeting R2-D2

R2-D2 whirled and beeped.

Ford helped Paul assemble a metal ramp to wheel the two-hundred-pound robot up our front steps and into the house. Beads of sweat covered the top of Paul's bald head, and Ford was nearly out of breath by the time they were inside.

"Man, that thing is heavy," Ford said, massaging his arms.

Lindell and Owen ran to their shared bedroom to change into *Star Wars* costumes. Lindell put on an orange flight suit with sewn-on black boots like Luke's from *Episode IV*. Owen put on a beige tunic and brown belt to be like Anakin in *Episode I*. My father-in-law reclined in the corner of the couch, a book teetering on his rounded belly, and watched the parade of costumes.

"Ah, boy, look at that," Phil said. "It's Darth Vader."

Ford rolled his eyes. "That's not Darth Vader. Lindell is Luke and Owen is Anakin. Don't you know Darth Vader, Grandpa?"

Phil raised his eyebrows behind wire glasses and smiled through thin lips. "Where's your costume, Ford?"

Ford shrugged as he knelt down to zip the back of Lindell's costume. "I probably don't have one that fits anymore," he said. "Is that good, Lindell?" He patted Lindell on the back, and then he turned to walk away, toward Paul, who was taking off R2-D2's head and adjusting a mass of red and yellow wires. Lindell and Owen dueled with light sabers in the background.

"When I get this all fixed up," Paul said, "I have something to show you guys."

"Is it C-3PO?" Lindell screamed.

"No, not C-3PO. Even better." Paul was sitting on the ground, his head inside the hollow barrel of R2-D2's body. "You guys remember the hologram scene in the movie? When Princess Leia sends a message to Obi-Wan?"

"You have a hologram?" Ford said. "No way!"

"Well, we'll see," Paul said. He pulled what looked like a spark plug out of R2-D2's belly. "I just got the projector set up a few nights ago. I hope it works."

Paul closed the door on R2-D2's body and pushed his box of tools on the floor closer to the door. All three boys hovered around him. Lindell bounced up and down with excitement. Paul adjusted a lens on the front of R2-D2's head and moved the robot into the middle of the room so that a beam of light shining from the top of the dome was pointed directly at the blank spot on our wall.

"Oh, boy. What's this? A movie?" Phil said.

Robin and the boys shushed him as they sat down on the sofa.

On the wall, Princess Leia, draped in a cloak, came into focus. Her crouching image shone in an eerie blue-white beam of light. "Help me, Obi-Wan Kenobi. You're my only hope," she said.

The boys jumped and clapped. "Oh my gosh, that's it! How did you do that?"

"Good job, R2," Lindell said, patting the silver dome.

When Princess Leia disappeared, Paul returned to R2-D2's side and adjusted the lens. "Sit still, Jedi," he said. "Because I have another important message for you."

The beam of light on the wall flickered for a minute. Then the rough outline of a man came through in the same blue-white color. It was full of static and flashing erratically. Then, all at once, we could see that it was Dustin. He was wearing his khaki-colored desert camouflage uniform.

"Help me, Lindell, Ford, and Owen Kenobi," he said. "Your mom is graduating, and I'm not there to congratulate her. Please tell Mom congratulations for me. I love you guys. Have a great dinner with R2-D2. Bye."

The beam of light zipped back into the lens, like it was being pulled by a string.

I was speechless and overcome with emotion, but everyone else started screaming.

"That was Dust!" Phil yelled.

"Oh my!" Robin said. "Did you see your dad?"

"It was Dad! It was Dad!" Owen said.

I asked Paul to play it again.

Although I had seen Dustin on Skype, and I had heard his voice through the computer, there was something about seeing his image on the wall. I tried to touch the beam of light. I knew exactly the way his shoulders would feel, how the patches of his uniform would prickle my cheek if I could lay it against him.

Behind me, Paul explained how he had gotten Dustin's e-mail address from Senator Collins's office, and that he had asked Dustin to take a video of himself relaying a message to the boys. Paul did not realize how clever Dustin would be to include my graduation and reenact Princess Leia's *Star Wars* scene. He chuckled as he told Phil how many hours he had spent tinkering with the video image to make it look like a hologram. "I'm just so glad I could do this for them," Paul said.

We watched the message on our wall about a dozen more times.

The next day, I put on my black cap and gown and walked single file with my classmates into the university's ice hockey arena, which had been fitted with a nonslip floor. I looked up at the sea of faces in the bleachers and searched for the boys. I wanted to see Dustin's face, too. A part of me wondered, *Could he be there? What if last night's hologram weren't the only big surprise? What if he had flown home?*

My heart rose at the thought.

Finally I saw Ford and Owen waving and holding flowers about ten rows up from the front. Lindell was sitting on Robin's lap.

Dustin wasn't there.

I saw the boys from the stage, too, when I received my master's hood, and I blew kisses at them.

When we got home, I had an e-mail message from Dustin and a bouquet from the local florist sitting on the front porch.

"I'm proud of you, and I wish I was there," Dustin's e-mail read. "You should feel really good about all that you've accomplished."

I bit my lip and opened the small envelope attached to the flowers. I guessed that they were from Dustin, and I felt like a little girl after her first dance recital. The card inside was folded and handwritten, not printed.

Happy Military Spouse Appreciation Week. From your friends at Chapel Hill Floral.

. . .

CHILDREN'S BOOK AUTHOR and illustrator Scott Nash is tall and lanky. Even his face, and especially his nose, is long and thin. His sandy-colored hair and beard, flecked with gray, is wispy around his ears. His eyes are kind and narrow and framed with deep lines, which has the effect of keeping Nash in what seems like a perpetual smile.

Scott's wife, Nancy, looks equally warm, but is about two heads shorter than her husband. Her hair, pulled into a loose pony-tail, is untreated and streaked with gray, and her face, even with-out makeup, seems to glow. She wore a soft green cardigan sweater with big, round covered buttons.

When Scott and Nancy arrived for the twentieth Dinner with the Smileys, they felt like old friends despite the fact that we had never met them before.

Scott walked easily to the kitchen table and peered over Owen's shoulder. "What are you drawing?" he asked.

Owen blushed. "Just some sketches," he said.

Lindell, whose head barely came to Scott's knees, jumped up and down for attention. "I read your books," he yelled. "You drew Flat Stanley."

"I did," Scott said, crouching to be closer to Lindell. "And I brought Flat Stanley with me today."

"Can I see him?" Lindell said, clapping his hands. "Is he flat?"

Scott put his hand on Lindell's head and smiled. His eyes twin-kled. "Flat as a pancake, and you'll get to paint him." He stood back up, looking first to make sure he wouldn't hit his head on anything.

We took Scott and Nancy to the mall to see the opening night of Owen's first art show. His drawing of a shoe had been selected by the school art teacher for an exhibit in the atrium. It hung from a wire display rack alongside artwork from other local students.

Scott knelt down to examine the sketch and asked Owen to talk to him about the techniques he had used.

"I just sort of drew my shoe from memory, first," Owen said. "And then I looked down at my shoe and made some changes."

Scott took pictures of the sketch with his iPad. He rubbed his beard and examined the work closely. "I love the way you kept it simple," Scott said. "The lines are fantastic."

Owen smiled bashfully, his chin lowered to his chest.

"Are these the shoes?" Scott pointed at Owen's feet. "Are these the ones you drew?"

Owen looked down and shifted his weight to stand on the sides of his beaten and dirty sneakers. He nodded.

"Let's see; hold your shoe up there," Scott said.

Owen lay down on his back on the tile floor and covered his mouth to stifle a laugh. He lifted his foot in the air and held his shoe next to the drawing.

"Congratulations," Scott said. "Your drawing looks exactly like your shoe!"

When we got back home, Scott brought in a box full of paints and a life-size cardboard Flat Stanley, cut into three sections. He led the boys through the French doors in the kitchen and out onto the back porch, where the sun had been warming the wooden deck. A red umbrella above the patio table squeaked as it moved in its stand with the breeze.

Scott passed Stanley's head to Owen. He gave Ford the waist and Lindell the pants. His rules were simple: Have fun and be creative.

But the boys were skeptical. They waited for more instruction, their paintbrushes held in the air at their sides.

Scott had his hands on his hips. He smiled and nodded. "Go for it," he said.

The boys looked at each other. Then Lindell said, "Let's do this!"

Illustrator Scott Nash

Owen gave Stanley orange sideburns and a goatee. Lindell made the pants blue-and-white striped. Ford painted an L on the shirt, just like the one on his baseball jersey. Scott smiled down on them as they worked.

Once Stanley was mostly dry and the pieces taped together, there was still some paint and cardboard to spare.

"What do we do with this?" Ford said. "Dump it?"

Scott motioned with his head for the boys to follow him. Then he walked down the wooden steps to the backyard, the leftover supplies hanging from each of his hands. The boys clamored behind.

Scott laid the extra cardboard on the grass and gave a minilesson about Jackson Pollock, the artist who splatters paint on canvas.

The boys looked at Scott, and then at me, as if they were unsure.

"So we can just throw this paint at the grass?" Lindell said.

"At the cardboard."

"Do we splatter it hard or soft?" Ford asked.

"Just have fun with it," Scott said. "Be creative."

Ten minutes later, the boys' hands and legs, plus Sparky's paws, were covered in blue and orange paint. Owen had painted his face to look like Scott's beard and mustache. "Look, I look like you," he said.

Not to be outdone by his little brother, Ford painted his entire face and hair blue. "Look at me," Ford said. "I'm all blue."

Lindell squealed with delight, and Sparky ran circles around the backyard, his tail beating vigorously back and forth.

After dinner, and before Scott and Nancy left to go back to Portland, Maine, Scott let Lindell play with his iPad, and he gave the older boys a sneak peek at his soon-to-be-released book *The High-Skies Adventures of Blue Jay the Pirate*. Ford, especially, delighted in being part of this "secret."

"Nobody has this book yet?" he asked.

"It's not for sale yet," Scott said. "So technically, no."

Lindell walked into the room, holding up the iPad. He was making a movie of himself. "We are the Smileys," he said. "Yes, our name is really Smiley."

He walked back out, still talking to the camera. Nancy smiled at me.

"We are a military family, and we have people over to dinner," Lindell said, walking down the hallway.

Ford sat on Owen's bed and ran his fingers over Scott's sketches of birds dressed as pirates in the freshly bound book. He bit his lip to hide a smile. "This is so cool," he said.

·   ·   ·

A FEW DAYS later, I stood next to the splintered bleachers at the
Little League field and talked to Shelley while Sparky tugged on
the leash in my left hand.

"You haven't gotten it at all? Not even any spotting?" Shelley
whispered so that the other mothers nearby couldn't hear. She was
wearing a bright yellow rain jacket that made her dark, curly hair
seem even shinier.

"Nothing," I said. "I'm officially two weeks late."

"Pregnant?"

"I can't see how I would be," I said. "That would fall under the
realm of 'impossible.'"

Behind Shelley, through the chain-link fence and in center
field, Owen hung his head and kicked his toe at the ground.

"Get your chin up, Smiley," a coach yelled.

Owen slouched his shoulders even more.

"Maybe stress made you late," Shelley said, but I was only half
listening. I watched Owen and looked back at the coach standing
outside the dugout.

"Head up, Smiley," the coach called out again.

Owen stared at the ground.

"Have you been to the doctor?" Shelley asked. But she must
have realized I wasn't fully listening, because she turned to see
what I was watching.

"Maybe we should take him out of the game," an assistant coach
said.

Information about what I was seeing and hearing came at me fast.
I was trying to understand. Owen had seemed fine earlier in the day;
why was he sulking in the outfield now? I left Shelley and peered
through the chain-link fence into the dugout. Ford was standing in
the dust-filled space with one foot propped up on a short, cement wall.

"What's going on with Owen?" I asked.

Ford looked up and over at me. "I have no idea," he said. "But he's embarrassing himself."

"Can you help him?"

"How can I help him, Mom? I'm in here and he's out there."

I walked back to Shelley. Owen stood in the outfield with his glove hanging at his side. His jersey hung from his shoulders like it was on a coat hanger. Strands of his thin, straight hair spilled out from beneath his baseball cap, and his ears were bent down from the sides of it.

"What's going on with him?" Shelley asked.

"I have no idea," I said. "He was fine earlier."

In between innings, when Owen came to the dugout, I called him to the fence.

"What's going on out there?" I asked.

"Nothing."

"So why are you pouting and staring at the ground?"

"You wouldn't understand."

Owen turned to walk away. I called him back.

"Tell me what's going on, Owen."

"I'm no good, Mom. All these kids are better than me."

"It's not a contest," I said. "You're still learning."

"I'd learn a lot more if Dad was here."

"But he's not, and—"

Owen looked up at me. Tears made tracks down his dirty face. "When I see all those other kids playing catch with their dads before the game, I feel so angry I'm hot inside," he said.

"Owen—"

"Leave me alone!" He turned and ran into the dugout.

Shelley put an arm around my shoulder and rubbed my back.

One inning later, Owen was back in the outfield. His shoulders and head still hung low.

"He's not ready," a player's dad said to the coach. "He's going to get hit by the ball because he's not paying attention."

My eyes stung.

"He needs to come out of the game," someone else said.

I choked on my breath.

For years, Dustin had always told me, "Do not go into the dugout." No matter how bad things get—no matter how unfair things seemed—moms and dads who weren't coaching did not belong in the dugout, he said. "It's all part of the game. Babies become boys in there, and there's no room for moms and dads."

But I had to go into the dugout. Just this once. Owen had no one—no one except for Ford and me. I gave Sparky's leash to Shelley, and I pushed open the gate to the field. Red baseball dirt kicked up around me as I ran down the concrete steps of the dugout. It was cool and damp down there.

Ford looked startled when he saw me coming at him. "Mom, what are you—"

"You have to help him," I sobbed. "You have to help your brother. Please! Dad isn't here to do it, so Owen needs you."

"Okay, calm down," Ford said. He looked around at the other kids in the dugout. "There's nothing we can do. Owen's just acting like a baby."

"Please, Ford!" The tears were coming faster now. I could barely talk. "Please! Dad has always been there for you. What would Dad say to Owen right now?"

"He'd tell him to quit crying or get off the field."

"Then tell him that, Ford. Tell him that because I can't. I can't do it. I can't bear to say that to him. Please!"

Ford stared at me. "Okay, Mom," he said, blinking slowly. "I've got this."

In between the next innings, Ford called Owen out of the dugout and behind the bleachers. He put one hand on Owen's bony shoulder as he talked closely to his face. Owen nodded and wiped at his eyes with his shirtsleeve. Ford patted Owen's back and smiled. Together, they ran back to the dugout. I don't know what Ford said to Owen, but my guess then was that it was no longer my business. When Owen got back on the field, he still looked sad, but he stood straighter and watched for the ball.

The next several evenings were filled with the familiar sound of a baseball hitting the leather palm of a glove. While I made dinner and steam moistened the kitchen windows, I listened through the screen:

"Should we go to the batting cages? Would that help?" Ford said.

"I don't know. I'm just no good."

"You're still young, Owen. I couldn't hit the ball when I was your age either."

"But Dad was home to help you."

"And now I'm here for you."

Thump. Thump. Thump.

"Are things okay at school?" Ford asked.

"I guess so."

"Who are your best friends?"

"Same as always."

Thump. Thump. Thump.

WHEN MY PERIOD was four weeks late, I went to the doctor. She asked if I'd been dieting or exercising more than usual. Unfortunately, I hadn't been doing either.

"Your husband is deployed, correct?" she said.

"Yes, he's been gone since November, so I'm not pregnant."

"And how are you holding up as a 'single' mom?"

I told her that I was mostly fine, but I had my moments, moments when things felt unmanageable. The hardest part was being both mom and dad. I never had a moment of rest. I was never off duty. Mostly, I said, I was tired and overwhelmed.

"Have you finished your master's?" she asked.

"Yes, earlier this month. The same week my basement flooded, actually."

The doctor put down her clipboard. "Wait a minute," she said. "In the past six weeks you've been dealing with a deployment, managing three children, working, finishing your master's, and your basement flooded?"

"And my in-laws left soon after my graduation," I said, smiling.

Until then, until the doctor said it out loud, I didn't realize how much had happened recently. I felt tired just thinking about it. *Had I really just finished a hundred-page research paper, graduated, helped my children through the loss of our neighbor, entertained out-of-town guests, and dealt with a basement flooded with sewer water?* Often it seemed like I was on autopilot. I couldn't stop to answer "how do you do it?" because I didn't really know. Without Dustin at home, I had no pinch hitter. There was no one to help when I was exhausted.

"This is a lot, Sarah," the doctor said, picking up her clipboard again. "You are under a tremendous amount of stress."

"Yes, now that you mention it—"

"And stress is a big factor in anovulation."

"Anovu-what?"

"Missing a period."

"So what do I do about it?"

"Let's wait a few weeks," she said. "Take care of yourself. Try to get some exercise. Hire a babysitter and have time to yourself. Then we'll see what happens."

A few nights later, Morgan took me to dinner at Fiddlehead to celebrate my graduation. We talked for a long time about being a military wife and how our experiences give us such respect for single mothers for whom this isn't a temporary situation. And I was glad to connect with someone who had been through it before, someone who could truly relate.

.   .   .

FORMER MAINE GOVERNOR John Baldacci crouched in our back-yard, the hem of his khaki trousers rising high and exposing white socks and New Balance sneakers. He put Dustin's old catcher's glove on his left hand.

"Okay, show me what you've got," he said to Owen. "Put it right here." He put his fist in the meatiest part of the glove.

Owen pulled back his arm and straightened his left leg. Grass stains covered his knee, and his shoes were gray from dirt. He looked up at John from beneath his green Lions cap. John nodded back. Owen released the pitch, and it smacked into the glove.

"That's great," John said, his narrow face brightening. He stood up again. "Get your arm into it more," he said, mimicking a pitch.

Former Maine Governor John Baldacci

"Like this." He pretended to throw the ball. Then he crouched back down again and said, "Alright, let's do it again."

John, Ford, and Owen played catch for nearly an hour. Lindell ran circles around them and periodically poked his head into the kitchen to ask, "Is dinner ready yet? We're starving out here."

I was talking to John's wife, Karen, an oven mitt in my hand. "Go ask everyone what they want to drink," I told Lindell, and he ran back across the porch.

John is one of the most famous Italians in Maine. His family used to own an Italian restaurant in Bangor. I hadn't given much thought to that—until I opened the oven and pulled out my steaming, homemade lasagna.

Who makes lasagna for someone named Baldacci?

"Would you like me to set the table?" Karen asked.

John and the boys filed in through the open screen door.

Ford and Owen took off their baseball caps and threw them in a basket beside the door.

"What's for dinner, Mom?" Owen asked.

"Lasagna," I said quietly out of the corner of my mouth.

"What?"

"Lasagna," I said again, this time louder.

"You know, my family used to have an Italian restaurant," John said.

I smiled and looked at the floor. "I've heard that."

Ford helped Karen set the table while Owen and John took their seats. Usually our guests sat at the head of the table, in Dustin's seat. But John chose to sit near Owen instead. He was mimicking pitches again with his hands.

Lindell climbed into John's lap. "What does a governor do?" he asked, patting the sides of John's sunken cheeks, which seemed even more narrow next to his large ears and tall, rounded forehead.

"A governor is in charge of the state," John said. "You know how your dad is in the navy? Some moms and dads are in the National Guard, and the governor is in charge of them."

I placed the pan of lasagna next to a store-bought salad and bread on the table. I told Lindell to go to his seat, and he said, "But the governor is sitting in it."

"Should I move?" John asked.

"No, you can have my seat," Lindell said. "But just for tonight."

John cut into the hot cheese and said, "This looks wonderful. Who's ready for some lasagna?"

"Me, please," Ford said, holding up his plate. "I never turn down Mom's lasagna."

John placed a square on Ford's plate. Then he served really large pieces to Owen and Lindell.

Owen stared at the pile of cheese and sauce. He looked up at me.

"Just eat what you can," I whispered.

"I think I'll be governor when I grow up," Lindell said.

"Really? Well, you'd probably be a good one," John said. "In fact, I'm going to call you Governor from now on. Is that okay with you?"

Lindell grinned. "Yes."

"Alright, Governor," John said. "What's the first thing you want to do in the state of Maine?"

"Make sugar a vegetable!" Lindell clapped his hands in front of his face. "And then there will be no naps in preschool."

Ford sighed. "Governors don't do things like that," he said. Then, looking at John: "What's the hardest decision you ever had to make as governor?"

John put down his fork and wiped his mouth with a paper towel. "That's a great question, Ford, but I don't have to think long for the answer. The toughest decisions I ever made always dealt with using our National Guard. Those aren't easy decisions. I never forgot about the families, like yours, who were affected by my decisions."

"Can you make my dad come home?" Lindell asked.

"No, Governor, I'm afraid not," John said. He scraped at the last bit of lasagna on his plate. "Hey, this wasn't bad," he said, pointing to the lasagna. "It's quite good."

I blushed.

"Did you know that my dad plays soccer?" Lindell said.

"No he doesn't," Ford and I said in unison.

"Jinx! You owe me a soda," Ford said.

I smiled at Ford and then looked at Lindell. "Dad doesn't play soccer, honey. Why did you say that?"

Lindell shrugged. "I know," he said. "I just wanted to say 'dad' again." He climbed down from his chair and stood next to John's. "Do you want to see something?" he asked.

"Sure, Gov," John said.

Then, while I watched in horror, Lindell pulled down his pants and mooned the former governor of Maine.

"Lindell!" I snapped.

Lindell's face turned red with embarrassment. He pulled up his pants and started to cry.

"Oh my gosh!" Ford covered his mouth with his hands.

"Did he just? Really?" Owen said, laughing.

"That's Lindell for you," Ford said.

John winked at me, as if to say, "Don't worry. I'm a parent, too." Then he turned to Lindell: "Now look here, Governor," he said smiling, and he went on to tell Lindell how behavior like that wouldn't go over very well if Lindell were in office.

I had a long talk with Lindell that night about what's appropriate and what's not. "You are very comfortable around people, and that's a wonderful quality," I said. "You make people laugh, and you aren't afraid to talk to anyone. But you have to know the limits. Mooning everyone at the table tonight definitely was over the limits."

"I thought he would think it was funny," Lindell said, frowning.

"Mr. Baldacci was very gracious with you, but I don't want to see that behavior again."

As it turned out, my lecture was well-timed because our next dinner was with another politician, the congressman from Maine's second district.

Dinner with Representative Michaud required the boys to miss a day of school. That was the good news. The "dinner," however, would also involve walking around a graveyard. To the boys, that seemed like bad news.

"If we're going to miss school, can't we go to a baseball game, or something?" Ford said.

I smiled. "If it was a baseball game, you wouldn't be missing school."

The four of us were eating macaroni and cheese around the dinner table. Dustin's seat was empty. "Tomorrow's dinner—well, technically, it's a lunch—is an important one," I said.

"Aren't they all important?" Ford asked.

"Memorial Day is coming up, and the Veterans of Foreign Wars needs help putting flags on service members' graves."

"We won't see the dead people, will we?" Lindell asked.

"No, of course not. But do you know what a congressman is? Mike Michaud is a congressman."

Ford explained the role of Congress in a hurried, exasperated tone. Then he waved his hand at me like, "Okay, hurry up; tell us what we're doing."

"Mike is one of two representatives in Maine," I said. "We'll help him put flags on the graves, and then we'll go to lunch together."

"But we don't have to go to school, right?" Ford asked. "Even after we're done?"

"Right. But we do have to be on time. We're meeting the congressman at 9:00 A.M. He's a busy man, and we don't want him to wait for us."

Ford groaned.

Once, when Ford was younger, he complained to the school guidance counselor that I sometimes made him late to school. This, of course, was only partly true. Yes, I'm not a morning person, but getting out the door on time is made more difficult by three children who wait until the last minute to put on their shoes and gather their backpacks.

The school counselor met with me and said, "What we have here are two personalities, type A and type B."

All my life, A had been equivalent to excellence.

"You're type B," the counselor said. "Ford is type A. But Ford wishes you could be more type A."

It sounded as if I could buy a new type or train for it like a marathon. But, alas, I'm type B just as sure as I am 5 feet 4 inches.

Eventually, Ford and I came to an understanding: He'd help me be more organized in the morning, and I'd respect his evening tiredness after 8:30 P.M. (Meaning, basically: Don't expect Ford to be polite to guests after 8:00.)

"We will never be on time to meet the congressman," Ford said.

"Oh, come on!" I started clearing dishes. "It's not like we have to meet him at the crack of dawn. I'll be on time."

"Sure." Ford rolled his eyes.

I knew then that even if I had to leave the house in my pajamas, we would not be late. I wasn't going to let Ford win this one.

And, sure enough, the next morning, after listening to Ford say over and over again that "we're going to be late," and "I knew it," our van rolled into the gravel parking lot of the cemetery at the exact moment the clock changed from 8:59 A.M. to 9:00 A.M.

I smiled to myself.

Congressman Michaud, or Mike, as he insisted we call him, and his assistant, Chris, joined us in front of the Korean War Memorial at Mount Hope Cemetery. In their hands they had bunches of American flags, held like bouquets, on wooden sticks. Mike's silver hair was bright in the morning sunshine. He was dressed in a conservative blue button-down shirt, khaki pants, and a red tie. Chris, tall and slender, had on a navy-blue tie and blazer. Together, Mike and Chris's attire showed the boys that this was serious—like church serious.

Ford and Owen listened carefully to instructions given by a round man in jeans and a black Harley-Davidson T-shirt. He had a Vietnam vet baseball cap on his head with VFW pins on it. "Look for the word 'veteran' on the gravestones," the man said. "Or look for these special markers in the grass." He pointed at a nearby metal stake in the ground. "Every service member gets a flag."

Ford raised his hand as he squinted at the sun. "Does it matter which war?"

"No. Every service member gets a flag."

Ford raised his hand again. "Does it matter which branch of service?"

"No. Every service member gets a flag."

Lindell raised his right hand and spontaneously reached up with his left to grab Mike's.

"Yes, sir," the man said, pointing at Lindell.

"Um, when we poke the stick in the ground, will it hurt the people in there?"

Mike kneeled down to speak softly and privately with Lindell while the man in the black shirt continued. "Every service member gets a flag. But not their wives."

I bristled, looking left and right to see if anyone else's mouth was hanging open. Ford smiled knowingly at me when our eyes met. As everyone else turned to leave, dispersing into the hillside of the cemetery, Ford came to my side and whispered from behind his hand and out of the corner of his mouth, "You want to put some flags on the wives' graves, don't you?"

"Oh, we're totally going to," I said.

"Yeah, I thought so," he said.

Lindell held Mike's hand and walked ahead of me on the gravel pathway.

"So, Lindell, you'll be my helper," Mike said.

"Okay." Lindell half skipped, half walked.

"We're going to walk through this whole cemetery," Mike said.

"Okay."

"And we're going to read all the gravestones and find the ones with 'veteran' engraved on them. You let me know when you spot one."

Lindell stopped walking and looked up at Mike. "There's just one little problem," he said.

"What's that?"

"I don't know how to read."

Mike smiled down at Lindell. Clearly, he hadn't thought about that.

Owen went with Chris. Together, they made their way to the back corner of the cemetery.

Ford and I went right, and as soon as I was sure no one was near us, I whispered, "Operation Put Flags on Wives' Graves is now activated."

Ford smiled and gave me a thumbs-up.

We found several military wives' graves and nodded at each other as we put a flag in the ground in front of them and then in front of the veteran spouse.

When we were out of flags, we all met up again at the bottom of the hill, where Mike was reading tombstones to Lindell.

"It's so sad, isn't it, Mom?" Owen said. "There's this one guy back there who lived thirty years after his wife had died. Thirty years!"

"I know." I put my hand on Owen's shoulder.

"And this other grave was for a week-old baby. A baby, Mom!"

"It's hard to imagine, isn't it?"

"I'm so worried I forgot someone," Owen said, wiping at his nose. "What if I missed one of the veterans?"

"I'm sure you got them all."

Before lunch, we followed Mike to a nursing home, where he was presenting a veteran with an award. The setting reminded the boys of our trip to Gloria's assisted-living facility. They reminisced about Frank and Anita.

After Mike made a short speech to a small gathering of residents leaning on walkers or sleeping in their wheelchairs, a wrinkled and shrunken man sat down at a piano beside the boys and me. He played back-to-back ragtime songs, and never missed a beat. You would have thought a player piano was making the music, not a man, and a ninety-something man at that. Lindell danced around the piano to the delight of the elderly onlookers. Old ladies woke from their naps in their wheelchairs and clapped to the music. After four songs, the man got up and shuffled to the dining hall. He smiled and nodded as he walked past us. Not knowing what to say, I stood there disbelieving. I wanted the man to stay and play more. In fact, I wanted him to come to dinner.

A nurse wearing white pants and sensible shoes came closer and whispered in my ear. "That's Mr. Jones," she said. "He has Alzheimer's. Doesn't even remember his own name, but, boy, can he play that piano!"

A WEEK LATER, closer to Memorial Day, we had our twenty-third dinner with Owen and Lindell's principal, Lynn Silk. Lynn lost her son Brandon in a military helicopter crash two years earlier. She brought her daughter-in-law, Jaclyn, who is married to her middle son, also in the military and currently deployed.

The boys knew that Lynn (Mrs. Silk to them) had lost her son.

But I didn't know if they knew that he died in a helicopter like the one Dustin flies. I also didn't know how much Owen and Lindell, especially, understood that some people don't come back from deployment.

"It's okay to ask Mrs. Silk about her son," I told them the night before.

"Mom, that's terrible," Ford said. "Do you want to make our guests sad?"

"I would think that Mrs. Silk likes talking about her son, even if it makes her sad."

"That's the worst advice I've ever heard," Ford said. "I'm not going to be the one to bring it up."

"Me neither," Owen said, nodding at Ford.

The next evening, when we were all gathered around the table with Lynn and Jaclyn, I realized that my boys would never utter Brandon's name unless I brought it up for them. They stared at their plates and hardly spoke to our guests. The room was thick with uneasiness.

So I said quite abruptly, "I told the boys they could ask you about your son, but they are worried it will make you sad."

Ford banged his palm against his forehead. "Mom!" He looked at Lynn. "This wasn't my idea. I told Mom it was not okay to bring up your, um . . . well, uh . . . your—"

"Brandon," Lynn said gently. "His name was Brandon."

Neither of the older boys made eye contact with Lynn.

"I love talking about Brandon," Lynn said. "He was my boy, just like you are your mom's boys."

Ford and Owen stared at the table. Lindell chewed his food noisily.

"It's okay," Lynn said. "Talking about Brandon is probably harder for you than it is for me. It's okay to feel unsure about it. But do you mind if I tell you a little bit about my son?"

Neither Ford nor Owen dared answer.

"I'd love to tell you about him," Lynn said.

The room was quiet for one painful minute. Then Owen looked up at Lynn and said, "Did he like sports?"

"Brandon loved sports," Lynn said.

"And he was really good at them," Jaclyn added.

"You knew him, too?" Ford asked Jaclyn.

"I did. He was a great brother-in-law."

"Are you scared to have your other sons in the military now?" Owen asked.

"That's a great question," Lynn said. "It's a difficult one, too. But I believe in what my boys are doing. Would you like to see their pictures?"

"Yes!" Lindell yelled.

Jaclyn got up from the table and went to the front porch.

"I saw that Flat Stanley came to dinner with you," Lynn said as she watched Jaclyn go. "Would you believe that Jaclyn has a Flat Husband and I have Flat Sons?"

"What?" Ford's brow wrinkled.

"Are they flat like pancakes?" Lindell said.

Jaclyn came back into the kitchen carrying two life-size cardboard cutouts, one of Jaclyn's husband and the other of Lynn's third son.

"I have one of Brandon, too," Lynn said. "But I left him at home."

Then to me she whispered, "I decided it would be hard on the boys to see Brandon's."

Probably a good move, I thought.

"We wanted to bring you a Flat Daddy," Lynn said to the boys, "but we didn't have enough time, so we brought what we hope will be the next-best thing."

"Is it my real daddy?" Lindell said.

Jaclyn took a cake box out of a brown paper bag on the floor. She opened the lid, and there, settled between streams of red, white, and blue frosting, was Dustin's image, dressed in his navy dress whites, airbrushed onto the icing of a cake.

"Cake!" Lindell screamed. "I always hoped you'd bring cake."

"And it's an ice-cream cake," Lynn said.

"Ice cream? Really?" Ford was interested.

"How did you get Dad's picture on there?" Owen asked.

"The bakery did it," Jaclyn said. "I got the picture off your mom's Facebook page."

I got a knife from the kitchen counter to cut into the frozen-solid cake. And this is where things got weird. There is no good place to cut into a cake that has your husband's image on the front. Cutting off his head seemed really awkward. But so did cutting off his limbs. I was reminded of those decorative candles, the ones shaped like bunnies or Santa Claus. They always seem like a good idea until you light the wick and Santa melts and sinks into himself.

Especially given our recent conversation at the dinner table, I felt horribly uneasy about cutting into Dustin's image on the cake.

I hovered over the picture with the knife.

"Ummmmm," Ford said.

"Oh, well, this is uncomfortable, isn't it?" Lynn said when she realized.

I laughed nervously. "I'm not sure where to cut."

"I'm not eating any," Owen said. "I won't eat Dad. No way."

"The cake had seemed like a good idea at the store," Lynn said. She was beginning to laugh. "But now—"

We all peered down again at Dustin's smiling face and full-length body on the cake.

"Wow," Jaclyn said. "Really awkward."

I placed the knife above Dustin's head and winced.

"No, Mom, don't!" Owen yelled.

I moved the knife to Dustin's stomach.

"No, don't cut there," Ford screamed. "Not the stomach."

Cutting the infamous cake with Dustin's picture on it at dinner with
Lindell and Owen's principal, Lynn Silk

I moved the knife down a little farther. Jaclyn laughed. "Okay, now this is getting really weird," she said. "Has Dustin had his, um, surgery yet?"

"Any fourth child in the future?" Lynn said through tears of laughter.

I pierced the frosting with the knife and pushed down through the frozen ice cream.

"Oh, God!" Ford yelled. "I can't look."

"That's gotta hurt," Owen said.

Lindell screamed, "You just cut Daddy in the—"

I put up my hand to shush him.

Once I had successfully cut one wedge of cake with my

husband's private area on it, I realized the next predicament: Who would eat it?

"I think you're going to have to take one for the team here," Jaclyn said.

I flopped the piece onto a plate and doubled over with laughter.

"Somewhere across the world Dad is sitting up in pain," Owen said.

"I guess I'll take the face and head," Ford said. "I'd like to have a piece of Dad's mind."

We all laughed again, whether as a release or out of embarrassment I didn't know.

Lynn dried her eyes and said, "Brandon would have thought this was really funny."

Jaclyn added, "Yes, he really would have."

Later that night, after Ford and Lindell had already fallen asleep, Owen called me into his bedroom. The room was dark except for a small reading light clipped to the headboard of his bed. He had his patchwork quilt pulled up to his chin.

I sat down on the edge of the bed and smoothed hair away from Owen's forehead.

"Mom," he said, "is it true that Mrs. Silk's son—Brandon, I mean—died in a helicopter?"

"Yes, honey."

"Like Dad flies?"

"Yes."

Owen was quiet for a minute. Then he looked right at me and asked, "Will my dad die in a helicopter?"

Ford, Lindell, and Congressman Michaud at Mt. Hope Cemetery

Zookeeper John Linehan with Owen

CHAPTER NINE

June

I arrived late to the Little League championship game. Lindell had fussed about putting on his shoes, and I couldn't find Sparky's leash. By the time the three of us arrived at the field, Joe Bennett had already sung the national anthem and announced the starting lineups. The home team, Fox and Ginn, was on the field warming up. Ford and Owen were in the dugout with the Lions.

"Fox and Ginn is using their best pitcher tonight," Mike, another team parent, said as I tied Sparky's leash through the chain-link fence.

"You mean Alex, the one who pitches sixty miles per hour?" I asked.

"He actually pitches closer to ninety miles per hour," Mike said.

Lindell ran off to play with a friend in the dirt behind the bleachers. I turned around and looked at the boys on the field. It's amazing what a difference two years makes when it comes to middle school–aged boys. Owen and the boys his age were swallowed up by their billowing jerseys and baggy baseball pants. The older boys, nearly thirteen, were beginning to look like young men. Their bodies filled out their uniform, and their shoulders were about twice the width of their hips. Next to the younger boys, Alex looked like a grown man. I had heard that some people thought he shouldn't be playing Little League because he was too good. Parents were afraid the nine- and ten-year-olds could get hurt by his pitches. So far that hadn't been a problem, though, because Alex also played for the middle school team, and Fox and Ginn had been "saving his arm" for school games. But the school season was over now. Alex didn't have any other games to play besides this critical championship, so Fox and Ginn decided to pull out their not-so-secret weapon.

Alex pitched to the catcher crouched at home plate. His knee rose to his chest, and he stared out from beneath the brim of his cap. When he released the ball, it whistled in the air and smacked into the pitcher's glove.

The catcher fell back onto his heels, and then onto the seat of his pants.

"Wow, that is fast," I whispered to Mike. "Poor Owen must be scared in the dugout."

"You didn't know?" Mike turned to look at me. "Oh, right, you missed the lineup. Owen's batting first."

"What?"

"He's first in the lineup for the Lions."

"My Owen?"

Mike laughed. "Is there another?"

"Wait, what? They're batting him first? Against *him*?" I pointed to Alex.

Just then, Owen ran out of the dugout. He dragged a bat, nearly the length of him, in the dirt and adjusted the batter's helmet with his free hand. The elastic hem of his pants, which was supposed to ride high on his calves, fell to his ankles. His jersey was so big, with it tucked in, you could just barely see his number: 3.

"Oh. Dear. God." I put my hand to my mouth.

Mike laughed and patted my back. "I'm sure they have a plan," he said. "Maybe they want to get him out there first so he doesn't get scared watching from the dugout."

"Oh. Dear. God." It was all I could manage to say. I was tempted to run onto the field and carry all fifty-five pounds of Owen back home with me. I couldn't breathe as he stepped into the batter's box and kicked his toe at the red dirt. Joe, who had left the announcer's booth and was serving as umpire, patted Owen on the shoulder. Owen looked like he would fall over.

Joe returned to his spot behind the catcher, and with his hands on his knees, he shouted, "Play ball!"

Owen pulled the bat to his shoulder and swayed his hips side to side. He dug one cleat farther into the dirt. Alex stared from the shadows of his cap. He held the ball and his glove beneath his chin.

"This actually might be hard for Alex," Mike whispered to me. "Owen is so small he has a tiny strike zone."

"Oh. Dear. God."

The entire field was silent.

I spotted Shelley, in her yellow jacket, on the Fox and Ginn bleachers. She had one hand on her throat and the other hand over her mouth.

I stood in my seat and put my hands on either side of my head. The back of my throat was dry and sticky. "If Alex's pitch hits him, it will kill him," I said.

"Oh, stop it," Mike said, slightly laughing. "He's going to be fine."

"Shhh," someone behind us said.

Alex drew his knee to his chest. He pulled back his arm and released the pitch.

Owen swung and missed.

Alex pitched again. Another strike. After the third strike, Owen ran to the dugout like a kid jumping into his bed when he is sure the boogie man is on his heels.

I sat down and breathed.

"See there," Mike said. "He did great. He never even moved out of the batter's box."

For five of the six innings, no Lion could get a hit against Alex.

A couple of players, including Ford, who was the first to get on base, were walked, and a couple of them made it home. But by the bottom of the sixth, the Lions were losing 11–2. The boys ran defeated, shoulders hunched, from the field to the dugout. Many of the spectators who didn't have a child in the game had already left the stands. It was obvious that Fox and Ginn would win.

The Lions were up one last time.

Alex, who had run out of pitches, was sent to the catcher's position.

A new, less threatening pitcher took the mound.

The Lions got a hit. They scored a run. Then Carl, the fastest runner on the team, stole second base. Another player got a hit. Carl ran home. Another hit. Another run. Soon the score was tied 11–11.

The Lions had two outs.

Mike and I were speechless. I sent an e-mail from my iPhone to Dustin: "Bottom of the sixth. Lions down by nine runs. They come back to tie with eleven. But they have two outs. No one is making a sound. Just the crack of the bat and the thump of the ball into the gloves."

The boys in the dugout were on their feet and hanging on the wire fence. Even they were silent.

Murmurs rippled through the stands: "Oh my gosh" and "Can you believe it?" But no one dared speak more than that.

Carl was on second. Derrek was up at bat. The pitcher threw the ball. Derrek hit it to the outfield and ran to first. Carl ran to third just as the second baseman was throwing it there to hopefully get him out. But the third baseman missed the ball. Carl sprinted home and scored their twelfth run. The boys in the dugout ran out yelling and jumping in the air. They piled on top of Carl. They had won the championship.

After an award ceremony, during which Joe acknowledged the oldest boys who had just played their last Little League game, Coach Boyce called the Lions into a team huddle at first base. He congratulated them on a great season and an amazing game.

Lindell ran onto the field and stood just outside the huddle, peering up at Coach Boyce. He had dirt on the seat of his pants, and the cowlick at the back of his head made a tuft of hair stand on end. He clasped his hands low behind his back.

"Alright, let's all get in here for our last team cheer," Coach Boyce said.

Ben, one of the older players, spied Lindell and said, "Hey, what about him?"

Coach Boyce looked down at Lindell and smiled. "It's a Smiley," he said. Then he picked up Lindell, and Ford and Owen's teammates crowded around both the coach and Lindell. They were a circular wall of forest-green jerseys and gray baseball pants.

"Who are we?" Carl yelled in a deep, low voice.

"Lions," the boys chanted.

"Do we ever quit?"

"No!"

"One, two, three . . ."

"Lions!" they yelled as the center of the huddle opened up. The boys stepped back and held their hands in the air.

Through the opening, Coach Boyce tossed up a giggling Lindell. When he caught him in his arms again, both of them were mobbed with hugs and cheers from the team.

The first thing Owen said to me when he came off the field with his bat bag slung on his shoulder was, "Can you believe I was up against Alex?"

The first thing Ford said was, "Dad would have loved that game."

. . .

MY PARENTS, WHO have a camp on Phillips Lake twenty miles east of Bangor, arrived in June to spend the summer there. Our days were still busy, as the boys were not yet out of school and the Lions had advanced to the citywide Little League play-offs. But since my graduation in May, a new sense of calm came over me. I had time to do laundry and wash dishes. I was exercising and not eating on the run as much. Sometimes, when the boys were gone in the morning, I even sat and did nothing. My head and mood were filled with the anticipation of long, warm summer days spent on the lake. Like a room that doesn't seem dark until someone turns on a light, I didn't realize how hectic my life had been until the slow and wonderful month of June.

Naturally, then, my period returned.

The boys and I spent every warm afternoon at my parents' camp. The mountains surrounding Phillips Lake like a bowl were lush and full of green leaves again. On the weekends, when we spent the night there, we woke to rings of fog hugging the mountaintops, and by afternoon, shadows from white, puffy clouds slid across the green backdrop.

Being at camp and on the lake brought lots of memories of Dustin. In the last seven months, our home had already been washed over with new memories that didn't include him. We had been there with him and without him. But camp was different. Camp, which had been boarded shut since the previous September, was still full of Dustin.

"Can we get out the kayak?" Ford asked, and I remembered how the summer before Dustin taught him the correct way to hold a paddle.

"Where are the boats?" Lindell said, the screen door of the shed slamming behind him. "I want my boat."

Dustin loved to do radio-control boats with the boys in the

alcove of water between the rocky bank of my parents' yard and the boat dock.

Owen pulled out a deflated, turtle-shaped float from under the house, which sits on concrete pilings. "Oh, no . . . The turtle!" he said. "Can you pump it back up?"

I took the limp float from Owen and searched for the air valve. Dustin was so much better at these things. In summers past, I was the one who packed lunches and spread sunscreen over the boys' shoulders. Dustin carried kayaks to the dock and filled up deflated rafts. I lay in the sun and told the boys to be careful jumping off the swim dock in the middle of the lake. Dustin swam with Lindell on his back to the rock poking out of the water, where schools of fish liked to swarm.

"Mom, blow up the turtle," Owen said again.

"Hold on, Owen, I'm trying to find—"

Suddenly, there was a splash. Ducks honked frantically and beat the water with their wings. Owen and I turned around and saw Sparky chasing a mother and seven ducklings through the water.

"Mommy, get Sparky!" Lindell screamed. He was standing at the end of the dock, a round inner tube around his waist. "Get him, Mom! He's going to drown!"

Sparky is a bird dog and a fantastic swimmer. I knew he could swim to the other side of the lake and back without panting. The ducks probably could, too. So despite Lindell's frantic, tearful screaming, I knew this was not an emergency. Had Dustin been there, we would have divided and conquered. But I was on my own and completely outnumbered. I could handle only one "crisis" at a time.

"Just a minute, Lindell," I said. "I don't even have a bathing suit on."

"No, Mommy! Get him now!" Lindell yelled. He was crying and jumping up and down. "Sparky is going to drown. Hurry, Mom!"

"He's not going to drown!"

"I got this, Mom," Ford said. He was coming down the hill behind me, pulling on his life jacket as he went. "Owen, help me get the kayak down to the water," he said. "I'll paddle out and get Sparky."

Sun danced on the lake as Ford cut through it with the yellow kayak. Sheets of water fell from the paddles as he moved them up and down. Sparky and the ducks had made it to the wooded island in the middle of the lake.

Lindell screamed and cried, his hands on either side of his face. "Get him, Ford! Get him! Don't let him drown!"

"He's fine," Ford yelled back as he got closer. "He's actually having fun. So are the ducks."

It took a while, but Ford finally corralled Sparky back to our side of the lake, and, eventually, to the shore.

When Sparky got out of the water, he shook vigorously, and arcs of water flew from his fur.

"Sparky, I thought you were going to drown," Lindell said, hugging Sparky's neck.

Ford sighed and smiled at me as he unbuckled his life jacket.

I put my hand on Ford's wet shoulder. "Thank you, Ford. That was a big help."

After the sun set, the boys and I lay on our backs at the end of the dock and stared at the stars that looked like pinholes in black paper.

"A shooting star!" Owen said, pointing up at the night sky.

"Darn, I missed it," I said.

"Do you think Dad is looking at these same stars?" Lindell asked. He had his arms behind his head, just like his older brothers.

"No, it's daytime for Dad," Owen said. "Dad's in a different time zone."

"What's a time zone?" Lindell asked.

"Technically, though, the stars are still there," Ford said. "The sun just drowns out their light."

"But it's not these same stars," Owen said.

"No, different ones."

"What's a time zone?" Lindell asked again.

Ford explained time zones to Lindell, but when we saw the first bat swoop down at the lake and back up to the pine trees, we all clamored across the deck and ran to the camp's screened porch like we were being chased by one of the bats. Lindell and I slept on the sleeping porch, where the wall of open windows let the breeze rustle through the sheets and we could hear the haunting echo of loons on the lake. Ford and Owen slept in the loft.

The next morning, I woke with Lindell snuggled against me. His small, round mouth was open, and drool seeped onto the pillow. His knees were tucked into himself, and his bare chest rose and fell with each small breath. He stirred when he heard me moving in the room.

"Is it morning?" he asked with his eyes still closed.

"Yes, but it's early," I said. "You can go back to sleep."

"Does Daddy come home today?"

I froze. "No, why?"

Lindell sat up in bed and rubbed his eyes. "I had a dream last night that Daddy was home."

In fact, Dustin *was* coming home soon for his two-week, mid-deployment rest and recuperation, or R&R. But I couldn't tell Lindell that yet. Dustin was due to arrive July 1, but the date could always change, and we decided it was best not to set up the kids for disappointment until plans were solid. Plus, we had considered sneaking away together for two nights first and then surprising the kids.

Lindell lay back onto the bed and rested his round cheek on his clasped hands. His eyes slowly closed again.

I watched him for a minute and wished I could say, "In just a few short weeks, you'll wake up and Dad *will* be here."

OUR FIRST DINNER in June was with Noel March, the president-appointed US marshal for the state of Maine, and his family.

Now that our days were easy and filled with family on the lake, Dinner with the Smileys seemed less necessary. Throughout the winter and the wet, muddy spring, the weekly dinners had been like beacons of hope. We clung to anticipation of the next dinner.

Now that it was summer, though, and especially because my parents were in town, we needed our community less. Or, so it seemed.

I considered taking a break from the project and starting up again in September. Keeping up with the weekly dinners seemed more like a nuisance during the fun-packed days of summer. Isn't this why so many civic and social groups take the summer off? People are just too busy with family and other activities.

And, indeed, I had canceled our dinner with the US marshal once already when summer plans got in the way. Then, on the afternoon of the rescheduled dinner, the boys and I were at the lake again.

My dad took Ford and Owen tubing behind the boat, and for lunch, I paddled out to the island with them for a picnic. Our hair was stiff and dry from the sun and lake water. We smelled like coconut-scented lotion, and our feet were brown with dirt.

"Do we have to go home for the dinner?" Ford asked. "Can't we do it another time?"

I was thinking the same thing. But we couldn't cancel again.

At 4:00, we loaded the car, and my mom followed us into town to get ready for the 5:30 dinner. I made lasagna and salad while the boys watched *Star Wars* in the living room. They were still wear-

US Marshal Noel March

ing their swim trunks. When Noel, his wife, and three children knocked on the door, it seemed like the boys might not even get up.

Luckily, however, Noel March, with his booming, spirited voice and broad, six-foot-two stature, commands attention. He fills up a room both physically and metaphorically.

The boys swung their feet off the sofa and stood up at the sound of Noel's deep hello. He was wearing perfectly ironed khaki pants and a forest-green button-up shirt with the Marshal Service emblem embroidered in gold on the breast.

"Men, who wants to be a junior marshal?" Noel asked.

"Oh, I do," my mom said, stepping up to take one of the silver badges in Noel's hand. "I was hoping you'd bring some of these." Mom admired the pin in her hand. "Just like in the old westerns," she said.

"I want one," Lindell said. "Do you have one for me?"

"I sure do," Noel said.

Ford watched with a smile sneaking across his face, even if he didn't take one of the junior marshal badges.

"Alright," Noel said, his eyes twinkling behind his glasses. "Who likes to laugh at others' expense?" Noel's bald head shone beneath the overhead light.

"I do," Lindell said, holding up his hand.

"Well, young sir," Noel said, "tonight I'm going to tell you about the time I chased a bad guy across the top of two buildings and split my pants in midair."

"You ripped your pants?" Owen giggled behind his hand covering his mouth.

"Right in half," Noel said.

"Oh my gosh," Lindell laughed. "I've gotta hear this one!"

At the dinner table, Noel delighted the boys with his stories of "catching the bad guys." He used dramatic voices and big, exaggerated hand movements. He even had sound effects: pounding on the table for a *boom!* and slapping his hands together to startle us.

The boys were riveted.

"Tell them about Bruno," Noel's daughter said. "Tell them that one!"

Noel got up from his seat and stood beside the table. He moved in and out of an Italian accent as he shared what his family kept referring to as "the Bruno story": "It was late at night, and I was the lone officer breaking up some fighting drunks at a local bar. These guys joined forces and turned on me. I tried to call for backup on my walkie-talkie, but it was useless. There was too much background noise from the jukebox they had me pinned against. Then, out from the shadows emerged this looming, bearded, leather-jacketed giant."

"Bruno!" Noel's daughter shouted.

Noel crouched down. He looked intensely at each of the kids' faces. "The crowd circling around me made a path for the giant.

He came to stand inches from me, face-to-face. He looked down at me."

Noel broke character for a moment and resumed his usual speaking voice to say, "Now, remember, I'm six-two," he said. "Not many people look downwards at me. That's how big this guy was."

All the children—Noel's and mine—stared up at Noel as he rolled up his sleeves and got back into storytelling mode again.

"So I thought, 'I'm gonna have to shoot this guy.' But instead, the giant winked at me and bellowed, 'Which ones do you want, officer?'

"I pointed to the three drunk combatants, and the giant—"

"Bruno!" Noel's daughter yelled again.

"The giant grabbed all three men and dragged them outside to my police car. When I thanked him, he said, 'Name's Bruno; do you remember me?'"

Noel pulled at the belt loops on his pants and did an impression of the big and gruff Bruno. "I didn't remember him," Noel said. "But Bruno tells me that once, when he was passed out on the street, I helped him get home. He appreciated the respect I had shown him, quite unlike his other encounters with police officers. So he shakes my hand and says, 'We're even now,' and he walked away."

"Whoa," the kids said in unison.

"Tell us more," Lindell said.

And Noel did. He had dozens of stories just as captivating as the first one.

After dinner, Noel played guitar for the boys and went into the basement to hear Owen on his drums.

Outside, there was bike riding and a game of chase as the late summer sun set behind the pine trees.

By the time the March family left, I felt energized. It was as if I had been recharged, and all at once, I realized why I could not stop Dinner with the Smileys for the summer: Even when our dinners weren't necessary (as in, we weren't especially lonely or lacking for something to do), it still was incredibly enriching and invigorating to meet new people, learn about different ways of living, and, basically, to share an evening with another family in our community.

I was glad I had not canceled the dinner, and for a long time afterward, I used the memory of our evening with Noel and his family to fuel me when I felt too tired to cook another meal or host another guest. No matter how stressed or tired I was at the beginning, the feeling of renewal and connectedness at the end of dinner could not be matched.

Our next dinner was with the Lunch Bunch, a group of four women, plus my mom, from Virginia Beach, Virginia, who I have known since I was Lindell's age. Mom, Mrs. Tace, Mrs. Walters, Mrs. Owney, and Mrs. McCoy all were in the Parent Teacher Association together when I started kindergarten. They have been best friends and weekly lunch buddies ever since. In June, the Lunch Bunch rode the train from Virginia to Maine to spend time at my parents' camp. The boys and I had them to our house for dinner on one of their last nights in town.

Quite frankly, this dinner should have been a disaster. A half hour before the Lunch Bunch was supposed to arrive, I realized the meat I had bought for the taco ring was spoiled. I raced up to the store to buy more and pulled into the driveway—panting, out of breath, and with a pounding headache—seconds before the Lunch Bunch. But these were my mom's friends, and, in many ways, surrogate mothers for me. I knew they, more than anyone else, would understand. What I hadn't expected, however, was that the Lunch Bunch would help me cook, set the table, and clean up afterward. It felt like a family Thanksgiving—in June. We women crowded my small kitchen as the boys ran under our feet and Mrs. Tace danced and sang the theme song from *Barney and Friends*, just like she always did when I was ten.

"Uh, that's kind of like a baby song," Ford said, even though he couldn't help but laugh at Mrs. Tace, tall, gray-haired, and lanky, leaping across the kitchen floor in her gold-colored flats.

"Honey, Mrs. T. will sing that to you no matter your age," Mrs. Owney said as she dried the pizza stone I had used for the taco ring.

"I love you. You love me . . ." Mrs. Tace sang over and over again.

"We're a happy family," Lindell added.

After dinner, the Lunch Bunch gave each of the boys gift bags filled with mementos, like a Rubik's Cube from the 1980s, the decade in which they all met, and souvenirs, like saltwater taffy from my hometown in Virginia. For me they brought a dozen buttery, melt-in-your-mouth cookies from the Plaza Bakery, an iconic favorite place to stop when I was out of school for a dentist appointment or doing errands with my mom. They also had with them pictures from the year they first met.

The boys laughed at Mrs. Tace's large round glasses and Mom's perm. As they stared at the grainy black-and-white photograph, they tried to make connections to their own life.

"So this would be like you and Mrs. Fahey still being friends thirty years later?" Ford asked me. "Because you guys met when Owen was in kindergarten, right?"

"Actually, I met Shelley when Owen was in third grade," I said. "But, yes, close enough."

Mrs. Owney put her arm around Ford's shoulder. "Honey, we have known your mom and your memaw for a mighty long time," she said. "In fact, I remember when your mom was in second grade, and the elastic in her tights broke."

"What are tights?" Owen asked.

"What women wear under dresses," I said.

"Mommy ripped her pants?" Lindell clapped with excitement.

"Her pantyhose fell around her ankles in the middle of class," Mrs. Owney said. "And your momma cried. She was always kind of sensitive, you know? And our other good friend, Mrs. Katabian, was your mom's teacher. She told your mom to go into the bathroom and put her underpants on the outside of her tights to hold them up underneath her dress."

"Kind of like Wonder Woman," I said, blushing.

"Oh my gosh," Lindell laughed. "Mommy lost her pants!"

Mrs. Tace told the boys how I used to cry at school, and she, as the acting PTA president, would sneak me away and take me to get Krispy Kreme donuts or cookies from the Plaza Bakery. Mrs. Walters and Mrs. McCoy told the boys about meeting Dustin for the first time, being at our wedding, and meeting Ford, Owen, and Lindell when they were just infants.

We sat around the kitchen table—a table the Lunch Bunch remembered well from when it was in my mom's kitchen—and shared stories as we laughed and snuck just one more cookie from the white Plaza Bakery cookie box that had grease spots on the bottom.

After the Lunch Bunch left that night, Ford sat down on the sofa with his new Rubik's Cube and said, "That was a lot of fun. They are really nice."

"They are, aren't they?" I said.

"And Dinner with the Smileys is really fun, too," Ford said. "I can't believe our next dinner will be the halfway mark."

"Incredible, huh?" I sat down beside him and patted his knee. "We've met a lot of people."

Owen sat across from us, on the smaller sofa, and turned the dials on his Rubik's Cube. "I miss Dad and all," he said. "But I think I'll miss the dinners when they're done, too."

I thought about Dustin's upcoming two-week visit, just a few weeks away now, and tried not to smile. The boys still didn't know. Lindell crawled into my lap and rested his cheek on my shoulder.

"I wish Dad could come to a Dinner with the Smileys," Ford said.

"You know, it's pretty neat that our name is Smileys," Owen said, still turning his Rubik's Cube. "Because Dinner with the Johnsons or something just wouldn't have the same ring to it."

Lindell, who was very near falling asleep, lifted his head and said, "Yeah, neither would Dinner with the Poopsies."

"No, Dinner with the Poopsies would not be good," Ford said.

A week later, our babysitter, Kara, who was seventeen at the time, arrived at 8:00 in the morning hugging a pink flannel pillow to her chest and carrying a flowery Vera Bradley tote filled with clothes. Her shoulder-length, curly brown hair was still wet from her shower, and she smelled like sweet soap. Lindell ran to the front door to greet her. "Kara!" he yelled, wrapping his arms around her long, skinny legs. "I'm finally going to a zoo tomorrow!"

"I know," Kara said. She bent down to pick up Lindell, and when he rested on her hip, it seemed like he might topple her over. At five years old, Lindell weighed at least half as much as Kara.

"Are you going with us?" Lindell said, pulling on Kara's curls.

"I am. See? I brought my stuff. We're even going to stay in a hotel tonight." Kara looked at me. "There's a pool at the hotel, right?"

I was running back and forth throwing more clothes and snacks into a bag. "Oh, I'm sure of it," I said. "What's a hotel without a pool?"

Ford and Owen were in their rooms sulking about the fact that I thought we needed a babysitter with us on the weekend trip to Boston. "The babysitter is for Lindell, not you," I told them. Plus, we had decided to invite each of our four babysitters to a Dinner with the Smileys over the summer, just as we had had a teacher each month during the school year.

Ford groaned. "I'm almost twelve," he said. "I don't need a babysitter."

"Then think of Kara like an older sister."

We loaded the car and left for Boston at 9:00 A.M. We were headed to the Franklin Park Zoo, just outside of Boston, but first, we'd spend one night at the swanky and totally-out-of-our-price-range Hotel Commonwealth in Boston's Back Bay. When John Linehan, president and former zookeeper of the Franklin Park Zoo, heard about our project and the fact that Lindell had never been to a zoo, not only did he invite us to come have lunch with him at the park, but he and others affiliated with the zoo arranged for us to have special accommodations at the Hotel Common-wealth as well.

After four hours of driving and one hour of missed turns and backtracking, Kara, in the passenger seat beside me, deftly used the map function on my iPhone to bring us to the front entrance of the hotel with red awnings. The landmark building in the middle of the historic urban district towered beside us.

"It's a mansion!" Lindell screamed.

"No, it's a hotel," Ford said from the middle seat. "Can we get out now? I feel like I'm going to puke."

"You think you're going to puke?" Owen said. "I had to sit in the way back for the last two hours because someone [he stared at Ford] had to be a brat about giving up his seat."

"Okay, guys, stop it," I said, opening the sliding doors of the minivan.

The boys spilled out onto the busy downtown sidewalk. Ford and Owen elbowed each other a few times and complained. Then they stopped and joined Lindell staring up at the building and the red-carpeted entryway.

"Whoa," Owen said. "This really might be like a mansion."

Cabs honked on the street behind us. The brakes on city buses released air with a shrill screech. People in business suits and carrying briefcases zigzagged past the boys and talked on their smartphones.

"Do you want me to take them inside while you deal with the valet?" Kara asked through the open passenger door.

The valet? Despite being thirty-five years old, I'm very much still a child when Dustin and I travel. He is the worldly, firstborn type who knows when to tip and how much. Dustin doesn't need a GPS to get around a city, and he can confidently hail a cab.

On previous family vacations, I didn't have to think about tips or parking. My job was to keep the kids from beating each other, and Dustin dealt with the rest. Now, however, I was technically the only adult. Three children and my teenage babysitter were depending on me to know what to do.

Before Kara left with the kids, I asked her, "How much do I tip the bellhop? Do you think they take debit cards?"

Kara smiled and shrugged her shoulders. "I have no idea," she said.

It seems silly, but this was a big moment for me. I was nervous as the valet dressed in black pants and a white shirt came closer. I didn't have a clue what to do, and I felt stupid. I reached into my purse and pulled out a crumpled twenty. "Will this cover it?" I asked.

The man motioned for me to put away my money. "You can tip us once you get your car back at the end," he said, smiling out of the side of his mouth. He looked over his shoulders and waved for me to come closer. "The bellhop will probably expect a tip once he gets your bags to the room, but twenty dollars is too much. The standard is one dollar per bag."

I was so grateful for the help. "What about room service?"

"With all those kids, don't get room service," he said. "Too expensive. There's a bagel place a block away. I'll get directions for you."

I found Kara and the boys inside the lobby with the bellhop and our luggage. Lindell rode on the bottom of the gold luggage rack into the elevator and up to one of the top floors of the hotel. Our room with a view overlooking the city was larger than our kitchen and living room at home. The boys hopped onto one of the king-size beds and ran in and out of the bathroom with up-dates. "They have soap shaped like seashells, Mom," Lindell said. "Like seashells! This place is so fancy!"

When I handed the bellhop his tip, I asked, "What time does the pool close?"

"Which pool?"

"There is a pool here, right?"

Behind me, Lindell streaked across the room swinging his swim trunks over his head. The kids chanted, "Pool! Pool! Pool!"

"Ma'am, I'm sorry, but we don't have a pool here at Hotel Commonwealth," the man said. "But I'll see what the concierge can do for you."

The bellhop left, and I turned around to face an angry mob of boys already dressed in their bathing suits.

"No pool? What kind of hotel doesn't have a pool?" Ford said.

"The fancy kind," Kara said.

I found the valet outside again and asked for help. "We need a pool," I said desperately. The kids and Kara followed closely be-hind me. They had towels draped around their necks and flip-flops on their feet.

Passersby stared as they moved past us in the red-carpeted lobby with thick molding and gold chandeliers.

The valet flagged a taxi and asked the driver to take us to the Boston University pool. Then he turned to me and said, "If you run into any trouble, call the hotel and ask for me."

"We are so fancy," Lindell said as he slid into the backseat.

It was his first time in a taxi.

Early the next day, after a day of swimming and a night of watching movies in our hotel room, we met John Linehan at the stone-walled entrance to the Franklin Park Zoo.

"This is my first time at a zoo," Lindell said, pointing to his shirt that read CAREFUL, I BITE.

"So I've heard!" John patted Lindell's head with one hand and shook my hand with the other. His gray, wavy hair was brilliant against his rosy face and contrasting dark black eyebrows.

We followed John to the middle of the zoo, where a picnic was waiting for us in the shade next to the donkey exhibit.

Over turkey-and-cheese sandwiches, John shared stories about working at a zoo.

"Do you have any favorite animals?" Ford asked.

"Please don't tell me it's the camels," Lindell said. "Because I don't believe in them."

John looked puzzled by Lindell, but without hesitation he said that the zoo's best and most notorious escape artist, a male gorilla named Little Joe, was among his favorites.

John told us about how Little Joe first escaped his rock enclosure in August 2003. He didn't leave the park, but ventured to a monkey exhibit, had a bowel movement outside the glass, and then put himself back into his own enclosure.

"He pooped on another monkey's house?" Lindell said, delighted.

"Lindell mooned a governor," Ford said helpfully, as if it would explain for John Lindell's enthusiasm over Little Joe's poo incident.

Then John told us about Little Joe's second escape two months later. This time, Little Joe left the park and was "hunted" by police with tranquilizer darts and real guns.

"I didn't want the police to hurt Little Joe," John said. "He was scared, and I knew if I could get to him first, before the police, he was more likely to comply. Little Joe knows that he is safe with me. You'll see that when we go to his exhibit."

After lunch, John took us past the giraffes, where he was able to call the female giraffe to him at the fence.

"The animals know me," John said. "We're like old friends."

Later, we had the chance to hand-feed the giraffes from a raised perch that felt like a tree house. We also met Little Joe and watched in amazement as he and John seemed to communicate through eye contact alone.

The moment everyone was waiting for, however, was the camel exhibit.

"Lindell seriously doesn't believe in camels," Ford told John as we walked along the shaded pathways.

"But your dad is in Africa, right?" John said. "So he probably sees a lot of camels."

"Yeah, he's sent us pictures of them, too," Ford said. "And still, Lindell says they are fake. But, that's Lindell for ya."

John laughed. "Don't worry, we're going to make your brother a believer right over here." John pointed ahead of us. We came around a corner and saw camels resting in the distance.

"Here it is," Kara said to Lindell. "Camels, right before your very eyes."

Lindell stared through the fence for a minute and chewed on the side of his lip.

"Just like Dad sees every day in Africa," I said.

"What do you think?" Ford asked.

Lindell shrugged and turned on his heel to walk away. The rest of us looked at each other in confusion.

"Lindell! The camels," I called after him.

"Robots," he said over his shoulder. "They're just robots."

When we got home from Boston, the boys' summer vacation officially began. It was also Father's Day weekend but the boys didn't really know that, and I wasn't going to mention it. During the last few weeks of school, Owen's class had made Father's Day coupon books to give to their dads as gifts, but the boys and I hadn't talked about which day Father's Day would actually be. The point was for the students to commit to quality time with their parents. "This coupon good for one full day of working in the yard together," for example. But Owen knew that his dad couldn't cash in any of the coupons for at least six months. So he made all of his promises for the future: "This coupon good for a full twenty-four hours of catch when you get home." My favorite coupon was for "one week off from doing the trash." I said to Owen, "Honey, Dad has had a whole year off from doing the trash. Where's my coupon?"

We spent the first part of Father's Day at my friends Jenn and Aram's pool. There were other dads and children there, but still, my boys didn't seem to realize that the cookout was for Father's Day. During the summer, especially, they aren't aware of days and dates. Besides, they were too busy swimming with the other kids.

Later, we went to my parents' camp on the lake. The boys swam while I lay on the dock, and around dinnertime, our vet and friend, Dr. Dave, came by on a pontoon boat with his family. We joined them on a sunset cruise around the lake, and at some point, I asked Dave's wife, "Have you had a good Father's Day?"

Owen overheard. "Wait, today is Father's Day? Like, this actual day?"

My heart sank. We hadn't even been able to connect with Dustin on Skype, and we sent our Father's Day cards weeks ago because military mail is unpredictable and slow. The boys didn't pay attention to which day Father's Day would actually be, and I thought it was best not to make a big deal of it. But now Owen looked hurt and shocked.

"It's just a day, really," I told him as I reached out to touch his shoulder. "Did you miss Dad any more today than you did yesterday?"

"No, I guess not," he said.

"Then it was just another day."

This is a hard fact of military life: Although everyone thinks holidays, birthdays, and anniversaries would be the toughest times to be apart, in reality the loneliness is felt twice as much on the ordinary Saturdays or Sundays, when other people forget that your loved one is halfway across the world. Our Father's Day had been full of friends and family. I suspected we would miss Dustin more the next day, a regular Monday, when we had no plans.

Right then, however, on Dr. Dave's boat, I was tempted to tell the boys, "Guess what, your dad is coming home in two weeks!"

It took everything I had in me not to.

The end of June was busy, which was great because I could hardly wait for July and Dustin's R&R. All the kids from Ford and Owen's baseball team and their families came to the lake for our twenty-seventh Dinner with the Smileys.

The first dinner to revolve almost entirely around children, our dinner with the baseball team was a cookout filled with boys (lots of boys!), baseball, water guns, and a special cake with all the teammates' names on it.

Lucas, from our dinner with the orchestra, was there, and so was Mike, from the championship game. I was happy and relaxed as I watched the boys play with their friends and talk with this caring group of team parents and coaches.

When we got home from the lake that day, there was an envelope with Owen's name on it waiting for us from the Bangor School Department. The envelope was thin but looked formal, so, of course, I worried it contained bad news. Inside, however, was this: "Your son has been identified as Gifted and Talented in the visual arts."

Owen's dark eyes sparkled. "What does it mean?" he asked. "What does it mean?"

"It means that your school thinks you are very talented in art," I said. "They want you to be in a special program next year."

Owen read and reread the letter. He was processing this unexpected information. Then he looked up at me and said, "Can we write to Scott Nash and tell him?"

OUR LAST DINNER in June, and on the eve of Dustin's trip home, was with Doug and Nichi Farnham. Doug is an Air National Guard pilot who flies the KC-135, midair refueling tanker. Nichi is a state senator in the Maine legislature, once was Bangor's mayor, and served three years on the Bangor School Committee.

The boys had caught on to the fact that each dinner seemed to have a theme, so when they asked about our twenty-eighth dinner, I told them, "Colonel Farnham will take us on a tour of the KC-135, and then Mrs. Farnham will talk to you at dinner about working in the Maine legislature." As far as I could tell, those would be the themes of the upcoming dinner.

What Dinner with the Smileys was teaching me, however, was that one of the greatest outcomes to inviting members of the community to your family table is the unexpected experiences that come with them. So far, few dinners had gone as planned, and by that I mean, they had exceeded my expectations.

The Farnhams pulled up in a dark Suburban that dwarfed our small cape. Their three sons, Scott, twenty-one, Carl, eighteen, and Gary, thirteen, stepped out and stood along the sidewalk like stairsteps that mirrored my own three boys standing in the grass to greet them.

"Oh, gosh." I put my hand to my mouth. "My future just flashed before my eyes!"

I knew the Farnhams had three sons, and I had met Gary at the Little League field, but when I saw all three of the boys—excuse me, men—lined up together, broad shoulder to broad shoulder, I

Dinner with Col. Doug Farnham

had these thoughts in this order: (1) someday my little boys will be men, (2) someday my little boys will have big feet and hairy legs, and (3) someday I'll be Nichi—smaller, and hopefully as delicate and radiant, standing next to three grown sons.

"Crazy, isn't it?" Nichi said as she hugged me hello. "Looking at your three young boys sure does bring back a lot of memories for me, too."

All nine of us went to the Air National Guard base to tour the KC-135. Then we came home for spaghetti. The evening was mild, and songbirds flitted noisily across the backyard. The kitchen had steamed up from the boiling noodles, and the hair at the nape of my neck was drenched. I suggested that it might feel better outside, where we'd have more space and the nice summer breeze.

"Would you like us to help you carry the table outside?" Scott asked.

"I'll get the chairs," Carl said.

Scott asked Ford to grab the other end of the table, and together, Nichi's firstborn and mine carried the old farm table through the French doors and outside to the back porch. Nichi and I sat together at one end of the table across from Doug. The Farnham boys were lined up on one side, and mine were on the other. I watched as Scott helped his mom pass the bowl of salad and, later, clear the dishes, and I wondered if Ford and I would ever have that kind of relationship. At the beginning of the deployment, when Ford was struggling so much, that would have seemed unlikely. But certainly, I thought, things hadn't always been so easy for Nichi and Scott. Hadn't time and maturity played a hand in shaping this grown-up version of a mother-son relationship? After all, Ford was only eleven. Scott was twenty-one. Ford was still a boy, Scott, a man.

"You'll get there," Nichi told me as we talked at our end of the table, beneath the noise of little-boy voices and the deep sounds of grown men. "But the stage you're in now goes so fast," she said. "You'll miss this, too."

I looked across the table at Ford.

He was smiling and chewing on a slice of bread as Scott told him about working on Nichi's campaign for state senator.

"Did you, like, go to school for that, or something?" Ford asked. "It sounds like fun."

"It was fun," Scott said. "So, who do you have for school next year, Ford?"

"I'm going to kindergarten next year," Lindell interrupted.

"Oh, wow!" Nichi said. "Mom's going to have all three kids in school during the day. That's huge." She smiled warmly at me. "I remember those days."

Our evening ended relatively early because Doug and Nichi and their boys knew what Ford, Owen, and Lindell did not: Dustin was flying home the next day. I was meeting him at the airport at 10:00 P.M., and we were headed to the Samoset Resort in Rockland, Maine, for two nights alone before surprising the boys.

The kids thought I was going to Augusta to speak at a conference. Buddy was staying with them until I returned on July 3, just in time for dinner twenty-nine, which I told them was with a city councilman. Ford, especially, thought it was irresponsible of me to plan a dinner so close to my trip. "What if you don't get home in time?" he asked.

"Buddy's wife, Lily, is going to have the dinner all prepared," I said. "So when I show up, we'll welcome the councilman and then sit down to eat."

"You're just going to come in at the last minute?" Ford was horrified. "I don't think this is a good idea, Mom."

"Well, I have to go speak at this conference, and it's too late to cancel the dinner," I said, continuing the ruse. "It will all work out, Ford. Don't worry."

What Ford didn't anticipate was that by the time they saw who the real guest of dinner twenty-nine was, our meal would probably be just an afterthought.

Lindell and Owen playing after dinner

Dustin's surprise visit for his R&R

CHAPTER TEN

July

Shelley texted me at 10:00 P.M.

"Excited?" she asked. "When does his plane land?"

I wrote back: "It's been delayed to 10:45."

"What did you decide to wear?"

I sent her a picture of myself wearing my new dress: navy blue, empire waist, with a low V-neckline to show off the necklace Dustin had sent me from overseas. Then I took a picture of my shiny new high heels with the peep toes for my bright red manicured nails.

Now it was 10:30.

I was working on my hair and choosing earrings.

My phone dinged.

"Are you pacing at the terminal?" Shelley wrote.

"No, I'm actually still at home getting ready," I wrote back.

A minute later, my phone rang. It was Shelley. "Sarah!" she screamed. "You know there's construction at the airport, right? Aren't you worried about being late? You better get your butt in the car! Like now!"

My heart started to race. I threw my overnight bag into the back of the car and screeched out of the driveway. Our house isn't far from the airport, and the terminal is small, but with the construction, I'd be cutting it close. Too close.

At 10:40 I was stuck in a line of cars outside the airport. A man in a reflective vest held a stop sign in front of the cars.

I texted Shelley: *Track his plane. Please tell me it's late now. I'm stuck . . . in the construction!*

Shelley wrote back: *It's landed :(*

At 10:45 the sliding doors of the airport terminal parted with a *whoosh*, and I ran across the grated floor. The airport was surprisingly busy for nearly 11:00 at night. Passengers pulled wheeled suitcases in front of me and cut off my path. I ran left and right to keep from being blocked. The long necklace bounced and hit my chin. I had a cardigan sweater draped over my arm. I ran past couples hugging and grandchildren running to grandparents with outstretched arms. And then, as a crowd of people at the luggage carousel parted, I saw him. He was smiling that familiar smile, with two deep lines on either side of his mouth like parentheses. He began jogging toward me. He was so close now I could hear the change jingling in his pants pocket. When I finally had my arms wrapped around his neck, I buried my face into his shoulder and laughed and cried at the same time. He smelled exactly the same. Squeezing me tight and turning me around, he whispered into my hair, "I've missed you so much." I could feel the prickliness of his unshaven beard—left over from thirty-six hours of transatlantic travel—against my cheek.

It was a nearly two-hour drive to Rockland. We held hands the whole way, like two teenagers on a first date. Dustin drove with his other hand. I stared across the middle console, at the sharp lines of his jaw illuminated by the amber light of the dashboard. It seemed incredible to think that less than a day ago he wasn't there. And now he was. Forty-eight hours ago he had been a bodiless, pixelated face on the computer screen. Now I was rubbing the calloused places on his knuckles and the hair going up his arm.

There was so much to say, so many things that wouldn't have translated well across Skype or e-mail—so many things that in the past eight months I hadn't wanted to waste precious conversation time on. All these months I had kept my anxieties bottled up. It would have been impossible to function otherwise. But now I felt like I could rest. I didn't have to be the only responsible person. I could sleep with both eyes shut.

With my guard let down, a flood of worries came over me in the hotel room. There was so much to do in the short two weeks of Dustin's R&R. I needed help with the taxes. The porch door was sticking. The garage was leaning to one side. The living room window had leaked. All these things had been weighing on my mind, and now, finally, I had someone to share the burden.

The familiarity of being with my husband again caused me to reflexively unload my list of worries. Dustin was taking off his shoes and unbuttoning his shirt as he listened. He had dark circles under his eyes from traveling. The top of his dark hair was messy from the airplane headrest. And I felt guilty for blabbering on, but I could finally let go of some responsibility, and that was very tempting.

Dustin got up from the stiff hotel chair and walked over to me in his sock feet. He put one hand around my waist and took my right hand in the other. Then he swayed me back and forth like we were dancing. With a goofy, boyish grin—the same one I've fallen in love with a million times before—he started singing the words to Bob Seger's "We've Got Tonight": *We've got tonight . . . who needs tomorrow . . . we've got tonight, babe . . . why don't you stay.*

We danced like that for a while on the rough hotel carpet. I was taking in Dustin's familiar, musky smell and the feel of my cheek against his shoulder.

And then he pulled back to look at my face and said, "I've been thinking a lot about having a fourth child."

"A what?" I nearly choked on my shock and surprise.

"Another baby," he said. "What do you think?"

I struggled to understand, searching his face in the dim light. I was just barely keeping my head above water with three boys, and he wanted another one?

"Ummm—" I said.

"Well, maybe not *right* now," Dustin said. "But we do make pretty great kids, don't you think?"

That's when I realized that for eight months, my husband had had time to idealize parenthood. I'd sent him only the perfect moments: Lindell's funny quips, Owen's drawings, pictures of Ford pitching in Little League. We didn't Skype when the kids were fighting or when Lindell was kicking the walls in his room during a time out. I didn't send Dustin pictures of the whining or fighting.

Dustin had forgotten all these things.

"Is that a no?" he asked, his smile slowly fading.

There were two beds in the room. I jokingly pointed at each one and said, "So, that bed is yours, and this one is mine."

Dustin laughed.

Two days later, we drove home to Bangor. We parked a block away from our house, and I texted Buddy and Lily so that they would bring the kids outside. Buddy told them what we had rehearsed as part of the plan: "The city councilman is late, but Mom's on her way and she has a surprise for you in the front yard."

When Dustin and I came around the corner, we saw all three boys standing on the sidewalk. But they were looking in the wrong direction. I walked behind Dustin, getting video with my iPhone. A couple of times, he looked over his shoulder at me. His smile was so broad, the lines beside his mouth deepened and lengthened, until they met the laugh lines coming from his eyes.

Over Dustin's shoulder, I could see the boys ahead, at the end of the sidewalk. They were still looking the wrong way.

We were about three driveways from our house when Owen

turned around, peered down the street, and saw Dustin walking toward him.

"Dad! Dad! Dad!" Owen screamed. His voice was guttural and jagged, like he might be close to crying. "Dad! Dad! Dad!" He yelled it over and over again as he ran up the sidewalk.

Ford followed him saying, "What? What? I don't get it. What?"

Owen jumped into his dad's arms and hugged his neck. His lanky legs hung from Dustin's waist stiff and straight, like the knobby limbs of a hoofed animal.

Dustin pulled Ford to him with his left hand, and Ford put his face into the side of Dustin's collared shirt. Lindell ran behind Ford, but once he was standing in front of Dustin, he got shy. He hugged Sparky instead.

"Come on over," Dustin said, waving at Lindell. "Let me give you a hug."

Lindell released Sparky and ran to Dustin, who pulled him in with his last free arm.

Owen clung to Dustin's neck and waist like a monkey.

"I don't get it," Ford said again, laughing. "Is this the dinner with the councilman? Have you been planning this all along?"

"There is no dinner with a councilman," I said. "Your Dinner with the Smileys 'guest' tonight is Dad."

The boys hung from Dustin's arms and side as we walked into the house. *Our house.* Dustin was inside our house! I could hardly believe it.

Lily was in the kitchen finishing the lasagna. I stepped to the side, filled up from our two-day honeymoon at the Samoset, and let the boys clamor for Dustin's attention in the living room:

"Come look at our new fish, Dad."

"Dad, I got a letter saying I'm gifted in art."

"Dad, wanna go play catch?"

"I can say my ABCs, Dad. Wanna hear?"

"Dad, look at this math test I did."

At dinner, Dustin took his usual place at the head of the table. He beamed as he looked at each of the boys, and then at me. But I noticed that the rest of us hadn't fallen into our usual places. I was in Ford's seat. Owen was in mine. Ford was in Lindell's seat, and Lindell was across from me. Things were different, a bit uncomfortable even.

But hadn't we all changed in so many ways, besides where we now sat?

Later that night, I lay on the couch, exhausted to my bones, and listened to Dustin in the other room reading stories to the boys. The clock in the living room ticked softly. The sofa pillow was cool against my head. The house smelled like warm lasagna. And in that moment, for that one second in time, everything was perfect.

I had planned it so that Dustin would be there for our thirtieth dinner, which we were calling the Basement Reunion, the following weekend. When the basement flooded with sewer water in April, our community came to support us. Dustin, in particular, was grateful because he had felt helpless so many miles away. I knew he wanted to be there to say thank you in person when everyone who had been involved—from Julie, who loaned us her industrial dryers, to Marion and Mort, who were my first responders—joined us at the lake for lunch, instead of dinner, so that everyone could swim.

We picked up sub sandwiches on our way to my parents' camp, and, of course, I hadn't planned accordingly. We were running late. Ford and Dustin joked with each other about my perpetual tardiness as I maneuvered our van through the winding camp road in the woods.

"Is Mom always this late for the dinners?" Dustin asked. He was half-joking, half-serious.

"The dinners are usually at home," Owen said. "So, no, not really."

"Thank you, Owen," I said.

"But she's late to a lot of other things," Ford said.

"Dinner with the Smileys is supposed to be casual. Remember? No pressure?" I said. "So let's all just relax."

Sunlight filtered through the pine trees, casting yellow, mottled spots on the curvy road. Occasionally, when the trees parted at the driveway to a camp, we caught a glimpse of the lake beyond. Boats sped past, churning the water into frothy, white foam. Swim docks bobbed up and down and slowly turned on the rope attached to their anchor.

When we pulled into my parents' gravel driveway, we were fifteen minutes late. Some of the guests were already there. We could see them through the trees on my parents' screened-in porch.

"Late to our own dinner," Ford said. "That's a Dinner with the Smileys first."

I was pulling boxes of sandwiches and bags of chips out of the car. I poked my head through the back window and said, "We haven't had many Dinner with the Smileys with Dad either, so why don't we just focus on that?"

In fact, however, it was kind of strange to have Dustin in my new world, with new friends and old friends I'd gotten to know better since he was gone. It reminded me of awkward wedding receptions, in which a person finds himself drinking beside the bride's childhood best friend, college roommate, and cousin from the Midwest. People were talking about things Dustin didn't know about. He was on the outside of inside jokes and memories. I was the lone bridge between my old life, which Dustin knew better than anyone, and the new one from the last eight months.

"Did you and the kidlets ever go to Salem, Mass?" Marion asked as we sat down for lunch. She was balancing a plate of salad on her lap in one of my mom's adirondack chairs.

"No, we didn't have time," I said.

"Oh, Pookie," Marion said. "You're working so hard, trying to fit it all in."

"Pookie? What?" Dustin asked. "Wait, you guys were going to go to Salem?" His voice was full of the guarded curiosity of a stranger. "I don't remember that."

"We thought about it," I said. "On our way home from Boston a couple of weeks ago. But it didn't work out."

Shelley, who had taken care of all three boys the day the basement flooded, was beside us, sitting on an overturned log. She mentioned something about one of the previous baseball games. "Did Mike tell you about Lindell at the concession stand?"

"Oh, yes," I said laughing. "I heard all about that."

"I thought it was the cutest thing," Shelley said.

"What's this about Lindell at the concession stand?" Dustin asked.

"I think I sent you an e-mail about it," I said. "He's too short for the concession stand, and no one inside can see him when it's his turn in line. They just see this little hand reach up and smack down a dollar bill, and they know—"

"Lindell wants a hot dog," Shelley finished for me.

Dustin rubbed at his prickly chin. "No, I don't remember that being in one of your e-mails. Maybe, though."

By the end of the lunch, Dustin had a migraine. I knew it even before he told me because I saw him rubbing at his left temple with his index finger.

Back home, he went into our bedroom to sleep off the pain.

I fixed dinner and tried to keep the kids from pestering him.

"But I want to see Daddy," Lindell whined. "Why can't I see him?"

"Because he's getting rid of his headache."

"But he doesn't have much time at home," Ford said. "I feel like we're wasting a day."

We were in fact already one week into Dustin's two-week

R&R. For the first seven days he was home, we avoided all talk of the inevitable good-bye. I made a concerted effort not to know what day of the week it was. I wasn't counting. I didn't want to know the details of his departure. I was happy to be completely lost and oblivious, caught up in the emotion of that first week. But at some point the tide shifted. Dustin was beginning to talk about what time he needed to leave for the airport on the following Sunday. He had been doing laundry and packing his suitcase with clothes he wouldn't need in the days he had left at home. He was in departure mode again. And I was again aware of time and date. The upcoming good-bye loomed heavy in my mind.

I couldn't say it aloud—not in front of the kids—but I also thought we were wasting a day.

A few days before Dustin left, we went to Acadia National Park, hiked the 3.3-mile loop around Jordan Pond, and had lunch at the Jordan Pond House, famous for its warm popovers served with butter and jam on a hillside overlooking Bubble Mountains and the water.

Lindell held Dustin's hand for most of the hike and sat next to him at lunch so they could share a lobster.

The kids were antsy and impatient, as they always are at a restaurant, but Dustin and I were quiet. I felt heavy with dread. I couldn't stop thinking, *This time next week, he'll be gone again.*

After Dustin paid the bill and left a tip, we walked in silence to the car. There was very little time left now.

On Saturday night, we sat down together as a family at the wooden farm table that is the center of our lives, and had, at this point, been host to nearly one hundred Dinner with the Smileys guests. Dustin said a prayer for us. Then he looked up at me and smiled softly.

I held his hand as we ate. In one week's time, I thought, someone else—one of our weekly dinner guests—would fill Dustin's seat, and he would be halfway across the world again.

Early Sunday morning, on our thirteenth wedding anniversary, we drove to the airport.

The kids were quiet now, too. We had all been here before; we knew the drill. I wondered if any of us would cry. I was beginning to feel hardened to the coming and going. I was tired from it, actually. Then I felt something totally unexpected: excitement. I was glad that Dustin was leaving because that meant we were one step closer to his actual homecoming. Also, my life had been on hold the past two weeks. I was ready to get back into a routine. For fourteen days, Dustin had felt like a visitor, with his suitcase open on the bedroom floor and his travel toothbrush next to the sink. And although I was grateful for the time we had, it was a two-week vacation, not a life.

So I didn't cry when we said good-bye. Not even when Dustin whispered "happy anniversary" into my ear as he hugged me. The boys and I stood outside the security line and watched as Dustin boarded the plane and turned around for one last wave.

"Can we go home now?" Lindell said impatiently. "I'm hungry."

I took a detour, through a back road that leads past the airport's flight line, and where, when the timing is right, you can watch jets take off and land. The airplanes fly so close overhead, you can see the landing gear and read numbers under the wings.

I pulled off the side of the road and rolled down the windows. An engine whistled and rumbled in the distance.

"What are we doing, Mom?" Owen asked.

"I'm hungry," Lindell said.

I turned around and put a finger to my lip. "Listen," I said. "That's Dad's plane."

The boys unbuckled and jockeyed for position next to the side windows. The whistle and rumble grew louder. It seemed like even the asphalt beneath the car was shaking.

"Move, Ford. I can't see," Lindell whined.

"You don't need to see," Ford said, elbowing Lindell. "There's nothing to see yet."

"But, Ford, I can't—"

"Look!" Owen pointed out the window. "There it is! Here it comes!"

The airplane barreled toward us.

Ford moved to the side and let Lindell get on his knees on the bucket seat to see better out the window. Before the plane got to the chain-link fence on the side of the road, the nose lifted up. It climbed into the air so close, it seemed like we could reach up and touch it.

"Dad!" Lindell shouted. "It's me, Lindell!"

Ford waved out the window.

"Do you think he can see us?" Owen asked.

The plane went overhead and toward the other side of the street.

The boys clamored for positions at the opposite windows.

The airplane climbed farther into the clouds, farther out of view.

"Dad, come back!" Lindell said. "Come back!"

The rumbling grew softer. The shaking stopped. The plane approached the clouds.

Owen sat back in his seat. "I miss him already," he said.

"I do, too," I said.

When the airplane slipped all the way into the clouds, I turned the key and started the engine again. "Well, where to now, boys?" I said, adjusting my rearview mirror.

"Home," Lindell said. "I'm hungry."

"Yeah, I'm kind of hungry, too," Ford said.

Having Dustin home for two weeks was like a safety net. I slept better and worried less. I wasn't the only adult responsible for three children and our home. So the next few days after Dustin left were filled with mild anxiety. It wasn't the full-blown panic I felt when he first left, but I definitely had a sense of being alone again.

Every creak in the house kept me awake, and in the morning, I lay in bed going over our day in my head, worried I would forget something on my to-do list. Everything had to be coordinated again. No more sneaking out alone at 7:00 P.M. to shop in peace and silence while another capable adult handled the children's bedtime routines. I could almost feel the tension rising in my shoulders again.

Our first Dinner with the Smileys after Dustin left was with Shelley and her family. Like the Basement Reunion, I had strategically planned this dinner and its timing. I knew we'd be reeling from Sunday at the airport, and I was worried about having guests. *What if I don't feel like entertaining? What if I can't get my act together? What if I haven't been to the grocery store?*

Shelley suggested we come to their house, and let her husband, Jim, a game warden, cook "mystery meat" for us. Aside from the last part, Shelley's plan sounded like a comfortable way to ease back into our pre-R&R routine.

The Faheys' house is tucked deep in the woods in Maine. On a clear winter day, you can even see Mount Katahdin, ninety-five miles north, in the distance. Their basement, with wood paneling and fur throw rugs, looks like a small hunting lodge. It is filled with the heads and antlers of animals their family has shot. A giant stuffed bear claws at passersby, and Shelley's first moose antlers hang proudly just below the ceiling.

My boys and Shelley's, who are roughly the same ages, ran through the basement in their sock feet playing a game of tag. It was good to see the boys laughing with their friends. I knew their minds were far from thinking about the airport. As I watched them, however, I also eyed the animals on the wall and wondered which one we'd be eating for dinner.

"None of these," Jim said casually. He riffled through a box of

Shelley Fahey, wife of game warden Jim Fahey

fishing lures, looking for one to give Owen to use at the lake. "Part of our dinner was shot a few months ago and is in pieces in a freezer."

"Lovely," I said.

"The other part is in the back of my truck. Caught it this morning."

I was a little afraid. But our dinner—moose and fish—was actually better than I had expected. And anyway, the real gift was the company.

Thirty-one dinners into our journey, an important lesson had emerged: no one comes to dinner for the food. Not really. They come for company and conversation. As far as I know, no one has ever left Dinner with the Smileys and said, "Gee, I wish I hadn't come because the lasagna was cold in the middle." Likewise, although I might not order moose burgers again, it wasn't the meat but the friendship that buoyed us at our thirty-first dinner.

It didn't take long after Dustin left for the boys and me to get back into a routine. In fact, I welcomed the structure. We spent many long summer days at camp on the lake, and I had become quite good at filling Dustin's roles. I towed the boys' kayaks with mine when they got tired paddling. I dove down into the lake water to assess the depth before they jumped off a rock. I lugged our picnic through the woods of the islands. And, on a daily basis, I chased Sparky as he went after the ducks in the water.

I tried to let Ford enjoy his summer. I was mindful of letting him be a kid, and not asking him to take the place of his father. However, there were some things I couldn't do alone, things like lifting the eighty-pound Old Town canoe out of the water and onto the grass. Sometimes Ford groaned when I asked him to come in from swimming and help me with the canoe. Other times, he swaggered across the wooden dock and used his older-brother voice to say things like, "I think I'm getting some good muscles from this."

I'd smile and nod, but as we raised the red canoe out of the water, I was still lifting at least seventy of the eighty pounds.

Whenever another, older male was around, such as when Morgan and her family spent the day at camp with us, Ford reverted back to his boyish grinning and scratchy voice. I resisted the urge to let other people help me with things that Ford could easily do, and, in fact, had already been doing. When Morgan offered to carry one end of the canoe, I made Ford do it instead. I wanted to show him that he wasn't helping me solely because Dustin was gone. He wasn't just filling in. Rather, he was on his way to becoming a man.

All Ford's help and experience with the canoe and kayaks became important for our thirty-second dinner, which could only be reached by boat. We had a virtual flotilla of watercraft (four kayaks, one canoe, one motorboat) to get the thirteen diners from my parents' dock to the wooded island in the middle of Phillips Lake.

My older brother Van and his wife, Kelly, were visiting from Virginia, where Van is a fireman. My other brother, Will, his wife, Cindy, and their daughter, Makena, were up from Florida as well. But our official guests that evening were Andrew, a Bangor fireman, and his girlfriend, Tanya, who works for the city of Bangor. We called this dinner Fire on the Island with Two Firemen because we roasted hot dogs and s'mores over a bonfire that the two firemen struggled (yes, struggled) to make.

"Hey, I put out fires," Andrew said. "I don't make them."

We ate our charred hot dogs on paper plates balanced on our

Roasting hot dogs with the firemen and their wives

knees, and we sat on overturned logs or massive granite rocks. A resident bald eagle chattered overhead as it glided above the treetops like a kite.

At dusk, Van and Andrew gave the boys a lesson in steam as they let each of them douse the bonfire with buckets of water. We packed up the boat and kayaks and headed back to my parents' camp before nightfall. The wind had picked up quite a bit while we were sheltered by pine trees on the island. Whitecaps dotted the dark waters, and those of us in kayaks rocked back and forth with each surge of waves. Lindell had gone on the motorboat with my parents. Owen was in the canoe with Will, and I had Sparky in a kayak with me. Andrew, Ford, and Van paddled alone in kayaks. When we got to the middle of the lake and the wind was no longer buffeted by the island's trees, Ford's kayak began to tip sideways and back and forth.

"Do you need me to tow you?" I yelled across to him, but he couldn't hear over the wind.

He dug the paddles into the water and grimaced as the wind blew against his face.

"Ford, do you need me to tow you?" I yelled again.

"No, I can do it," he yelled back.

"Are you sure, Ford?" Andrew came up beside him. "This is really rough paddling, buddy."

"I've got it," Ford said. He pushed the paddle into the water like he was digging into rocky dirt.

Sparky, sitting in between my legs, whimpered and shifted his weight from hind leg to hind leg. I was afraid he'd jump out. Then what would I do? My heart quickened, and I had an urge to curse Dustin. *Why wasn't he here? Why did I have to do all of this alone?*

Van came up on the other side of Ford's kayak. "Andrew and I will be on either side of you," he said. "We won't leave you. Just keep paddling."

Ford pushed against the wind while the larger, grown men on

either side of him paddled seemingly with ease through the strong wind. They were going slow, pushing with long, deliberate strokes, to stay beside him.

Van called over to me: "Sarah, you go ahead with Sparky. We'll stay with Ford."

Sparky continued to whimper, but I couldn't leave Ford. Waves spilled over the side of the kayak.

Up ahead, I saw my dad coming back in the motorboat.

"Climb onboard," he called out to Ford when he was close enough. "Uncle Van can tow your empty kayak back."

"No, I can do this," Ford shouted over the wind.

"Are you sure?" my dad asked.

"Yes, I've got this, Pop," Ford said.

I let Sparky jump into the motorboat with my dad, and they drove back to the shore. Van and Andrew stayed on either side of Ford, and I stayed just ahead of them.

Together, the four of us crept across the lake, pushing against the gusts.

Everyone else was waiting for us on the shore when we pulled into the cove in front of my parents' camp. My kayak scraped against the pebbles in the sand as it ran aground. Will held out his hand and pulled Ford to the side of the dock. Then he helped lift him out of the kayak. My fingers and toes were numb from adrenaline.

Ford simply wrapped himself in a dry towel and said wistfully, "Well, that was a lot of fun, wasn't it?"

Fun?

Later that night, as I was tucking him into bed, Ford said, "Mom, I can't believe I did that. I really can't. Will you be sure to tell Dad if you e-mail him tonight?"

"Yes, Ford." I kissed his forehead.

A week later, we had a houseful again at my parents' camp for the thirty-third dinner, which featured a bluegrass band made up

Bluegrass band, with Sarah's brother, Will, on the far right

of guitar instructors Bill Thibodeau and Jeremy Shirland. Bill and Jeremy were accompanied by Will, who plays the fiddle and mandolin. Far into the dark hours of the calm summer night, the tinny sound of bluegrass music echoed across the lake, along with the boys' laughter and singing. Neighbors walked over to hear the music and try some of the barbecue from our local favorite, Moe's Original BBQ, delivered to us by the owners, Dewey and Emily.

I didn't know Dewey and Emily very well. I had only briefly talked to them when we were in the restaurant for dinner. But I asked them to stay for the music, and by the end of the night, Emily and I realized we have much in common, from our Alabama background to our self-deprecating sense of humor. The coming winter would be Emily's first in Maine. I thought back to my first

New England winter four years ago, and I gave her tips: Stay busy. Get a therapy lamp. Embrace the early darkness. And reach out when you need to hear another voice.

In the weeks and months that followed, Emily and I became great friends. But that night, as our friendship was beginning—set to the joyful sounds of bluegrass music, and with the boys running barefoot through the grass and catching fireflies in a jar—we were basically strangers. Later, I'd look back and think that if I hadn't had the nerve to ask Dewey and Emily to stay for dinner, I would have missed out on a fun new friend.

After the band left and our guests were gone, the boys went to bed in the loft of the camp with black dirt covering the soles of their feet and dried sunscreen in their hair. At close to midnight, I sat in a rocking chair on the screened porch with Will, and we watched the game warden's boat putter across the lake. The boat's green and red lights cast an eerie glow on the still water. Loons moaned in the distance.

Dustin's R&R already seemed like a lifetime ago.

We ended July with a potluck lunch organized by the Maine Troop Greeters, an organization of men and women who greet every plane, day or night, coming into Bangor International Airport with troops from overseas. It was difficult to get the boys focused on this dinner because they knew what was coming next month: dinner at Fenway in Boston. They struggled to be patient as the mostly elderly members of the Troop Greeters got close (to hear better) and asked them about school.

"It's summer," Ford said, shrugging. "But I guess school is okay."

It was a back-soaking hot kind of day, and lunch was outside in one of the members' yard. The boys were anxious to go swimming, and they whined about being so hot and thirsty. I hissed at them out of the corner of my mouth, reminding them to be polite.

For all of the lessons learned so far, it seemed patience was still a work in progress. One of the greeters rescued them by inviting them inside, into the air-conditioning, to see his Civil War memorabilia.

He had Ford at, "Do you like history?"

Back outside, the Troop Greeters, many of them wearing WWII baseball caps with various pins on the front, asked the boys about Dustin, but Ford, especially, didn't want to talk about him. I reasoned we were all still in separation mode, adjusting to the idea of Dustin being gone again. Talking about him made the absence too fresh.

But Ford stayed cheerful, if not overly polite, and, at this point, that was all I could hope for.

When we got in the car to go home, Ford said, "That was fun, but I miss having dinners at our house."

I thought about that for a minute. When was the last dinner at our house? I counted in my head. Seven of our last ten dinners had been away from home.

"There were too many troops for our house, though," Lindell said.

Owen corrected him. "Troop *Greeters*, Lindell. Those people from today *greet* the troops."

"What do you like most about eating at home?" I asked.

"That the people get to see where we live," Ford said. "And they sit in Dad's chair."

I thought I was making things more interesting for the boys by mixing it up. I hadn't considered that nothing can replace being at home, around our dinner table.

The car was quiet for a while, except for Lindell talking aloud about the difference between "troops" and "Troop Greeters." I inventoried our upcoming dinners—two in Boston, one at Acadia National Park, one at Mount Katahdin—and wondered if we should change course.

"Should we cancel some of the August dinners and make more of them at home?" I asked.

"What?" Ford screamed from the back of the van and stomped his foot on the floor.

I was startled. Wasn't that what he had just said?

"Are you crazy, Mom?" he said. "You want us to miss Fenway? No way!"

"Yeah, no way, Mom," Lindell added, even though I wasn't sure he knew what we were talking about.

Fair enough. Our plans would remain unchanged. But I made a mental note anyway. Nothing beats being at home, huddled around our small wooden table, joined in conversation with our guests.

Sarah and Ford

CHAPTER ELEVEN

August

When Elisabeth Dean said that she wanted to take me and the boys to "climb some rocks" for our thirty-fifth dinner, I thought she was referring to something along the lines of one of our family's frequent day trips: walking across boulders on the rocky shoreline of Acadia National Park on Mount Desert Island. It's one of the boys' favorite things to do. Even Lindell, who has to be hoisted onto the larger boulders, has become skillful at finding just the right footing and avoiding the slippery rocks covered in green moss at low tide.

When the sea level goes completely out, the boys search tidal pools for abandoned seashells and crab legs. At high tide, they skip rocks across the water.

For all the earthiness of climbing rocks at Acadia National Park, however, it isn't particularly hard physical labor. It's possible to not break a sweat. It's less climbing and more walking carefully on rocks. So I dressed for our dinner in a khaki skirt, black shirt, and a wind jacket (just in case, because sometimes it is cool on the coast).

I hadn't met Elisabeth yet. The only thing I knew about her was that she worked at Acadia Mountain Guides in Bar Harbor. I had seen the store many times along Main Street. I think I even bought a pair of wool socks there once. But that wasn't why we were having dinner with Elisabeth. Early in the spring, Bangor High School raffled off a Dinner with the Smileys as a fund-raiser at a silent auction. Elisabeth had the winning bid. When I called to coordinate her prize (dinner thirty-five), she said, "I thought it would be fun to take you and the boys to Acadia to climb some rocks." And that's exactly what I told the boys.

"So, we're just going to walk on the rocks like we always do with Dad?" Owen said.

"Sounds like it."

"And where will we eat?"

"Elisabeth says there is a restaurant across the street from the store."

The boys were cautious.

"The rocks part sounds fun," Ford said. "But what if we don't like the restaurant?"

"Can we get a souvenir at the store?" Owen said.

Outside the car windows, pine trees made a blur of green. Highway 1A was like a snake in my rearview mirror, stretching as far back as I could see, and then disappearing behind the tree-covered mountains near my parents' camp. Soon, the trees would get sparser, and the coastline would open up. We'd see Frenchman's Bay hugging the rocky edges of the island, with Cadillac Mountain rising up in the distance. Lobster shacks lined the roadway, their pots releasing steam into the foggy morning air. Antiques stores with weather vanes and piles of lobster buoys displayed out front, were just beginning to open.

"Will we go up the mountain?" Lindell asked.

"Maybe," I said. "I don't know where Elisabeth plans to climb rocks. But it's possible."

There are easy walking paths on top of Mount Desert Island's tallest mountain, and we've spent many afternoons jumping from rock to rock there. I figured Elisabeth would take us to the coast or to the mountain.

"I hope we go to the coast," Owen said. "I want to skip rocks."

We passed Pirate's Cove, the boys' favorite place to play minigolf.

"Can we do putt-putt after?" Lindell said.

"If it's not too late."

The road hugged the rocky cliff of Mount Desert Island. On the left, sailboats and tall ships bobbed up and down in the harbor. A foghorn blew in the distance, but the morning sun was just beginning to burn off the mist. We pulled into downtown Bar Harbor, where shoppers were already walking up and down Main Street and peering into shop windows. Acadia Mountain Guides is on the high part of Main Street, farther away from Frenchman's Bay, but closer to Mount Desert Island Ice Cream, the boys' (and President Obama's) favorite ice-cream shop.

"Will we get ice cream after?" Lindell said.

"I don't know. Maybe."

Inside the small store with wooden floors, Elisabeth was standing at the back wall, behind the sales counter. She was tall and had a long, brown ponytail. With her multipocketed hiking pants and sporty green tank top, she looked like she stepped out of the pages of an L.L. Bean catalog.

"Hello, Smileys," Elisabeth said, coming around the counter. "How was the drive?"

"Can we get ice cream?" Lindell asked her.

Elisabeth patted his head and said, "That's up to your mom." Then to me: "Jon Tierney, who is an internationally certified climbing guide, is going to join us, but he's running a little late."

Climbing guide? I was confused and curious, but still, I had not put two and two together. I continued to believe we were going to "climb some rocks."

Then Elisabeth said, "While we wait, let's go upstairs and get you guys fitted for your gear."

"Gear?" Ford whispered to me.

I shrugged. "Maybe walking sticks? Hiking boots?"

"Everyone will need a harness," Elisabeth said. "And I'll need your shoe size for the rock climbing shoes."

My stomach dropped. *Harness? Rock climbing shoes?*

We walked up narrow, creaking steps to a loft where harnesses, carabiner clips, shoes, ropes, and helmets were neatly stowed on shelves.

"Oh God." I put my hand to my mouth. "We're rock climbing, aren't we?"

Elisabeth smiled. "What did you think we were doing?"

Jon Tierney has a soft, gentle voice, but when he speaks, he is deliberate and thoughtful. His wispy brown hair shows very little gray. The only signs of age are the smile lines around his eyes. His forearms and hands are solid and tanned. Like Elisabeth, Jon was also wearing hiking pants and boots.

I looked down at my skirt and felt embarrassed.

We drove to Bubble Mountains, which borders Jordan Pond, where Dustin, the kids, and I hiked just a month earlier.

Jon led us through the woods, over boulders and across well-worn footpaths, until we reached a clearing under a canopy of trees. In front of us was the bald side of the mountain. It rose up before us like a wall—a sixty-foot, completely vertical wall.

"This is the spot," Jon said. He lowered his shoulder and set down bags filled with gear.

"Ummmm," Ford said. His hand shielded his eyes as he looked up to the top of the cliff. "I'm not so sure—"

"Grab the end of this line, Ford." Jon tossed a thick, braided rope, and Ford caught it against his chest like a football. "Owen, grab some of those clips over there." He pointed to a pile of metal carabiner clips at my feet.

"Mom, are we actually climbing this thing?" Owen whispered as he bent down to get the clips.

I tried to be calm. "It will be fine," I said. "It's character building." Inside, however, my stomach was in knots and my heart felt like it was beating in my throat.

"Let's do this," Lindell yelled, clapping his hands together. He started to climb the rock with his tennis shoes.

"First, you need to get on your gear," Elisabeth said. She waved Lindell over to her. "We're going to put a harness around your waist, and a helmet on your head. Then, you're going to wear these special shoes." She held up a tiny pair of soft climbing shoes.

"Okay, then," Lindell said. "Let's put them on."

Jon, who was already in his gear and helmet, scaled the side of the rock to set an anchor at the top. He moved up the vertical cliff like Spiderman, easily finding places for his feet and hands.

"He makes it look so easy, doesn't he?" Elisabeth said. Then I think she saw the fear on my face, because she began to tell me about Jon's credentials—how he's climbed almost every mountain in the world and that he is world-renowned for his teaching abilities. "You are in very capable hands," she said.

I figured as much as I watched Jon. He moved effortlessly, like he was climbing stairs or an ordinary ladder. His straight posture and deliberate, steady voice calling down to us were reassuring.

Still, I suddenly felt like I could use the bathroom.

Jon slid down the side of the mountain using the rope and kicking his feet against the rock as he went. "Should we go oldest kid to youngest kid?" he asked.

I looked at Ford. He was chewing his thumbnail and trying not to smile or make eye contact. I thought about times at the pediatrician's office, when the doctor holds a needle in her hand, ready

Ford rock climbing at Acadia National Park with Jon Tierney

to give a flu shot, and says, "Let's do this oldest to youngest," or "Can you set a good example for your brothers, Ford?"

Ford looked at Owen, then Lindell, and back at Jon. He shrugged. "Sure, I'll go first," he said. "I guess."

I watched from the base of the cliff, my hand covering my mouth, as Ford awkwardly straddled the side of the rock, trying to find a place for his feet. His knuckles were white from gripping so hard. He kept his body close to the rock, as if he was hugging it, and he moved slowly up the mountain. When he was about six feet off the ground, he looked down. "Whoa," he said.

"Don't look down," Jon told him. He was dangling from a rope beside Ford.

So Ford looked up to the top instead. "I'm not sure I can do this," he said.

"You're doing great," Jon said. "Just take your time."

Owen hovered close to my side. Occasionally, he buried his face into my shirt and said, "I can't look," and "Tell me when it's over." I rubbed his back and called out encouragement to Ford. "You look great! I'm so proud of you! You're doing fine!"

When Ford was about ten feet away from the top, he looked out, away from the mountainside, and saw how high up he was. "I can see the water!" he yelled. "I can see the mountains."

"Just don't look down," Jon said, still hanging beside him.

But, of course, the next thing Ford did was look down at us below.

His face turned white. "I can't go any farther," he said. "I want to go back down."

Jon put a hand on Ford's back. "Just take a breather here and see how you feel in a few minutes."

"Keep going, Ford!" I yelled. "You're almost there!"

"No, I want to come back down," he said. "I'm done."

"Are you sure?" I asked. "You're so close."

"Yes, Mom. I want to come down right now."

Jon showed Ford how to rappel. He bounced with his foot off the side, like he was on a giant swing. When he was back on the ground, and after Jon unhooked him from the rope, Ford came to me. His face was flushed, but his eyes were bright. He was trying not to smile again. When he was directly in front of me, he put his arms around my waist and his head on my chest.

I hugged him tight.

"I can't believe I did that," he said. His voice was muffled in my shirt. "I can't believe it!"

I patted his back. "I am so proud of you," I said. "I can't wait to tell Dad."

Owen was next. He got about twenty feet off the ground before he looked down. Then he wanted to stop. It seemed that looking down was the wrong thing to do. Owen had a harder time rappelling because he is so thin and flexible. His knees buckled against the rock, and the rope seemed to be lowering him more than he was lowering it.

Lindell went ten feet off the ground, which was impressive given his size. His favorite part was rappelling because he did it hanging from Jon's rope, as if he were on a ski lift between Jon and the mountain.

So far, no one besides Jon had been to the top of the mountain. If Dustin had been there, he'd go to the top. I was sure of that. Dustin is not afraid to try anything once, even if it makes him look silly.

One of my favorite memories is of Dustin trying to ice skate and sliding across the rink like a bag of sand. He got back up, dusted off the ice from his knees, and tried it again. He never gave up.

"Well, I guess I'm next," I said before I could stop myself.

The boys chanted, "Go, Mom! Go, Mom! Go, Mom!"

Right away, I could see that rock climbing looked easier than it actually was. The mountain seemed to become more vertical and smooth the moment I was standing in front of it looking for a place to put my hands and feet. I was worried about my skirt, so I tucked it between my legs and into the harness until it looked like a cloth diaper.

Jon stayed beside me, just as he had done with the boys.

Down below, I could hear the boys still chanting. Dustin spoke to me in my mind. *You can do this. Keep going. Do it for them.*

I did not look down. When I got above the tree line, I looked out, just as Ford had done, and I saw the spectacular view. Cadillac Mountain was in the distance, and Jordan Pond was below. I could see where the ocean met the horizon. "Wow," I said, truly breathless. And then my heart sank as I thought, *My son was up this high.*

It hadn't looked so high and unsafe when I was watching Ford from the ground. Suddenly, I wished that I hadn't encouraged him. I should have told him to come down.

I climbed to the spot where Ford had stopped. I was ten feet away from the top.

"Keep going, Mom!" Ford shouted. "Go past me! Do it for Dad!"

I was terrified. My kneecaps trembled. I just kept thinking, *Dustin would have gone to the top.*

"Do you want to go farther?" Jon asked.

I nodded. Then I looked above me to find the next foothold.

As I came to the top of the cliff, I felt my chest lighten. Blood rushed to my head. I had done it! I went to the top.

The boys were screaming and cheering below.

"That's my mom," Lindell said. "Look at my mom!"

After I rappelled down and was safely on the ground, Ford came to me and put his arms around me again. "You did it, Mom," he said. "We both did it."

We ate dinner in Bar Harbor, at a place called McKay's across from Acadia Mountain Guides. I was still high from the excitement, and so were the boys.

We chattered about what it looked like and felt like. More times than necessary, we said, "That was amazing."

I looked across the table and smiled at Ford.

He smiled back and nodded.

Our next two dinners were both in Boston. We traveled again with a babysitter, Kara's older sister, Becca, and our first stop was Fenway for a Red Sox game. We met Bangor city councilman Ben Sprague and his fiancée Malorie, plus Becca's family, for hot dogs, french fries, and ice cream. Ben used to work at Fenway after college, which wasn't that long ago, so he was able to give us a behind-the-scenes tour of the booth where announcers and media sit. Before the game, the Red Sox invited us onto the field to watch batting practice.

Owen shaking hands with Jarrod Saltalamacchia from the Red Sox

From the red, dusty baseball dirt of the sidelines, Ford, Owen, and Lindell watched with awe as Jarrod Saltalamacchia, Adrian Gonzalez, and Carl Crawford stepped into the netted batter's box and practiced their swings. When the players walked back to the dugout, they stopped to meet the boys and sign their baseball caps. But we hadn't seen Red Sox star Jacoby Ellsbury yet, and the boys were craning their necks to see if he was in the dugout or somewhere in the outfield.

A lady with a badge hanging from her neck came to us and said, "Are you the Smileys?"

"Yes, and this is Dinner with the Smileys," Lindell said. "At the Red Sox!"

"I have someone I'd like you to meet," the lady said. She motioned for us to follow her.

The concrete steps down into the dugout were thankfully cool and shaded. It was high nineties outside, and sweat streamed down my back and from the sides of my hair.

A tunnel leading below the stadium was dark and even cooler. I pulled at my shirt to let the cool air onto my skin.

Just before we got to a hallway that led to the locker rooms, Jacoby Ellsbury came to greet us. Ford and Owen were speechless. They stood against the wall and smiled. But Lindell, whose baseball cap pushed his large ears down and out, ran up to Ellsbury and slapped his hand. Ellsbury smiled. He offered to sign hats and balls. Ford and Owen were still frozen and smiling against the wall.

We walked out of the dugout and back into the hot, bright sun of the field.

The boys ran to Ben and showed him the signatures.

"That's really cool," Ben said, his smooth, boyish face breaking into a smile.

"He signed my hat!" Lindell yelled. "And he gave me five!"

Ben nodded and continued to smile as he ushered us toward the stadium to find our seats before the game. We had quite the crew with Kara and Becca's parents, their other sister, Brianne, and her husband, Jamie.

But Ford chose a seat right next to Ben. He pulled out the score sheets Dr. Peterson had given him at the University of Maine baseball game.

"Do you know how to keep score?" Ben asked.

"Yeah, one of our guests taught me," Ford said.

"Cool. I always liked to keep score when I was your age, too."

"I can't wait to keep score with my dad."

"Do you like math?" Ben asked.

Ford shrugged. "It's okay, I guess. I'm good at it, but it's not my favorite."

A little later, after a conversation about embarrassing things that happen at school, Ben said, "I was pretty geeky when I was your age, Ford."

Ford tried to hide a laugh. "You were? You?"

"Yep. I had big, Coke-bottle glasses and everything. I was the most awkward kid in every situation."

Ford smiled up at Ben. "I can't picture that," he said.

"Yeah, well, it's true."

"What makes someone awkward anyway?" Ford asked.

"Sometimes, people think it's not cool to be smart. So they think smart people are awkward. But that's not true. Don't believe it."

"Mom says my dad was awkward when he was little, too."

"Your dad sounds like a good man," Ben said.

In between innings, when we left our seats to get food and drinks, I often found myself walking behind Ben and Malorie, who, just one month away from their wedding, were totally in love and couldn't be parted. Ben kept his arm around Malorie when he wasn't holding her hand or lightly touching the small of her back. Malorie sank into Ben's arms and walked confidently in his embrace. They reminded me so much of Dustin and me when we were newly married. And no other thing—not Dustin's empty dinner chair or his shoes collecting dust in the closet—made me miss him more. I longed to hold his hand or walk beside him, holding on to his arm. If I closed my eyes, I could almost remember the way that felt. But when I opened my eyes again and saw Ben and Malorie, I felt completely alone.

The Red Sox lost that night, and the boys were disappointed, so the several miles' walk back to our hotel was painful.

Everyone was tired and hot. I carried the boys' souvenirs in my tote bag, which was overflowing and felt like a suitcase on my arm. The backs of my heels had blisters. Still a mile away from the hotel, Lindell refused to walk any farther. He sat down on the sidewalk and cried into his knees.

I picked him up with my one free arm, and tried to carry him.

"Here, let me," Ben said, coming up behind me. He took Lindell and hoisted him onto his shoulders.

"Would you like me to take your bag?" Malorie asked.

"No, I'm fine, but I think I'll ask Ford and Owen to carry their own stuff," I said, looking at them.

Ford and Owen moaned. "But we're tired," Owen said.

I didn't ask again. Instead, I handed each of the boys a handful of their belongings. They grumbled more, but I kept walking. Eventually they followed, still unhappy and dragging their feet, but now accepting the fact that I couldn't carry everything.

While we were away at the game, the hotel had accidentally given away our hotel room because we hadn't checked in yet. It was close to midnight, and we had nowhere else to go. I laid my forehead on the marble counter of the receptionist's desk in disbelief and annoyance.

But the man in a suit behind the desk laughed. "That's no way for someone named Smiley to act," he said in a thick, foreign accent. "Chin up. I have surprise for you."

His fingers clicked rapidly on the computer keyboard in front of him. "For your trouble, we put you in the President Suite."

"The what?" Ford said.

"Tonight, we call it the Smiley Suite," the man said.

"I don't get it," Owen said.

"It means we just got upgraded to a really big, fancy hotel room," Becca said.

"I've never seen your house," the man said. "But I guess this suite is at least three times your room at home."

The boys' eyes were wide with curiosity and excitement. They ran to the elevator and we rode it to the top floor of the hotel, of which our suite took up half. The view of Boston was incredible. Lights from the city twinkled below. We could see Fenway's Green Monster in the distance. And, indeed, the suite's bathroom was probably three times the size of the boys' bedrooms at home.

"I have never been anywhere so fancy," Owen said as he crawled into one of the many beds. His eyes were heavy and already closing. "This is the best day ever."

The next morning, we traveled to Lexington, Massachusetts, where a man named Jim Shaw, who during a family vacation to the lake earlier in the summer was coincidentally rescued from a broken-down boat by my babysitters' family, had a historic day planned for all of us (me and the boys, plus the babysitters and their parents, Rick and Dawn).

We started with a trolley tour of Revolutionary battlefields. Our tour guide was a woman dressed in traditional colonial aprons and a bonnet. Unfortunately, however, she wasn't equipped with a sense of humor or very much patience.

The day before had been long and hot for my boys. We were already exhausted. So my expectations for behavior were considerably low. I wouldn't have been surprised if the boys misbehaved during the tour or found it hard to listen to the guide's narration. But, in fact, just the opposite happened: The boys were riveted. Even Lindell. He sat in the trolley seat, his feet dangling high above the floor, and listened with an open mouth to the woman speaking into the microphone. Occasionally he leaned over to Ford beside him to whisper a question. Ford patiently answered Lindell in a low voice. At one point, Ford put his arm around Lindell and smiled down at him.

Outside the trolley window, a group had gathered alongside the road for a political rally. They were carrying flags and holding signs.

Lindell looked at the protesters, and not understanding what they were doing there, asked out loud, "Is today a holiday?"

Our guide stopped midsentence and glared at Lindell, then at me and back at him. "If you continue to talk," she said, "I can't hear myself think. Please keep your mouth closed."

Lindell nodded silently.

The woman continued her dialogue into the microphone. I gasped and looked around the trolley to see if anyone else was shocked.

Ford grimaced over Lindell's head at me.

We exchanged glances, and, having read my mind, Ford shrugged and patted Lindell on the back.

I was mad. Furious, actually. This time, my kids were actually behaving.

Lindell had only asked a question. Yes, he forgot to raise his hand or wait for a break in the woman's sentence, but he's five.

I held up my hand to interrupt the woman.

She looked at me with surprise. "Yes?" she said. "Do you have a question?"

"Actually, my son did," I said. "He wants to know if today is a holiday because he saw the protesters back there with the flags and signs."

Ford gave me a secretive thumbs-up behind Lindell's back.

I looked at Jim, our host, at the back of the trolley and smiled apologetically. We were his guests, and suddenly I felt bad for making a scene. Then I looked at Rick and Dawn, several seats in front of Jim.

Dawn nodded with approval. Rick jokingly shook a finger at me and said *tsk-tsk*.

Lindell said thank you after the woman answered his question, and we continued with the tour.

When we got off the trolley, Jim took us on a walking tour through Lexington. Rick and his daughters took turns carrying

Lindell on their shoulders. Dawn helped carry waters and count children. "Do we have everyone?" she said as she counted heads.

I had forgotten to bring food for the boys, and I knew they were getting hungry. Still, they were polite as our guides spoke to them about history. Ford asked thought-provoking questions that surprised the guides but not the Cowans or me.

Ford remembers trivia and historical facts like most people remember song lyrics.

"Weren't there actually two Boston Tea Parties," Ford stated more than asked. And: "I think I've read that Captain John Parker never said, 'If they want a war, let it begin here.'"

At the gift shop, Jim offered to buy fake muskets for the boys. Lindell and Owen ran to the display of guns to select theirs. But Ford wanted a book about history instead.

Jim said that Ford was a boy after his own heart, and he bought him a book of American history.

On the town's center green, another guide told us about the "first shot" that began the Revolutionary War.

Owen and Lindell were beginning to lose interest. They chased each other through the grass and fired their fake guns.

Ford found a spot of shade beneath a tree and sat down to read his new book.

We had been touring the city for at least five hours, and the boys didn't have lunch. I knew I was on borrowed time, but I was amazed at the way Ford, Owen, and Lindell hung on. This never would have happened six months before, when Dinner with the Smileys was just beginning, when the boys hadn't yet experienced the week-by-week crash course in social graces.

Then, when we were just moments away from finishing the last tour, Owen collapsed on the ground and cried, "I can't walk another step. I can't do it. I'm so tired."

Too often I expect Owen to silently and agreeably keep up. I'm usually busy dealing with Ford or Lindell, and Owen is left following along in the background. But when he hits his wall, so to speak, there is no turning back. If Owen breaks down, he's done. And Ford and Lindell are soon to follow.

Jim noticed what was happening. He told our tour guide we'd have to sneak out of the group, and quietly but quickly, he led us to the parking lot. I thanked him and apologized for Owen's whining.

Then we followed Jim to his house, where we met his wife, Laurie. She had a backyard barbecue—complete with a tent and tables—waiting for us. Two men dressed in full colonial British uniforms made of wool greeted us at the opening to the tent.

"Good day, young sirs," one of the men with a white wig said as he bowed down to the boys. "Your party awaits inside."

The boys laughed.

"Ummmm, okaaaay," Ford said.

Lindell asked if the man's hair was real.

"But of course," he said. "The king would allow nothing less."

"Do you have wooden teeth?" Lindell said.

"A gentleman doesn't talk about such things, young lad."

Laurie and Jim had an amazing meal laid out for a few of their neighbors and us. There was barbecue, corn bread, vegetables, and strawberry shortcake for dessert.

Jim shared with the group the story about being rescued by my babysitter's family when his boat broke down in the middle of a lake. We talked about the spirit of community and helping neighbors. Occasionally, one of the British soldiers poked his head in and acted confused, like he didn't understand our modern world. The boys would laugh again, and then they ran around the yard chasing each other with the wooden muskets.

On our way home from Lexington the next day, Becca and I stopped at a water park in Old Orchard Beach, Maine, and we let the kids loose in their bathing suits and sunscreen. They ran from water slide to water slide, and they acted like typical young boys, knowing that this day—this stop—was entirely for them.

I was happy to give them a day of truly no expectations and no lessons.

Becca and I took turns staying with Lindell in the wading pool while one of us followed the older boys on the slides. With an extra pair of helping hands, I was able to play with Ford and Owen, when recently I had found myself saying too much, "No, I can't do that right now because I can't leave Lindell."

On our way back to the car, I got an e-mail on my iPhone. I recognized the sender. It was a message I had been waiting for, so I stopped walking to read it.

Then I sighed.

It wasn't good news.

One of our most anticipated guests had written to decline our invitation. There had, of course, been others who had turned us down over the past eight months. Some of the boys' teachers declined because they didn't want to be so "public," and one guest canceled just minutes before his dinner. So I knew the boys were capable of accepting the disappointment. Still, I dreaded telling them, because this guest was especially exciting, and for a while, it seemed like he was actually going to come to dinner.

The boys were quiet in the backseat as we pulled out of the amusement park parking lot. Their hair fell in clumps from chlorine, water, and sunscreen. Becca was in the passenger seat checking messages on her phone.

"So, boys," I said, looking in the rearview mirror, "we had a great day—a great weekend, actually—but I have some disappointing news." I went on to explain that the would-be guest was very kind and polite, and that the decision wasn't personal.

No one said anything at first.

Owen stared out the back window. And then Ford said, "Do you think some people say no because they don't like us?"

"No, I don't think that at all," I said.

"Some people just don't like being in the public eye," Becca said, turning around to see the boys behind her. "You guys are used to that because of your mom's column, but not everyone likes being seen and written about."

"Yeah, I guess so," Ford said.

"And besides," I said, "look at all the people who have said yes. Let's not focus on the ones we didn't get to meet. Let's look at the ones we did get to meet."

The declining guest is somewhat of a celebrity. I knew that played into the boys' disappointment. So I added, "It's fun to meet famous people, but it's not everything. There are more than one hundred and fifty people who have already come to dinner and want to be part of your lives. Most of them aren't famous, but when you graduate from high school, I bet all of them will say, 'I remember when I had Dinner with the Smileys with him.' In the end, having a community of adults to support you—not just now, but always—means more than meeting a celebrity."

"And shoot, you met Jacoby Ellsbury this week," Becca said. "What more can you ask for?"

I wanted to add that Dinner with the Smileys was never meant to be a way to meet important people, but the boys were already playing with their handheld game systems and not listening anymore. I thought instead that it was time to take the dinners back to their roots: the community.

Of course, as luck would have it, the next dinner guest that we had *is* somewhat of a celebrity, especially in Maine. So my speech in the car seemed ill timed. I didn't want the boys to now treat "celebrities" differently because I had said that the "ordinary" guests mean more in the end. There are so many exceptions and foot-notes in life. It's a wonder any child can make sense of it all. Ultimately, I decided to trust that my boys, after more than thirty dinners, could understand the difference and treat everyone—no matter their position in life—with respect and interest.

· · ·

THE BOYS HAD been excitedly awaiting our thirty-eighth guest, Donn Fendler, since January.

When Dinner with the Smileys was still just an idea, Donn was one of the first guests the boys asked to invite. They knew his story well—how he was lost on Mount Katahdin without food or water for nine days—because Donn's book, *Lost on a Mountain in Maine*, is required reading for most schoolchildren in Maine. Ford read it in fourth grade, and the year before that, I read it to all three boys as a bedtime story. But Donn's story of surviving in the wilderness happened in 1939, when he was twelve years old. Today, he is in his mideighties. I wondered if Lindell, in particular, would be able to make the connection between the man and his younger self.

Donn arrived in a navy-blue blazer, perfectly pressed khaki pants, and a striped tie. Despite his silver hair and sunken cheeks, the resemblance to his twelve-year-old self, as seen in a picture in the book, was obvious. His shoulders were still high, meeting his long, narrow face without much neck in between. His ears stuck out, just as they had in the pictures. But when Donn smiled as he came through the door, magnificent, upward-arced lines came from the edges of his eyes. His grip was firm and dry as he shook each of our hands. And just like at the nursing home for dinner seventeen, the boys were instinctively more mellow and quiet around Donn. His professional clothes and silver hair commanded respect, and the boys responded with attentiveness.

Owen took Donn on a tour of the house, stopping to show him their Little League trophies and fish tank in the bedroom. Lindell showed Donn a Darth Vader mask and tried to explain the movies, as if Donn would not know them otherwise. Ford pointed to his copy of *Lost on a Mountain in Maine* on a bookshelf, and Donn noticed Ford and Owen's other books—*Harry Potter, H.I.V.E., The Mysterious Benedict Society*, the Percy Jackson series—many of

Maine legend Donn Fendler from Lost on a Mountain in Maine

which Donn had read as well. The three of them talked about books while Lindell drove a Matchbox car in between them and up and over their arms.

At dinner, the boys interviewed Donn about specific parts of his book.

"Mr. Donn Fendler," Lindell said, "didn't you see a bear?"

"I saw three of them, Lindell. But they left me alone for the most part."

"Why wouldn't you eat any fish from the water?" Ford asked. "Weren't you hungry?"

"I was hungry. But I've never liked fish. I didn't think I was going to start then."

Our back door was open so that a breeze could come in from

the yard. Through the screen, over Donn's right shoulder, a robin's nest lay on the high beam of our pergola. The baby birds had hatched the week before, after weeks of us watching the mother sit on her eggs. Now the babies propped their wobbly, fuzzy heads on the edge of the nest, and the parents flew back and forth with increasing frequency and with worms dangling from their beaks.

Owen heard the familiar sound of the mother's wings flapping against the air as she came in for a landing on the nest. He ran to the screen door to watch. "See our birds," he said to Donn. "They build a nest there every year."

Donn turned in his chair to see the mother feeding the babies.

"You never saw birds while you were lost on the mountain, did you?" Owen said.

Donn seemed surprised that Owen would remember such a small detail from the book. "No, in fact, I didn't," he said.

The mother robin flew away again, and after a few minutes, the babies quit bobbing their heads up and down. They settled into the nest to rest.

"Mr. Donn Fendler," Lindell said, "we're going to Mount Katahdin next week for a Dinner with the Smileys."

Ford chuckled. "Yeah, I didn't think about that before. Kind of ironic. First we have dinner with someone who got lost on Katahdin, and then we go there ourselves."

"Mr. Donn Fendler, how can we not get lost?" Lindell asked.

Donn's eyes sparkled as he smiled. "Just stay with your mom," he said. "Stay with the group, and you'll be okay."

RAE WREN, a local schoolteacher, was our guest for the Mount Katahdin dinner. Rae is what people call a typical Mainer. Petite, but strong, she wears her brown hair in a boyish pixie cut. She dresses comfortably, in sporty shorts with lots of pockets and comfortable shoes. On the weekends, she hunts moose, deer, and rab-

Night before Mount Katahdin hike

bit. Once, she shot a bear, and she saved the skin, fur, and head to use as a costume. She'll eat practically anything, and she's climbed Mount Katahdin more times than she can recall.

This dinner had two parts: first, a planning meal at my parents' camp, and then the hike the next day. To help us with the boys, Rae brought her friend Doug Comstock. Doug has also climbed Mount Katahdin more times than he can count, and he even got married at Chimney Pond, a stopping point for hikers just below the tree line. Doug is tall, athletic, and nearly bald. His voice is low, but soft, and his arched eyebrows move dramatically as he talks. For the planning dinner, he brought a box full of magic tricks and puzzles. Rae also brought a box, but hers was full of hiking gear and maps. Together, Doug and Rae laid out the materials on the floor of my parents' screened porch overlooking the lake. Rae fitted each of the boys for backpacks, and issued them canteens and safety supplies. Doug had a backpack carrier for Lindell, just in case he couldn't walk the entire length of the hike, but Lindell didn't want to use it.

"I'm going to walk by myself," he told us.

Our third guest on this trip was our other babysitter, Alyssa, the one who discovered our basement flooding in April. So the ratio of adults to children would be sufficient, but I still wasn't sure about doing an all-day hike.

At the planning dinner, after I saw Rae's and Doug's gear, I tried to talk them out of a *real* hike.

"So, how far are we going?" I asked tentatively.

"We'd like to take you to Chimney Pond," Doug said.

"It's about 3.3 miles there, and 3.3 miles back," Rae added.

"Is that uphill, downhill . . . ?"

"It will feel almost level," Rae said. "If there is any elevation, it's gradual."

"But, still, almost seven miles with three kids?"

"Yeah, I agree with Mom," Ford said. "We'll never make it."

"Is there something shorter?" I asked. "Something that's just a mile, maybe?"

Doug and Rae looked at each other.

"Well, there's Sandy Stream," Rae said, wrinkling her nose. "But there's not much to see there. Maybe a moose, if we're lucky. No guarantee."

"I think we should do that one," Ford said. "How far is it?"

"It's a mile, maybe," Doug said. "But it's nothing like Chimney Pond. You'll never see anything else like Chimney Pond. Some people say it's the most beautiful place in the entire Northeast."

"Yeah, but seven miles?" Ford said. "No way."

Just then, as I watched my oldest son lobby for a shorter hike, I changed my mind. Had we not climbed a rock at Acadia National Park? Had we not been through eight months alone without Dustin? Why were we going to wimp out now?

I don't want to be the mom who thinks things are impossible.

I don't want to teach my kids that doing less is better. I don't want them to think that anything stands in their way.

Ford and Rae were still talking about the two hikes. Ford's arms were crossed, because he had already shut down. He tried to talk over Rae with his own arguments about why an all-day hike wouldn't work.

"We're going to Chimney Pond," I said, interrupting them.

"What?" Ford looked at me with angry eyes. "Mom! Do you know how long that will take?"

"Probably all day," I said. "And it will be okay."

I left to help my mom set the table, and Ford followed at my heels. "Mom, you've got to be kidding me," he said. "Do you realize what this means?"

I didn't answer him.

"Fine, I'm not going," he said.

"Neither am I," Owen said.

I turned around to look at them, a handful of forks in my hand. "Actually, you're both going because it's not Dinner with the Smileys unless all four of us are there."

"I'm not going," Ford said again.

Owen nodded in agreement.

Lindell held Rae's hand and said, "I'm going, and I'm going to walk all by myself."

Ford was mad all through dinner and the rest of the night. He was even still mad when I woke him up at 4:45 A.M. We had to be at the ranger's station by 7:00 A.M., and we had a nearly two-hour drive ahead of us.

Alyssa spent the night at our house so that she would be ready for the early morning. While Ford followed me through the house complaining, Alyssa helped Lindell, half-asleep, get out of his pajamas and into clothes.

"Mom, this is ridiculous," Ford said. "What happens if Lindell can't walk the whole way?"

"Doug said he'll carry him in a backpack carrier."

"I'm walking by myself," Lindell called out from the other room.

"Do we even have food? Water?" Ford asked.

"Rae said she has everything we'll need."

"I can't believe you're making us do this. Why can't we just do the one-mile hike?"

I turned around on my heel to look at Ford. "Because we're not quitters," I said. "Last night, we were about to throw in the towel before we'd ever begun."

"Yeah, because we know that seven miles up a mountain is insane."

"It's not insane."

"Yes, it is."

"Look, Ford," I said. "Earlier this month, if you had known that Elisabeth was taking us rock climbing, what would you have done?"

"I don't know," Ford said. "But Mom——"

"I'll tell you what I would have done: I would have said no. I would have told her it was impossible. I would have said we couldn't do it. I would have said we needed to do something easier."

"Yeah, well, maybe we should have."

"No, Ford. Remember that feeling coming off the mountain? Remember how satisfied we all felt? We never would have had that if we'd quit before we tried it."

Ford never saw my point. But he didn't have to. He was getting in the car anyway, because I couldn't leave him alone at home. He sulked in the backseat as we drove north in the silver morning light. And when Ford sulks, Owen does, too. Both of them glared at me in the rearview mirror.

As it turned out, the hike was not as easy as petite, athletic, capable Rae had made it sound. There were gigantic boulders to climb and steep steps made into the side of the mountain with rocks. There were endless footpaths and bubbling brooks and chipmunks skittering across the pathway.

At the halfway point, it already felt like we had walked seven miles. Ford and Owen were still angry. They groaned and complained, even when Doug and Rae told them silly jokes or did magic tricks with their hands for them. But Lindell—well, Lindell was in his element. He marched through the forest and climbed over boulders twice his size. He never once asked to stop or to ride on someone's shoulders. He stayed close by Doug, Alyssa, and Rae, and never was affected by his brothers' bad moods.

When we finally got to Chimney Pond, Mount Katahdin rose up before us and glistened in the sun. It was the most magnificent thing I've ever seen. With snow, it would have looked like Switzerland. A quiet pond in front of us reflected the mountain's colors and the clouds in the sky. We sat along its shore to have our lunch, and when I propped my feet on a rock and leaned back, I could feel, for the first time, my soles and arches throbbing in my shoes. My legs ached. Sweat moistened the sides of my face, and I had long quit caring what I looked like. Then I saw Alyssa. Tall and slender, she sat gracefully on a rock and quietly ate her sandwich. Her hair was pulled back into an easy ponytail. Her skin was luminescent, her sparse makeup perfect.

I felt old.

When it was time to hike back, I wasn't sure my aching feet would move. My legs felt like tree trunks.

"Once we get going," Doug said, "the fluid will move around again."

Ford and Owen grimaced as they moved.

At a wooden overpass, above a babbling brook, I stopped to take a video for Dustin. I was narrating, saying, "We're on a hike at Mount Katahdin. It's beautiful up here. We should do this when you come home. Except Ford and Owen think it's the worst thing I've ever asked them to do."

"What?" Ford said, interrupting me. He moved so that his face came into full view in the camera lens. "It's actually not that bad, Dad. It's nice up here. I'm just tired. That's all."

Lindell continued to walk on his own, unwilling to ride on someone's shoulders or in the backpack carrier. "I want to walk on my own feet," he said. But when we were one mile away from the finish, he started to look pale. Dark circles formed under his eyes. His hair was matted down with sweat. He had already hiked more than six miles, and I was afraid he might pass out or throw up. I wondered if he was dehydrated. I gave him water and asked Doug to put him in the backpack carrier. After brief resistance, Lindell grudgingly agreed. He slept on Doug's back until we were just outside the entrance to the trail. There, we woke him up and put him on his feet again so he could go through the "finish line" himself.

As I watched Lindell race to the end and cheer for victory, Rae, walking behind me, said, "You know, one mile in Mount Katahdin is really equal to two miles because of all the hills and boulders."

I stopped in my tracks and turned around. "So, you're telling me we really walked the equivalent of fourteen miles?"

Rae nodded and smiled.

"Rae," I said, "that was information I could have used twenty-four hours ago."

She laughed and moved in front of me with her walking stick. "But wasn't it great?" she called out over her shoulder.

Indeed, it was. I was glad to have done it. And judging by the red, happy looks on Ford's and Owen's faces, I knew they were, too.

Later in the year, once the kids were back in school, Owen's language arts teacher asked them to write about a time when they challenged themselves. I found his rough draft and outline, where he listed several possibilities to write about: (1) winning the Little League championship, (2) climbing a rock at Acadia Mountain, and (3) hiking seven miles at Mount Katahdin.

. . .

OUR LAST DINNER in August, like the one with Donn Fendler, was highly anticipated. It was also with another celebrity. Although you would not guess by appearances alone that Matt Stairs is a former Major League Baseball player. There is no swagger in his walk, and he smiles easily. He talks about his home and his family more than he talks about his career. All this despite the fact that he holds the record for career pinch-hit home runs in the MLB. Matt played for Dustin's favorite team, the San Diego Padres, as well as eleven others across the country. He is a powerful, accurate hitter, but nothing else except his thick, strong arms would give that away. Matt is so humble that when we met him at the local batting cages, he worried that he might disappoint the boys.

"Go in the fastball cage," Owen said excitedly.

"I haven't hit a ball in over a year," Matt said, laughing. "I probably need to warm up with something slower."

The boys were shocked: a record-holding MLB hitter wasn't overly confident in his ability to hit the ball cold? They hung on to the outside of the wire fence and cheered for Matt.

"My coach always says to keep the eye on the ball," Owen said.

"Be quiet, Owen," Ford hissed. "Let him concentrate."

Matt looked over his shoulder and smiled.

The machine released a ball, and Matt, holding the wooden bat as if it were made of light plastic, swung effortlessly and smacked the ball into the back side of the cage.

The chain-link fence clinked as it shook from the impact.

"Whoa," the boys said.

"Now do the fast cage," Lindell said, clapping his hands.

"Actually, I want to see you guys hit," Matt said.

We moved to a slower cage, and Matt coached each of the boys on their batting stance and grip. Ford and Owen both hit balls toward the middle of the cage. Matt patted them on the helmet and gave words of encouragement and guidance: "Get your feet a little wider . . . There you go . . . Come up on the bat a little . . . Okay, now watch the ball . . . You've got this."

When it was Lindell's turn in the cage, Matt turned off the pitching machine and instead tossed the balls to him under-handed.

The heavy bat swung Lindell around, and he fell on the ground multiple times. With a round, pudgy hand, he'd push the helmet up from his eyes and laugh. "That was a good one, wasn't it, Matt?"

Matt nodded and tossed Lindell another ball.

Before we left the cages, Matt got in the fastball cage and wowed the boys with powerful hits that sounded like they might break the bat. The wood smacked against the ball and made a wonderfully satisfying *thunk*.

The boys hung on the fence again and watched while alter-nately laughing with excitement and gasping in awe.

Former Major League Baseball pinch-hitter Matt Stairs

Afterward, we came back to the house for dinner.

While I made pizzas in the kitchen, the boys showed Matt an MLB bloopers video from our collection. Two of the reels feature Matt.

From the kitchen I heard Lindell say excitedly, "Keep watching and you'll see you! You'll actually see yourself—on that TV!"

"Oh, this part is really cool," Ford said. And I knew, without looking, that he was operating the remote control.

"What about the other one?" Owen said. "Go back to the other one."

"No, Owen. Just wait."

It's a wonder Matt could watch anything at all, because from the sounds of it, the boys—specifically Ford—were skipping back and forth across the video and talking over the sound.

Matt patiently told them the backstory to some of the clips. "That guy's really great," I heard him say, and, "Oh, yeah, I remember that play."

I moved from the cutting board at the sink, where I was slicing onions and peppers, to the rolled pizza dough on the stove. I was humming "Take Me Out to the Ball Game" beneath my breath. Sparky was outside in the backyard, and the screen door was open. I could hear his dog tags clinking as he ran from tree to tree chasing squirrels.

I had my mind on several things: the new school year just about to begin, our upcoming guests in September (to include a US senatorial candidate, a comedian, and my boss), and the fact that fall would be the last season we had without Dustin at home.

Then suddenly, there was a horrific commotion outside.

The mother robin with the nest on the back porch squawked and beat her wings rapidly. Sparky's tags clinked louder and faster. Paws scampered across the back porch, and there was a shrill cry I had never heard before. In an instant, I knew what had happened. The baby birds had fledged, and Sparky got one of them.

I ran to the screen door, a kitchen towel still in my hand.

Sparky had the tiny gray bird between his lips, and he wagged his stubby, erect tail as he ran across the porch.

I yelled for him to "drop it," and although he seemed stunned, Sparky laid the bird at my feet and then darted off to hide in a corner of the backyard.

The small bird was frozen stiff, but he was still breathing. He shivered as I came closer. His wings looked fine, and there was no blood. Bird dogs like Sparky instinctively hold prey with a "soft mouth." But the mother robin dive-bombed my head as I knelt down next to her baby. She squawked and frantically swooped low through the air.

"It's okay," I called out to her, as if she could understand. "I'm going to help you. I'm going to help both of you." I cupped my hands and slid them beneath the baby bird. He beat his wings slightly and then stiffened again as I carried him upward. I walked to the waist-high picket fence and lowered the bird onto the grass on the other side. The mother still shrieked at me and flew at my head. I knew she needed time and privacy to help the baby get to shelter, so I shooed Sparky back into the house and closed the door behind us.

Inside, no one seemed to realize what had happened. They were still watching the MLB bloopers, completely oblivious to the life-or-death drama unfolding outside in the backyard.

I moved away from the windows so that the mother bird wouldn't feel threatened. After twenty minutes had passed, I went back outside to see if the bird had moved. Both the baby and the mother were gone.

I let Sparky out into the yard again, and I said a little prayer that the mother and her three babies were by then safe in a faraway nest with their dad.

.   .   .

IN A NORMAL year, when Dustin is home, he and the boys close out the summer camping on Phillips Lake's largest island over Labor Day weekend. In a normal year, we also make at least one trip to Great Pond, the navy's outdoor camping and recreation facility in Aurora, Maine. I didn't think I could camp alone with the boys, so they'd have to wait until the next summer for that. But I could take them to Great Pond and provide a little bit of summer normalcy before the school year began.

We spent one night in Great Pond's most remote log cabin, where the gravel and dirt road dead-ends into the thick forest. While it was still daylight, we walked through the woods to the shore. Ford climbed a boulder and sat down to read his book. Owen and Lindell skipped rocks in the water. The sun set on the horizon ahead of us.

Back at the cabin, Ford and I built a fire for roasting s'mores. I had never built a fire before, and neither had Ford. Dustin usually did it for us. I wasn't sure how to begin, but I sent Owen and Lindell into the woods to find sticks and logs. Ford searched the cabin for a lighter and newspaper for kindling. Then, in the rock-lined sandpit, Ford and I made a roaring-hot fire that crackled and popped. Owen and Lindell waited with their marshmallows and graham crackers, their faces increasingly highlighted by the flames' red glow.

"I guess we didn't need Dad to start a fire after all," I said to Ford.

"Actually, he'll probably need us next time," Ford said. "Because this fire rocks."

I laughed.

"No, seriously," Ford said. "We made a great fire. I mean look at it. Dad couldn't have made it any better."

"No, I guess not," I said.

Then, as Ford ran off into the woods with Lindell and Owen carrying flashlights, I sat back in the wooden adirondack chair and wished that I could reach over and grab my husband's hand.

Senator Angus King

September

When Angus King, former Maine governor and then candidate for the US Senate, arrived at our house for the forty-first dinner, the boys were outside fighting each other with light sabers and foam swords. Angus had a long, brown bakery bag under his arm, and his wife, Mary, followed closely behind.

Owen ran through the front bushes, his sword held high above his head, while Ford leaped over my potted plants and attacked him from behind. They tumbled into the path in front of Angus and Mary.

I held my breath and regretted not asking the boys to put away the swords before our guests' arrival.

"Now wait just a minute," Angus said with a serious face as he looked down at the boys. "Are we sword fighting here?"

I stood at the doorway with my hand at my neck. *What a horrible way to start*, I thought. I glared at Ford and Owen.

Then Angus reached into the bag under his arm and pulled out a baguette of French bread. He held it at the bottom and pointed it upward in front of him. Then he crouched down into a squatting stance, and said, "Okay, I'm ready now."

Ford and Owen looked at each other first. They were unsure.

But Angus was smiling, his sandy-colored mustache spreading above his lips.

"Get him," Lindell yelled, coming out from behind the bushes. He drew his light saber and smacked the side of the baguette.

For the next several minutes, Angus and the boys had a battle in the front yard between swords, light saber, and French bread.

Mary, dressed in a nautical, blue-and-white-striped shirt and neatly pressed, cropped pants, came inside and offered me a strong but warm hug. She talked in overlapping sentences about her excitement to be at Dinner with the Smileys.

When Angus and the boys came inside, they were breathless and had rosy cheeks.

I reminded Ford and Owen to leave their weapons on the front porch, and Owen said, "But Mr. King brought his bread inside."

"*Owen*," I said in a stern voice.

"Okay, okay, I'm going," he said.

The day after Angus's term as governor ended, he and Mary and their two children set out in an RV to travel the country. They wrote a book about their experiences titled *Governor's Travels*. Mary presented the boys with a signed copy before we went into the kitchen for dinner.

Owen flipped through the pages, admiring the photographs, and he laughed when he saw a picture of Angus with a full, bushy beard.

Compared to the man in front of us—refined, clean-shaven (aside from the neatly kept mustache), and wearing a navy-blue zip-front cardigan over a button-up, collared shirt—the Angus in the book looked—well, not like a politician, but a dad. There were pictures of him with his son next to a campfire, and pictures of him driving the large RV or hiking in the west. The photographs looked like pictures of Owen's own dad. And yet, there Angus was in front of us—a candidate for the United States Senate.

This had been another unexpected lesson of Dinner with the

Lindell and Senator Angus King

Smileys. Our guests—whether a senator, a legend, a teacher, or an artist—are still just people around the dinner table. They have families and friends. They laugh. They like ketchup on their chicken or no ice in their water. They tell jokes. They share stories. They play tic-tac-toe while they wait for the waitress to bring the food. And around my three boys, who have no real understanding of the grittier side of politics, our guests are completely stripped of their titles and position in society. Which isn't to say the boys aren't aware of our guests' offices and jobs. But when we're passing the butter to a US senator or showing him where to find the bathroom after dinner, it's hard to treat him as anything less or more than simply human.

Of all the boys, however, Ford has the most sophisticated, if newly emerging, understanding of politics. While Lindell still refers to the presidency as "the job that George Washington did," Ford has a more global understanding and is aware of subtle nuances in the political world. He's beginning to realize that politics is often a game. He knows policies and leaders are not static over time. So Ford had some questions for Angus, sitting at the head of the table in Dustin's seat.

"Why is Maine a liberal state but always elects Republican senators?"

Angus smiled and said, "I hope Maine is about to elect an Independent."

"What's an Independent?"

"Someone who thinks for themselves rather than following a party."

"Why did we used to have the Whig party, and now we don't?" Ford asked.

The questions and answers went on for about an hour, long after Lindell had left the table to play a video game. When it was time for Angus and Mary to leave, Ford seemed truly disappointed that the dinner was over. "This was a lot of fun," he said as he shook Angus's hand. And then, while Angus and Mary walked down the front walkway to their car, Ford called out the door, "Thanks for coming."

The kids were back in school now, and the leaves were beginning to rustle high up in the maple tree outside our front window. The days were shorter, not only because of the sun setting at an increasingly earlier time, but also because our schedules were filled with the business of the back-to-school routine. Ford had begun his first year of junior high school, and although I worried every time I dropped him off in front of the two-story building with the chilly exterior, he seemed to be doing well. In the afternoons, when I picked him up, he walked to the car with his best friend, Noah, and alongside (although not speaking to) girls who are his same age but who had somehow, over the course of the summer, grown to be about five inches taller than the boys.

Owen was in fourth grade and had moved from the ten-room primary school to the slightly more intimidating (for him) elementary school across the schoolyard. His language arts class was reading Donn Fendler's *Lost on a Mountain in Maine*, and Owen liked making connections between what Donn had shared with us at dinner and what he was rereading in the book. But fourth-grade math had become significantly more challenging, and I, as the creative type in the family, was little help with nightly homework. Owen grew frustrated. He laid his head on the kitchen table and moaned, "I just don't get it!" Sometimes, Ford tried to help, but that usually ended in a fight. "Stop hovering over me," Owen would say, pushing Ford away.

"I'm just trying to help, Owen. Geez."

"You can help me without hanging over me."

When the timing lined up, Owen Skyped with Dustin to do his homework. With the computer set up before him on the kitchen table, and Dustin's bodiless face set against the bland, yellowed background of his living quarters, Owen worked through math problems with his dad. But if Dustin was already asleep during homework time, Owen Skyped with my dad.

Lindell had started kindergarten, so for the first time in nearly twelve years, I didn't have someone home with me during the day. This new freedom came with mixed feelings. I missed shopping for groceries with Lindell's chubby legs poking out of the seat at the back of the shopping cart. I missed stopping for lunch with him and listening to him try to sound out words. I missed rainy or snowy days when he and I would snuggle on the couch under a warm blanket and watch cartoons. Curled up with him, I could always smell the sweetness of his hair and the slightly soured scent of his breath. When his breathing grew deeper and slower, I knew he was asleep, and often, I would fall asleep, too.

Kindergarten changes boys. They enter as babies and come out as little boys. In my experiences with Ford and Owen, there is no other school year that involves such dramatic changes. I knew that in nine months, Lindell would be taller and thinner. His cheeks would have less fat and his hair would be less baby fine and slippery. He'd likely be able to read and write and tie his own shoes. He'd be less dependent on me.

Under any other circumstance, these realizations might have been heartbreaking. I would have cried to Dustin about losing my baby. I would have walked home from the school with rounded shoulders and wondered what to do with myself all day.

But these weren't ordinary circumstances.

Dustin wasn't here to cry to. There was no other adult to help me with the kids. I could use the six-hour break that the school day would give me. So in the end, when Lindell let go of my hand and joined the other kindergartners in a line to go into the school on the first day, I didn't cry.

Shelley, standing beside me, cried as she watched Lindell go, but I didn't. I had too much on my mind, too much to get done, now that I finally—finally!—had six full hours to myself.

I was teaching again at the University of Maine, but now I didn't have to coordinate child care for Lindell at the same time. I could go to the gym or to the library to write after work. I could sit in the house and do nothing. I could take a shower and not be interrupted. I could do all these things, but mostly, in those quiet hours of the school day, what I wanted most was to be with my husband. I imagined all the things we could do: go to lunch, take a walk, watch a movie, go back to sleep. Never mind that if Dustin were home he'd be at work.

As I sat in the quiet house and listened to the clocks tick, I could almost see Dustin on the opposite side of the couch, rubbing my feet as he read a book.

I felt the same sense of loss and loneliness in the pews at church.

Now that the school year had started, we were back to our usual weekly schedule, and that meant church on Sunday. For the first part of the service, the boys sat with me. I shushed them when they whispered too loud, and I glared at them when they elbowed each other. I passed crayons and coloring papers to Lindell, who kneeled in front of the pew and passed the time drawing.

Often, I didn't realize what a flurry of activity had occupied the pew until Renee called all the children to Sunday school, and the boys, along with their peers, left the sanctuary. All at once, the space around me was quiet and still. I'd collect Lindell's papers into a pile and smooth the jackets the boys had left behind. Then I'd settle into the dark green cushion of the pew and try to calm my mind. Ordinarily, this is when I'd reach over and grab Dustin's hand, lacing his fingers with mine. We'd sit shoulder to shoulder, and sometimes, I laid my head on him. Without Dustin, the pew seemed to stretch forever with endless empty space and no one beside me. When I felt alone or cold, I tried to imagine Dustin next to me.

Melissa, from our fifth dinner, sometimes saw me sitting alone, and crossed the aisle to join me. But nothing could replace the closeness of being next to Dustin, dressed in his nice suit and tie, and taking in the smell of his aftershave.

One day after church, the boys chased each other outside with their foam swords and light sabers while I made dinner in the kitchen. I heard their screams and laughter through the windows. Their feet crushed freshly fallen leaves. Sparky barked as he moved from window to window to see the boys.

Then Lindell ran inside screaming, "It's Dad! It's Dad! He's here."

"What?" I set down the spoon I was using to stir soup on the stove, and I went into the living room to see Lindell.

"Quick, come here," Lindell said. He ran back outside.

As I stepped out the front door, Lindell pointed down our

street, where Dustin's blue Ford Freestyle was coming slowly down the residential road. "It's Dad!" Lindell screamed.

My stomach sank. It was in fact Dustin's car, but we had sold it to our neighbor's granddaughter before Dustin left for deployment. She was coming to check on her grandfather Earle's house. The car slowed down to turn into the driveway that runs parallel to ours. Lindell stood and watched from our brick walkway.

I put a hand on his shoulder. "Honey, that's not Dad," I said.

"But it's Dad's car."

Everything about what I saw and heard in front of me—the car's brakes, the sloping roof rack, the tires turning against the pavement—brought back memories. How many times had we stood in our front yard and waited for Dustin to come home from work in that car? For me, the sight of the blue Freestyle always meant relief. To the boys it meant playtime. Dustin would gather them in the backyard to play catch or kick the soccer ball.

When our neighbor's granddaughter got out of the car and shut the door, it, too, sounded familiar. I could imagine Dustin coming down the sidewalk in his khaki uniform, his arms open wide for hugs. I could imagine the way his five-o'clock shadow would bristle against my cheek as he kissed me hello. I could imagine the way he'd smell like stale coffee after a day at work.

I sat down on the front step and pulled Lindell into my lap.

He was still staring at the blue car.

"That's Dad's car, but we sold it, remember?" I said. "Someone else drives that home now."

Lindell leaned his head back against my chest and reached his hand up to my cheek. "When will Daddy come back? It seems like forever already."

"I know, honey." I ran my hands through his fine hair.

.   .   .

SOMETIME LATER, WE went to a local apple orchard to visit the corn maze and buy our yearly pumpkins. The leaves were really beginning to turn. Their edges were yellow and orange, and, alongside the road, groups of them looked like upside-down candy corn.

The boys ran through the corn maze, and afterward we waited in line for ice cream.

I was busy putting change back into my wallet and passing out cones when Owen tugged on my coat sleeve.

"Mom, Mom," he said. "Isn't that Frank and Anita?"

"Frank and who?" I said absentmindedly while still rummaging through my purse.

"Mom, Mom, look," Owen said. "It's them, the ones from our dinner that was supposed to be with Gloria."

I looked up and saw Frank, with his curved back, shuffling across the grass strewn with hay. On his arm was Anita, standing as straight as a dancer.

"Oh my gosh, you're right, Owen," I said. "That's Frank and Anita."

Owen ran over to them. "Hi," he said when he got in front of Frank. "Do you remember me?"

Frank put a hand on Owen's shoulder. "Yes, you're one of the Smiley boys," he said.

"Hi, Frank. Hi, Anita," I said, coming up behind Owen. I knew Anita probably would not recognize us, but I talked to her as if she did. "It's great to see you," I said, taking her hand in mine.

Anita nodded and smiled while Frank came closer to give me a hug.

"How are your dinners going?" he asked.

"We're about to have dinner number forty-two," Owen said. "We ate with you at dinner number seventeen."

The boys were much better than me about keeping track of our dinner numbers!

"So your dad will be home soon, will he?" Frank asked.

"Yeah, but it still feels like a long time away," Owen said. "I'm in fourth grade now."

Lindell and Ford joined us to say hello to Frank and Anita. We talked for a few minutes, and then Frank asked us to come by and see them again for dinner.

"Can we, Mom?" Owen asked, looking up at me.

"I don't see why not," I said. "That sounds like a great idea. In fact, we could visit them with Dad, too."

"Yeah, you can meet my dad."

"I'll look forward to it," Frank said.

OUR FORTY-SECOND DINNER was with two of my bosses from the *Bangor Daily News*. Mark Woodward, now retired from the news business, was one of the first people I met when our family moved to Bangor in 2008. He is spry, with large round eyes, and he walks nearly as fast as he talks. When he tells a story, he moves his hands in big, exaggerated motions.

Mike Dowd, Mark's successor, is the opposite: subtle in manner and deliberate in the warm, even way he talks. Occasionally he slips reading glasses out of his front pocket and holds them to his eyes to read small print. Then he quietly drops the glasses back into his shirt pocket. He came with his wife, Ann, who is like a warm storybook grandmother. She hugged me as soon as she came in the door, and when we sat down to talk, she patted me on the knee. Ann is an ice breaker. She laughs from deep in her belly, and she cooed over the children. Sparky climbed into her lap, and she didn't push him away. She brought wrapped chocolates for everyone.

Also at dinner that night was Mark's friend Tim Caverly, creator of the Allagash Tails, a series of books about northern Maine. Tim had a presentation—an educational film shone from a projector onto a sheet hanging from our television cabinet—to show the boys, and I was disappointed when they didn't sit still for it.

Ford slid off the couch and onto the floor like a limp noodle. Lindell, fascinated by the projector, continued to poke at the beam of light with his foam sword, piercing the image on the sheet. I hissed at him under my breath and told Ford to sit properly on the couch.

Ann winked at me, as if to say, "It's okay. Let them be."

It's interesting how grandparents, with their larger perspective and hindsight, are often more tolerant of children's behavior. I took comfort in Ann's guidance to relax.

Plus, it was true that the kids had had a long day at school. Six hours of being told what to do is usually rewarded with at least three hours of running free in the backyard and using their outside voices. This dinner, and the boys' behavior, reminded me that instead of being frustrated, I needed to adapt better by anticipating conflicts and planning accordingly. In other words, I had set up the boys to fail. We weren't on a summer schedule anymore. Weekday dinners probably were too much. I had to respect the boys' need for free time after a day full of school.

In the middle of the presentation, Owen whispered to me, "Mom, I'm enjoying this, but I just can't sit still."

I remembered feeling that same way when I was a kid, when all of my muscles were twitching to move and I squirmed in my school desk.

I released the boys to the yard and the adults enjoyed the rest of Tim's movie without distraction, except for the echo of the boys' screams coming through the front windows.

Once we were at the dinner table, for reasons I will probably never fully understand, I began thinking about Dustin's lost wedding band, the one that slipped off his finger in the rapids at Mount Katahdin over a year ago. I shared the story with our guests, and my eyes teared up again when I thought about all that the ring had meant, all the memories it symbolized, and the fact that it was now somewhere tumbling down a rocky stream in Baxter State Park.

"You wrote a column about that last year, didn't you?" Mike said.

"I remember it," Ann said.

Under the table, I twirled my wedding band on my finger.

That night, as I lay in bed trying to sleep, I pictured Dustin's original ring in my mind. It was thicker in the middle than it was on the edges. The white gold had faded in spots, and sometimes the ring looked more gold than it did white. It was badly scratched on the outside, but still smooth on the inside. We had never gotten it engraved, but there was a small emblem, the jeweler's mark, in the center of the metal. I could still remember how cold the ring felt when Dustin and I were holding hands and I rubbed it with my finger. I remembered the way it scraped against wood as Dustin held on to stair railings or ran his hand across the dinner table. I could still hear in my mind how the ring made a pinging sound as it hit the porcelain sink when Dustin took it off before his shower.

Dustin had a new ring, yes, but it wasn't *the* ring, and it never would be.

OUR NEXT DINNER guest brought his wife and infant daughter— and his cameraman. Dan Cashman, host of a nighttime talk show in Maine called *The Nite Show with Danny Cashman*, planned to do skits with the boys and air them on his show later.

"Like, this dinner will be on TV?" Lindell asked.

"Parts of it," I said. "Mr. Cashman is a comedian. He'll cast you guys in skits that are funny, kind of like *Saturday Night Live*."

"Mom, Lindell doesn't know what *Saturday Night Live* is," Ford said. Then to Lindell: "It's like *MADtv*."

Lindell seemed nervous before Dan arrived. He was going to be in a skit, and he wasn't entirely sure what a skit is.

Dan is tall and lanky, with ears that point out at the tip and a chin that is much narrower than his forehead. He moves his long arms in a loose, rubbery sort of way when he talks, often putting a hand on his waist and then moving it to his pocket or rubbing his chin. He is unable to sit still for long, and he talks so purposefully and fluidly, that even his "ums" and "ahs" are well-placed.

Lindell was stunned. Speechless. And totally locked in on Dan. It was like a lightbulb went off for him: This guy—this Dan Cashman, whom Lindell would later refer to as Dandy Cashman—makes a living out of being funny.

"So, are we doing fart jokes in the skits?" Lindell asked.

Dan laughed. "Not a bad idea, but I've got some other things planned that I think you'll like."

"What is it? What's the skit?" Ford said.

Dan sat with the boys on the couch, and his long legs bent awkwardly so that his knees were nearly up to his chin. Dan's wife, Karen, and daughter sat on the other couch and watched quietly.

Dan told the boys the plan: They'd make a skit about making a skit.

Huh? The boys twisted their faces.

"While we're filming, I'll pretend I'm coming up with ideas for a skit," Dan said. "But you guys will say that all of my ideas aren't funny. Only, it will be funny, because that's the skit. Get it?"

Owen got up on his knees. "Oh yeah, this is great. We can just say, with a flat voice, 'Uh, that's not funny, Dan.'"

Dan pointed a long finger at Owen. "Yes! Just like that. That's perfect."

"And then we can beat you with foam swords," Lindell said.

"Excellent," Dan said. "At dinner, you'll tell me to go home. We'll act like I'm overstaying my welcome. It will be like I think I'm moving in with the Smileys. Owen will tell me to go home, but I won't move. Then we'll cut to you guys—"

"And we'll beat you with foam swords," Lindell said.

"Okay. Yes."

"So let's get started," Owen said, clapping his hands.

Karen and I watched from the sidelines as the boys—all of them—gathered in huddles, with occasional fits of laughter, and did retakes because someone spoiled their line or laughed too soon. Karen told me that Lindell reminded her of a young Dan Cashman.

"When Dan was young," she said, "he hosted pretend game shows in his basement. He'd shake the imaginary men's hands and kiss the women's cheeks. He'd do monologues and interview 'guests.'"

I looked across the room at Lindell. He stood on the sofa, to be more at Dan's height, and was completely animated—hands flying, expressions exaggerated—as he plotted with Dan for the next skit. I wondered then how these dinners were affecting the boys. Would I ever really know all the ways in which meeting a new person each week had changed them?

Later, in November, the boys' skit with Dan aired on the television show. We recorded it, and the boys watched it over and over again, amazed at their cleverness. Dan checked in periodically to see how the kids were doing. Lindell shouted, "It's Dandy Cashman," whenever he saw him.

I once asked Dan what it was like being around someone who mirrored his childhood self.

Dan said, "I can see that, yes, but more often, when I watch Lindell, I think of a young Will Ferrell."

By late September, our new school routine was well established. The boys' summer tans had faded, and goggles and beach towels were replaced with jackets and hats on the hooks on our front porch. Fall colors swept through the trees top to bottom. In the evening, there was a chill in the air, a sharpness that stung the lungs with each deep breath.

Marion, whom I met when the basement flooded, started leaving food on our front steps once a week. The boys and I called her the Food Fairy because we never could catch her in the act. She brought homemade French toast, cookies, pasta, and macaroni and cheese. On cold autumn nights, when the darkness was setting in earlier and earlier, those warm meals in aluminum pans waiting for me on the front steps were a reminder that we hadn't been forgotten.

We also spent a lot of time with Ben and Malorie, who had gotten married in September. Ben had a new role as a middle school youth leader at church, so every other Friday night, he picked up Ford and drove him to church for dinner. On the off Fridays, Ford would ask, "Is tonight a youth group night?" When I told him that it wasn't, he looked disappointed. He and Owen liked to ride their bikes to Ben and Malorie's house to play Risk or watch football. And when our printer broke the night before Ford's first social studies research project was due, he called Ben for help.

"Mom can't take me anywhere to get my project printed," I heard Ford say on the phone. "She's mad at me because I waited until the last minute, and now Lindell is already in pajamas, and it's late. But if I don't print this paper, I'll get an F. The teacher even said today, 'Don't use the my-printer-broke excuse.'"

Ben didn't have a printer at home, but he said, "I'll call you back in ten minutes after I track down someone who does."

Ben had fallen into the cool uncle role, which is ironic because he always described himself to Ford as "the most awkward person anywhere." Maybe that is why Ford felt so comfortable with Ben. He wasn't young enough to be Ford's peer, but he wasn't old enough to be mine, either. Ben was somewhere in between, with vivid memories of preteen angst, but still enough distance to offer Ford hope for the future.

My mother-in-law, Robin, came to visit at the end of September. Knowing that there was another adult in the house at night allowed me to sleep better and longer. My shoulders relaxed and fell down from around my ears. I could go to dinner with friends or stay in bed past 8:00 A.M.

One day, Robin and I took the kids to a nearby park, where Ben was already playing Wiffle ball. The boys joined Ben's team, and Robin and I walked laps for exercise. Early fall leaves crunched beneath our feet, and our pace was quickened by Sparky pulling on the leash, lunging at fattened squirrels scurrying across the sidewalk with a load of nuts for winter.

My phone beeped, and first I ignored it because it was only an incoming e-mail message.

When I peeked a few minutes later, I didn't recognize the sender's name. But something made me stop and read anyway.

> *Hi Mrs. Smiley—my dad, Greg Canders, read your article in the* Bangor Daily News *about losing your husband's ring last year. I drove up from Boston last night to spend some time with my parents, and my dad showed me the article this morning. We decided to attempt to find it. Could you please give me a call, as we have found a wedding band and would like you to identify it. Driving back from Millinocket now, we live in Bangor.*
> *—Zac Canders*

I stared at the screen on my phone, trying to make sense of the message. I wondered if it was a joke.

"What's the matter, Sarah?" Robin moved closer.

I continued to stare at the message.

"Is everything okay, Sarah? Is it Dustin?"

I handed the phone to Robin and let her read the message herself. Sparky whimpered, eager to get on with our walk.

Cheers erupted across the field, from the direction of the boys' ball game. I looked up and saw Lindell running the bases with his hands in the air.

"Hmm," Robin said skeptically, handing the phone to me again. "Do you think this is for real?"

"I don't see how it could be," I said. "Dustin and I couldn't find the ring right after he lost it. It's been more than a year. I'm sure it's long gone."

"Do you think it's a practical joke? Should you call the number?"

We started walking again, both of us in a daze, trying to figure out what motive someone might have for tricking me. Robin said that if I called the man back and met with him, I shouldn't be alone, and it shouldn't be at our house.

"You just never know," she said.

When we told Ben, he agreed.

So I called the phone number in the message, and I arranged to meet Zac and his dad in the parking lot of Moe's, Dewey and Emily's barbecue restaurant. There, the three of us plus Robin stood between our cars and made introductions. Zac's sandy-colored hair was tousled and damp. Greg's reddish skin was peeling at the bridge of his nose and across his forehead. They both wore plaid shirts with the sleeves rolled up.

"This probably sounds crazy to you," Zac said, leaning against his father's car.

I scratched at my head. "Yeah, I'm just trying to figure out—"

"Maybe we should explain," Greg said. "I read your column— the one about your husband losing his ring—last year, and I never forgot it." He pulled a tattered, folded piece of paper from his left breast pocket and unfolded it as he talked. I saw my column title, "Wedding Band Lost, but Love Found," and a head shot on the printed side of the paper.

"Dad is a professional scuba diver," Zac said. "He's done this before. He likes finding lost objects that mean something to someone."

"So we were going to hike the mountain today," Greg said.

"But the weather turned bad. So I said, 'Let's go find those rapids the columnist wrote about and see if we can find her husband's ring.'"

"I didn't think we had a chance," Zac said. He had his hands in his pockets, making his shoulders seem broader. "It took us a while to find the spot. We used your description from the column, about it being near whitewater rafting and a rope swing."

"Abol Falls," I said. "You saw the rope swing?"

"We saw it, and we knew we were in the right spot," Greg said. "So we got out the gear, and I went in. The water was really rough, as you probably remember from swimming there."

Zac smiled. "Yeah, I told Dad it was hopeless."

"And then, right before we were going to call it quits, my underwater metal detector beeped," Greg said. "I dug around in the silt and pebbles. My tank was almost out of air, and the rapids were pushing me against the rocks. I had to anchor myself."

"I thought it was time to give up," Zac said.

"And then, there it was." Greg smiled and his cheeks became rosier from the excitement.

"Dad came up with this ring in his glove, and I couldn't believe it," Zac said. He shook his head.

Greg dug around in his breast pocket again. "Before I show you the ring, though," he said, "I need to tell you that it's not—"

"It's not engraved," I said, nodding.

Greg and I stared at each other for a moment.

Then he breathed deeply and nodded back. He pulled out a small plastic bag from his pocket. "I think this belongs to you," he said. Greg emptied the plastic bag into my open hand, and Dustin's ring fell out. For a minute, I couldn't breathe.

There it was. Dustin's ring was in the palm of my hand. I instantly recognized the weight and feel of it. But the metal was spotted and dirty from being underwater for more than a year. I flipped the ring over in my hand. I couldn't stop touching it. Then

I held it out in front of me to look for the jeweler's mark engraved on the inside.

There it was. Dustin's ring.

"Go ahead, put it on," Greg said.

I slipped the ring onto my right ring finger. It felt just the way it always had when I wore it while Dustin washed the car or kayaked in the lake. I rubbed the sides with my other fingers, and it was like I was touching Dustin's hand in a dark movie theater or across the dinner table.

And to think Dustin didn't even know yet. He was halfway across the world, sound asleep, and completely unaware that I was holding the ring I gave to him thirteen years ago. It lay at the bottom of the river, frozen over in the winter and thawed again in the spring, and now it was on my finger.

Cars crept past us in the parking lot. A light rain began to fall.

I wanted to cry, but I was too embarrassed in front of Greg and Zac. My mother-in-law wanted to take a picture of us with her phone. I joked that passersby probably thought Zac and I had just gotten engaged. People stared out their car window, and I couldn't stop smiling and laughing.

"I still can't believe we found it," Zac said, shaking his head.

"It's a miracle," Greg said.

I stared at the ring. And then, suddenly aware of my surroundings, I said, "Oh my gosh, you guys have to come to dinner!"

"Oh, that's very nice," Greg said, "but—"

"But I'm on my way out of town." Zac looked at his watch. "Actually, I need to get going," he said.

"No, I don't mean tonight," I said. "Well, not necessarily tonight. But some other time, maybe? For Dinner with the Smileys?"

They both looked at each other. Greg said, "Dinner with the Smileys?"

Neither one of them had been following the weekly dinners.

I stayed up late that night waiting for Dustin, eight time zones away, to wake up and start his day. I couldn't wait to tell him about the ring. He usually checked his Facebook first thing in the morning, so I sent him a message there.

Dusty: You're not going to believe this, but guess what I have in my hand—or, actually, ON my hand? YOUR RING. Two guys—a father and son—found it while scuba diving at Abol Falls. Can you believe it? Isn't that crazy? I can't stop looking at it on my finger. I feel so close to you. Our wedding song couldn't be more true: The long and winding road DOES always lead back to you. ME

I stayed awake until after midnight waiting for Dustin, but he never came online.

Eventually I fell asleep with my head on the pillow next to the computer, and my hands on the keyboard.

The next morning, I woke up to a message from Dustin:

Sarah: Sorry, I didn't check Facebook before work this morning, so I'm just now seeing this. Wow, that is amazing about the ring! Incredible! How did they do it? How did they know? Was it in the same place? This is crazy! But honestly, Sarah, I always thought it would be found. I really did. How could it not? The road always leads me to your door. I love you, Dustin.

In the busy days that followed, whenever I felt stressed or anxious about day-to-day things (forgotten lunch boxes, dirty socks on the floor, an alarm clock that never went off), I looked down at Dustin's ring on my finger and thought, *How can I be anxious in a world where this could happen?*

And it wasn't just the miracle of the found ring. The realization that Greg and Zac would go out of their way to help someone and expect nothing in return was equally reassuring. Dustin and I tried to pay them. We offered to make a donation in their name to a charity. But Greg continued to insist that he didn't need anything.

"Make a donation to a charity if you'd like," Greg said. "But I should be thanking you, and especially your husband, for the sacrifices you make every day as a military family. Finding the ring was the least I could do."

Two weeks after we had met in the Moe's parking lot, Greg and Zac came to our home for Dinner with the Smileys. They brought the gear they had used to find the ring, and Greg helped Ford get into it. Standing in the living room, with Sparky running back and forth, leaping over scuba gear, Ford was all but swallowed up by the adult-size wetsuit, flippers, an underwater flashlight, and a metal detector.

Greg and Zac shared the story again about how they found the ring. They told us about other items they've found through the years. Greg once found a watch that had been lost for sixty years at the bottom of Phillips Lake, the same lake where my parents' camp is located.

The coincidences seemed to never stop.

Greg asked how Dustin and I met, and by this point, neither he nor Zac were surprised that it was another lost and found story. My dad and Dustin's dad were in the navy together in the 1970s. They were on deployment when I was born and Dustin was one year old. My dad came home seven months later, and I met him for the first time then. But I met Dustin long before that. So, in a strange twist of fate, I met my husband before I met my dad.

For a few years, Dustin and I lived around the corner from each other. There are faded and yellowed pictures of us standing on a pier in San Diego, California, waiting for our dads to come home on an aircraft carrier. Four-year-old Dustin has his arm around me. My mom likes to tell the story of Dustin calling me a baby for carrying a blanket. I threw my favorite blankie into the Smileys' kitchen trash to prove him wrong, and later that night, when I couldn't get to sleep, Mom had to go to their house and rescue it.

But Dustin and I didn't always live so close. Before my fourth birthday, my dad was transferred to Naval Air Station Oceana in Virginia Beach, Virginia. Dustin and his family moved to Guam. We briefly went to school together again when Dustin was in fifth grade and I was in fourth, because Dustin's dad was stationed in Virginia.

But the Smileys moved yet again, this time to Washington, DC, and I didn't see Dustin—except for in his family's yearly Christmas card—for about ten years. After Dustin graduated from the Naval Academy in 1997, and before he went to flight school in Pensacola, Florida, he called my family's house and asked me out on a date.

"Dustin Smiley?" I thought out loud. "The one who made me throw away my blankie? The one in all those pictures in my scrapbook?"

"Just go and be nice," my mom said. "He's a family friend. It's not like you have to marry him."

But by the end of the date, I knew: Someday I would marry Dustin Smiley.

And this is how our wedding song became "The Long and Winding Road" by the Beatles. There has always been a peace about Dustin and me. I felt it the first time I (re)met him in 1997. It was like we had always known each other. Sometimes it is hard to know where Dustin begins and I end. I can finish his sentences, and many times we think an identical, random thought at the same time. We have had our hard moments, of course, but we've always fallen in love again. Our shared history has shown that no matter where the navy sent our families, no matter how many years had passed, no matter how many hard times were to come, the road would always lead us to each other's door.

In the coming months, when I looked at Dustin's wedding band on my finger, terrible thoughts would cross my mind: What if something happened to him and he never made it home? What if I never had the chance to put the ring where it belonged? But just as quickly as the sickening thoughts came, they would vanish again when I remembered. One way or another, no matter which way the road leads, Dustin and I always arrive in the same place. With each other.

Lindell and Julie Williams at Sarah's birthday dinner

CHAPTER THIRTEEN

October

I had just finished teaching a class and was at my desk at the University of Maine when that night's dinner guest, Ric Tyler, the conservative half of Maine's popular radio program the *George Hale/Ric Tyler Show*, called my cell phone.

In his smooth radio voice, Ric said, "There's been a small change for dinner tonight."

"Okay. What's up?"

"Can you come to our house instead?"

"Um, I guess so. I mean I think so. I mean—"

"See, every Friday night, Elizabeth and I have friends to our house for dinner," Ric said. "They are friends who feel like family. And we were really looking forward to coming to your house, but then we realized just today that instead we'd like to include you and the boys in this family tradition."

I said okay, even as I knew in the back of my mind that Ford would protest. He thought we were having too many dinners away from home. "You've gotten away from the original idea of Dinner with the Smileys," he had told me before. "Our guests are supposed to fill Dad's chair. They can only do that at our house, not theirs."

After I hung up the phone with Ric, I remembered our tenth dinner, which felt like a lifetime ago, with Melissa Huston at the food bank. When the boys left for school that morning, I told them I'd pick them up early. But Melissa and I ended up getting them late. And then we went straight to the food bank, and I didn't have snacks. The older boys couldn't get over the sudden change of plans. Owen kicked at the back of my seat, and he and Ford spent most of that tenth Dinner with the Smileys confined to their bedrooms.

Was our forty-fifth dinner with Ric and his wife, Elizabeth, headed toward the same fate?

The boys had gone to school that morning believing they'd come home and help me get ready to welcome Ric and Elizabeth. Now I was going to tell them that the plan had changed, and I knew that if Ford resisted, Owen would follow, and there would be no recovery.

Luckily, though, Ford's school lets out at 2:30 P.M., and Owen's and Lindell's not until 3:00. So I had thirty minutes to get Ford on my side, to convince him that he was my helper, that together he and I would persuade the younger boys to adapt to the new plan. If necessary, I'd resort to quoting *Star Wars*: "Together we will rule the galaxy!"

Ford got into the car breathless from the crisp October air. His cheeks and the tip of his nose were red. "Hey," he said as he shut the passenger-side door. Middle schoolers, many of them twice as tall as Ford, walked in groups up and down the sidewalk. Yellow buses rumbled in the distance, idling in front of the school.

"Ford, there's been a small change of plans," I said, wishing that I had Ric's persuasive and smooth voice. Ric could probably convince me to walk across hot coals if he used his radio voice.

"Okaaaaaay?" Ford said.

"And I need your help making sure Lindell and Owen adjust smoothly."

"What do you mean?"

"Well, they usually follow your lead. If you're okay with the change, they will be, too."

"No, I mean what's the change of plans?" Ford said.

"Oh. Ric Tyler has invited us to his house for dinner tonight, instead of them coming to our house."

"That's all?" Ford said.

"Well, yeah."

"Dinners are better at our house, but, okay." He shrugged.

That was it? He wasn't going to flip out? He wasn't going to scream that he wasn't going and kick the seat?

"So you'll help me make sure Owen and Lindell are okay with it?" I said.

"Yeah, sure." Ford stared out the window. His binder was in his lap. "Is Ric Tyler the one who talks about politics on the radio?"

"Yes."

"Is he a Republican or a Democrat?"

"He's conservative."

"Okay, yeah, I've got some things I want to debate with him."

"But his wife, Elizabeth, is liberal."

"Really?" Ford said, his eyes getting big. "Oh, this is going to be good!" He rubbed his hands together.

Ric and Elizabeth live in a neighboring town. On the drive there, Ford plotted all the issues he'd take up with Ric. He wanted to know: What's the fundamental difference between Republicans and Democrats? How can you live peacefully with someone who has a different political view? Who was the best president that ever lived? How can we be sure we exist?

Owen and Lindell listened quietly in the backseat. Ford was happy, so they were, too. No one had an issue with the change of plans.

Ric and Elizabeth's house is more than twice the size of ours.

The wide, wraparound front porch leads into a grand foyer with a staircase and balcony that overlooks the entryway. Lindell dropped his coat on the floor and ran to the living room, where piles of toys waited in the corners, beside the long couch and next to the wide-screen television. Ric and Elizabeth's sons (one Owen's age, and one younger than Lindell) put down their handheld game systems when Lindell came into the room.

"Are you Wendell?" Colin asked.

"It's Lindell," Colin's older brother, Ian, said.

Ford and Owen stayed by the front door, each with thick, tattered novels tucked beneath their arms just in case things got boring.

"You guys are welcome to go into the living room," Elizabeth said. Her shiny black bangs fell around her eyes. "There are lots of toys and games."

Owen looked up at Ford.

"I actually want to debate with Ric," Ford said. His cheeks had turned red. "I have some things I need to argue with him."

Elizabeth laughed and put her arm around Ford's shoulder. "Oh, I love the sound of that," she said. "Have at him! He's in the kitchen."

Standing around the island in the kitchen were Ric and Elizabeth's good friends James (retired navy) and Melissa, and Melissa's father, Ron, who was visiting from Michigan.

Ford bounced on the balls of his feet as he walked into the room. But when he saw all the men there, he drew his shoulders around his ears and slipped onto one of the bar stools at the counter.

Owen's eyes twinkled beneath the lights and he smiled uncontrollably and shook everyone's hands. His back was perfectly straight.

"Men," Ric said in his deep voice and nodding at Ford and Owen. "Good evening."

I nudged Ford in the back. He pushed me away with his shoulder. Lindell's happy screams echoed from the adjoining room. I left to go see Ian and Colin, and once I was out of the kitchen, Ford began to talk.

"So, I have some things I want to ask you about, um, Mr.—"

"Call me Ric."

"Okay. Ric. I have some things I want to ask you about."

"Wait, wait, wait," Elizabeth said, coming out of the pantry. "I want to hear this. Wait for me."

I stayed in the living room while Ford and Ric bantered about politics and human existence. Ric's voice boomed and bounced off the walls. Ford's voice was thin and sometimes shrill. But he held his own against the grown men when Ron and James joined the conversation.

At dinner, Ron, who was seated to my right, leaned over and whispered, "Your son is very bright. And he's quite mature. I'm sure you and your husband are proud."

I looked across the table at Ford and wondered, *Do I give him enough credit?* I pictured him as he was when he was a baby, bouncing up and down in his crib and shaking the railings. I pictured him as a toddler dressed in a Superman cape and red rain boots. I pictured him as a kindergartner staring out the school bus window at me with tears in his eyes. Soon he would be a teenager. And then a man. Just then, however, he seemed trapped in between: no longer a baby. Not yet a teen. And far from being a grown man.

On the way home, I thanked the boys for their flexibility and for adapting to the last-minute change in plans. Then I turned to Ford in the passenger seat and told him that I appreciated his help and support.

He nodded and said, "You're welcome."

We seemed to be getting back on track.

Until . . .

Our next dinner was an early birthday celebration for me at our friends Julie and Brian Williams's house. Julie had been a friend of Dustin's first. Through the years, she and I had gotten close as well, and that closeness continued during the deployment.

In the early days after Dustin left, Julie checked in to see that the boys and I were okay. She invited us over for hot chocolate during the season's first snowfall. One night, when I was tired from finishing my degree and living like a single mother, Julie came over with a gallon of ice cream and two spoons. Then, when I graduated in May, Julie sent me a special homemade card that offered three options: (1) come to Dinner with the Williamses at their house, (2) leave the boys with them while I have a night to myself, or (3) let them pay for a sitter so they can take me out to dinner. I chose option 1, and we set a date for our Dinner with the Smileys (with the Williamses) on the week of my thirty-sixth birthday.

The gravel of the Williamses' driveway crunched beneath the van's tires as we drove around their colonial-style home to a parking area near the side breezeway. The boys had been at school all day. They were tired, and because the sun was now setting at 6:00 P.M., it felt later than it was. Somehow I had forgotten my plan to stop having dinners on weekdays. The clock blinked 6:00 just as I took the keys out of the ignition. We usually eat dinner at 5:30.

"Are we eating as soon as we get inside?" Ford asked in a rough, grumbly tone.

Lindell interrupted before I could answer. He had unbuckled his seat belt and was standing with his head poked between the front seats. "Isn't this the house I bought for a quarter?"

"Yes, it is, Lindell," Owen said from the back.

Once, when Lindell was four and had a quarter in his pocket but nowhere to spend it, he asked Julie if he could buy her house.

"How much are you offering?" Julie had asked.

"Well, I've got this coin in my pocket," Lindell said. "And I don't know what to use it for."

"So you're offering twenty-five cents?"

"Yes."

"Well, I can honestly say that is the best offer we've ever received." Julie winked at me. "Sold! To the little boy with the coin in his pocket."

Now, outside Julie's driveway, Ford groaned in the passenger seat again. "Mom, I'm really hungry. Are we going to eat as soon as we get inside?"

"Well, think about that for a minute, Ford," I said. "Do we usually walk into someone's house and eat right away?"

"Yeah, think about that, Ford," Lindell said, mocking me. "Usually we talk and all that stuff. And then we eat dinner. And then we have dessert. But, remember, I bought this house, so it's mine, and—"

"Shut up!" Ford screamed at Lindell.

"Hey," I said. "Would you like to spend this weekend in your room, Ford?"

"Whatever."

I took a deep breath and checked my hair in the rearview mirror.

"I bet we're not going to eat until 7:30," Ford said. "And I'm starving."

"I'm sure Mrs. Williams will have treats out for you guys."

"Yeah, but I'm hungry, Mom. Like, for dinner, not snacks."

"Then you should have eaten something before we left the house."

Ford kicked at the dashboard. "How was I supposed to know that we would be eating this late?"

I glared at him. "Do not kick the car again. And because of your attitude, you've just lost computer and Wii time for tomorrow."

Ford said something under his breath.

"What? What did you say?"

He grumbled again.

I still couldn't understand what he said. I puffed up my cheeks and blew out the air, so that the bangs falling across my eyes flew up. I tried to center my thoughts.

It was clear this dinner would be a disaster, but we couldn't back out. From the cold interior of the van, I saw yellow light coming from Julie's kitchen windows. Brian's silhouette moved across the large panes of glass as he went from the sink to the stove.

Brian and Julie don't have children. I prayed they'd understand whatever behavior was in store for them with Ford.

I started to open the car door, and then I turned around and looked at Ford. "And remember," I said. "This is my birthday dinner. So, please, for me, let this be a good night."

By the time we walked into the Williamses' kitchen, with its exposed high beams and wide-plank wood floors, Ford's face had turned stone-like. He wouldn't smile, and he barely said hello to anyone.

I began to panic inside. *How soon until Owen and Lindell followed his lead? How soon until the whole thing fell apart? What had changed since dinner at Ric's house and tonight?*

"Come on in," Julie said warmly. Her dark hair was pulled back into a smooth ponytail. She smiled, and the dimples in her cheeks appeared. "I have a surprise for you guys in the living room," she said. She waved her hand for the boys to follow her.

Lindell and Owen ran to catch up, but Ford, with his hands stuffed into the pockets of his pants, dragged his feet and stared at the ground as he walked.

Brian came around the island to give me a hug, with a spatula in his hand. Brian is thick and sturdy, but there is a softness to him, like a giant teddy bear. His hug reminded me of the strong, warm embraces from Dustin. He squeezed my arm as he pulled away. "How are you?" he said.

I told Brian that Ford was giving me trouble, and Brian, who has a brother, reminded me that Ford is about to hit those difficult teenage years.

"When does it end?" I asked.

Brian laughed. "I'm not sure it does."

Lindell and Owen ran in from the other room. They had cups and foam balls in their hands.

"Watch this magic trick, Mom," they both said.

"I want to show her first," Lindell screamed.

"No, Lindell, you don't even know how to do it." Owen elbowed Lindell out of the way.

"Oh! Is this the surprise?" I asked, trying to intervene.

"Yeah, Mrs. Williams gave us a whole box of magic stuff," Lindell said. "It's so cool. And I didn't have to buy it for a quarter."

Ford stood in the doorway and rolled his eyes.

Julie laughed. "Now remember, Lindell, I never did take your quarter that day. I think we are still on an IOU."

Lindell gave her a thumbs-up.

Before we sat down to dinner, the Williamses' friends Ben and Sarah joined us with their daughter Claire. Brian had made an impressive spread for make-your-own tacos. On the wood island, he laid out shredded pork, roasted chicken, ground beef, guacamole, peppers, and tortillas he had just fried in duck fat.

Ford went to the dining room and sat down without a plate.

"Aren't you going to eat?" Brian called after him.

"Nothing looks good," Ford mumbled.

I put down the plate I was making for Lindell, and walked quickly out of the kitchen to Ford's chair. I leaned over him and hissed under my breath, "Excuse me? You are being rude and inconsiderate. Change your attitude or you'll lose another day of computer and Wii."

"Fine, take it away from me," he yelled.

As I walked away, he said, "You're so mean."

My face turned hot. I blinked away tears. I was embarrassed, angry, and confused.

Julie was beside me and she rubbed my back. "I'll finish Lindell's plate," she said.

Eventually Ford ate. He even had seconds and thirds. But he never thanked Brian or Julie. On the way home, I yelled and cried in the car, "That was my birthday dinner, Ford! And from the beginning, you were set on ruining it, weren't you? How would you feel if I acted like that at your birthday? Huh? How would you feel if you were Brian or Julie and someone acted that way in your house? All I wanted was a birthday dinner. And Dad isn't here to do that for me. So you just had to ruin it!"

When we got home, Ford went to his room and closed the door. He didn't come out again until the next morning.

PANS AND SILVERWARE clattered in the kitchen below me. The toaster oven beeped and didn't stop. I could hear feet pattering about. I rolled over to a cooler spot in the bed and pulled the duvet cover around me.

Fish. That was all I smelled.

I opened one eye and saw Sparky's nose right in front of mine. He was panting hot, heavy breath. Beside him was Lindell, wearing only his underpants and no pajamas. His hair stuck up in all directions.

"Happy birthday, Mom," Lindell said. "We're making you breakfast."

"Lindell," Ford yelled from downstairs. "We need you in the kitchen!"

Lindell kissed my forehead. "Got to go. Bye," he said. He and Sparky ran out of the room.

With Sparky's dog breath gone, I could finally smell the burnt toast.

The boys came up the stairs singing "Happy Birthday." Ford carried the largest plate, filled with toast, yogurt, a bagel, cream cheese, and . . . Triscuits? Yes, it looked like Triscuits. Owen had a smaller plate balancing a bowl filled to the rim with soggy Cheerios and milk. Liquid sloshed from the sides and spilled onto the plate. He dropped the spoon on the floor. "Oops, I'll need to get you another one," he said.

Lindell followed Ford and Owen with a warm can of Diet Dr Pepper in his hand.

"Happy birthday, Mom," Ford said as I sat up in bed. He set the plate in front of me. "We have cards for you, too."

Lindell ran into the other room and came back with three sheets of computer paper folded in half.

"We couldn't go get cards for you," Ford said. "So we made them ourselves."

"I love them," I said, flipping through the papers.

Ford shrugged. "Maybe we can get you real cards once Dad is home. These are just until then."

"No, Ford, I love them. Really. These are better than any real cards."

All three boys climbed onto the bed and stared eagerly at me as I tasted the bloated Cheerios and opened the warm can of soda.

"We would have made eggs," Ford said. "But none of us know how to do that."

"Cereal is great," I said. "And you know I need my caffeine!"

"The Diet Dr Pepper was my idea," Lindell said smiling.

I gulped down a mouthful of wet Cheerios that disintegrated in my mouth. The boys smiled expectantly.

"Excellent," I said. I nibbled on the burnt, flaky toast. "You guys are amazing."

It was a Monday, so after I forced down the cereal and burnt toast, we had to get dressed and rush off to school and work. But as Ford got out of the car in front of the junior high school, he turned around and said, "I hope you have a good day, Mom."

"Thank you, Ford," I said. "And thank you for this morning. That was a fun surprise."

He swung his backpack over his shoulder and waved quickly before disappearing into a crowd of middle schoolers.

BACK IN AUGUST, as I was coming home from work one day, I saw my elderly neighbor across the street climbing into the back of an ambulance with paramedics on either side of him. He was wearing a bathrobe and pajamas, but he wasn't on a stretcher. So I didn't think much of it, although I guess I should have.

In September, I saw his wife, Anne, walking up the sidewalk, like she did nearly every day. We chatted about the weather and how much longer until the leaves would change, and then something caused me to ask about her husband.

"He died several weeks ago," Anne said. "I thought you knew."

I didn't. And suddenly, I didn't know what to say.

Anne invited Lindell and me to her house for cookies and milk. Inside, the carpeted living room was warm, and a clock ticked steadily in the background. Anne showed us woodworking her husband had made, and her eyes grew wet when she talked about the day he left in an ambulance and never came home again. Lindell stiffened as he chewed on the edges of an Oreo. I offhandedly mentioned that the Friars' Bakehouse, an iconic bakery in downtown Bangor operated by two Franciscan monks, has a Widows and Widowers dinner on the third Saturday of every month.

"You should check it out sometime," I said. "It's a way to be around other people who are going through the same thing. We could take you if you wanted."

Anne got up from her seat and went to a calendar hanging on the side of the refrigerator. "The third Saturday in October is the twenty-seventh," she said. "Would that one work?"

"Oh, I didn't mean that you have to go so soon," I said. "I mean, no pressure, but sometime, if you're interested—"

Anne took a pen from the kitchen counter. "I'm writing it down," she said. "October twenty-seventh. What time will you pick me up?"

As Lindell and I walked back across the street to our house, he held my hand and said, "She seemed really excited about going to lunch with us. I think she's lonely."

"Yes, Lindell," I said. "I think she is."

The Friars' Bakehouse is on a one-way downtown street nestled between a comic book store and a bustling restaurant with a bar. A wooden sign, shaped like a loaf of bread, hangs from the brick building and over the sidewalk. FRIARS' BAKEHOUSE it reads in scrolling script. The large picture window at the front of the store is filled with flowering plants surrounding a statue of St. Francis of Assisi sitting on a bench, his hand on a deer. The screened front door (which, oddly, is propped open when the shop is closed and slammed shut when the shop is open) lists the bakeshop's peculiar hours (sometimes they open at 8:02 A.M., for instance), which seem to change regularly. Inside the long, narrow store, where diners eat family-style and choose from one or two daily selections, there are statues of the Virgin Mary, crucifixes on the wall, and a sign that warns: NO CREDIT CARDS, NO CELL PHONES.

Brother Kenneth and Brother Donald, dressed in their dark brown monks' robes and sandaled shoes, will give you the hairy eyeball if your cell phone dares to beep or ring while you are inside the Bakehouse. And if you try to pay with a debit card, Kenneth—with his narrow red face—will silently shake his head no, and Donald—rounder and louder—will push his reading glasses up onto his bald head and say, "Read the sign. Cash only here." Soft church music plays in the background.

Once a month, the small space is filled with widows and

widowers from across the city who need the fellowship and support of people going through the same stages of grief. The Brothers serve them lunches like tomato soup and grilled cheeses, or
haddock chowder and artisan bread baked fresh daily. I was excited to introduce Anne to this new network of support, and the
boys were excited to help the friars in the kitchen, where they
thought a couple whoopie pies or homemade cookies might come
their way. It would be our forty-seventh Dinner with the Smileys.

We picked up Anne at 11:00 on the morning of the twenty-
seventh. A bad storm had come through overnight, and the sides
of the road were almost completely underwater.

Anne came to the car with an umbrella shielding her silvery
hair from the sideways rain. When she got into the passenger seat,
she smelled like sweet perfume and powder. We drove downtown
through puddles that made giant arced waves as the tires hit them.
Anne said she was grateful that we could take her, because she
doesn't like to drive in bad weather.

"This dinner will be a little different from our other ones," Ford
said from the backseat. "Because there will be so many people,
and I think Owen, Lindell, and I will have to help in the kitchen.
But hopefully we'll get some breaks to come visit you."

"I'd like that," Anne said over her shoulder.

Downtown looked uncharacteristically empty for a Saturday
morning. Vacant parallel parking spaces lined the storefronts.
"Guess we won't have trouble getting a close parking spot," I said.
But as we got nearer to the Bakehouse, I began to worry. No lights
were on, and the screen door was propped open.

"Do you have the right date?" Anne said.

"I'm almost positive. I talked to Brother Donald last week."

"Maybe we're early," Owen said. "Didn't the Friars tell us to
come early?"

I unbuckled my seat belt and told everyone else to wait in the car.
Rain pelted my hair and the tops of my shoulders as I peered

into the Bakehouse window, past the statue of St. Francis of Assisi and green plants with creeping tendrils. Every light in the small shop was turned off. There was no sign of Brother Donald or Brother Kenneth. I walked back to the car shaking my head and shrugging. Anne smiled anxiously from the passenger's seat.

"I have no idea what's going on," I said as I got back in the car.

"Well, we could wait a few minutes, I suppose," Anne said.

Just then, Brother Donald ran out the front door of the shop. His habit was tucked into his socks and he was carrying a rag in one hand. He waved the rag at us, and I rolled down the window.

"Our basement flooded," he said breathlessly. "Last night, with all that rain, it just flooded. Everything is underwater. We had to cancel this month's Widows and Widowers."

"Oh no," I said.

"Do you need any help?" Anne asked.

"No, you guys go get lunch somewhere else," he said. "We'll try again in November."

"Do you have any whoopie pies?" Lindell screamed from the back of the van.

Brother Donald poked his head inside the window. "Not today, buddy. You come back next week and I'll have one for you." Then he looked back at Anne and me. "See you in November?"

I nodded.

As we drove away, Owen told Anne, "Don't worry, we'll definitely bring you again in November." And then he asked me, "So, can we go to Nicky's for lunch today instead?"

Nicky's is a fifties-style diner with everything from a life-size Elvis cutout to Superman sporting a mullet on the walls. A jukebox shaped like an old pink Cadillac is at the center of the room. Diners sit in plastic booths or round tables with padded chairs. The menu is thick and offers a wide variety—from eggs and toast to cheeseburgers and fries. Unlike the Bakehouse, credit cards are welcome and a beeping cell phone goes mostly unnoticed against the pop music playing from speakers overhead.

There at Nicky's—over BLT sandwiches and, later, ice-cream sundaes—the boys and I promised Anne, dressed in a crisp plum-colored shirt and black slacks, over and over again that we would take her to the November Widows and Widowers' lunch.

Anne smiled. "I'm just happy to get to know all of you better," she said. But by the time we dropped her off across the street, I could see that a morning spent with three rowdy boys had certainly made Anne tired. "I think I'll go in and take a nap now," she said, smiling.

The boys and I pulled into our driveway. I closed the garage door behind us, and as it went down, blocking from our view Earle's brown-shingled house, we had no idea that we were about to lose him, too.

In late October, one of the boys' friends received bad news. His mom had breast cancer. I talked to Ford, Owen, and Lindell about the importance of supporting this friend when he was at our house, and helping him through what was surely a difficult, stressful time at home. "Remember to ask him how he's doing, or if he wants to talk about it," I said.

Ford grimaced. "I see what you're getting at, Mom, but sometimes having a friend not talk about it is more helpful. Like, when I'm missing Dad, I'd rather forget about it than sit around and talk about it. Talking about it makes it worse. All the adults say, 'Oh, you must be so sad about your dad being gone.' And I think, 'Great, I had almost forgotten how sad I was until you just mentioned it.'"

"I see," I said. "So what do you think this friend needs from us?"

"Distraction," Owen said.

"I can be that," Lindell chimed in. He was dancing around the living room.

"He probably just wants things to be normal when he's over here playing," Ford said.

Lindell came over and wrapped his arms around my neck.

"Okay, then, we'll try to be normal," I said, patting Lindell's back.

Over the next few weeks, I watched as the boys were especially conscious of how they treated this friend while he was at our house. Although they never mentioned his mom's illness, I could see that they gave him extra turns on the Wii, let him win sword fights outside, and asked him to pick the movie they'd watch at a sleepover. The boys, I realized, had learned compassion. They were taking what they knew about their own experience and applying it to someone else's.

As October was coming to a close, and Dustin's homecoming seemed closer and closer, I knew that I wanted to have a Dinner with the Smileys that honored Ford, Owen, and Lindell's friends. Clearly, it wasn't just the adults who were helping us through the year and teaching us lessons; the boys' friends had been a network of support for them, too. And, let's not forget, when the boys were busy playing with their friends, they weren't bothering me.

So, we decided to make our forty-eighth dinner, which would fall on the weekend before Halloween, a costume party after hours at the Briar Patch, our favorite independent bookstore downtown. The boys said it would be like the movie *Night at the Museum*, only, it was *Night at the Bookstore* instead.

The Briar Patch is a small one-room shop, where the heater is always on; books line eclectic, mismatched wooden shelving that is sometimes slanted or bowed in the center; and the thin-carpeted floors creak beneath footsteps. The storefront windows are filled with homemade displays that match the seasons, and the shopkeepers, Cathy and Gibran, always know the regular customers' names.

We are regular costumers. The boys are welcomed into the

Briar Patch with "Hello, Smiley boys," and "What are you reading these days?" Gibran, who is usually perched on a stool behind the wooden desk in the middle of the store, has bushy salt-and-pepper hair, a full beard and mustache, and square, black reading glasses. He knows exactly where every book is located, and as he moves across the creaky floors, his voice booms: "Excellent choice, Smiley boys. When you finish this book series, I have something new for you."

For our dinner, the younger boys and their friends dressed up as Power Rangers and *Star Wars* characters. Lindell was a bat. I threw together an orange turtleneck, plaid skirt, and brown wig to be Velma from Scooby-Doo. Ford and his friend said they were

Gibran Graham, bookstore manager, at Halloween dinner

too old for costumes, but I convinced them to at least wear adhesive mustaches. They put them on upside down.

When we pulled up to the Briar Patch, Gibran was standing outside the front door wearing a homemade Mad Hatter costume. He had a giant top hat covered in silk fabric over a bright-red wig. His suit jacket had silk ties spilling out of the pocket, and around his neck he wore a polka-dot scarf tied into a bow.

Finally Ford admitted, "Um, I feel a little underdressed now."

"I told you that you should wear a costume," Owen said through his plastic Count Dooku mask.

Gibran stood with outstretched arms and watched me parallel park. I maneuvered the van forward and back, in what felt like a twenty-two-point turn. Eventually, I parked with one wheel on the curb and one sticking out into the roadway.

Gibran knocked on the glass and said through the car windows, with his loud, robust voice, "Velma should not be allowed to drive the Mystery Machine. Lindell, why don't you take over?"

After we were all inside the warm store, Gibran locked the front door.

"Oh my gosh, it's like that movie," one of the boys' friends said.

"*Night at the Museum*," Owen said.

A local librarian named Rebecca, who is gifted with voices and storytelling, joined us for the dinner. Her long, red hair was piled high on her head and held in a bun with two long chopsticks. She had a silky scarf thrown dramatically around her neck. She carried a canvas bag full of books.

Lindell and his friend eagerly peered inside, digging through the books and yelling with excitement over the ones they recognized.

We ate box lunches, prepared by nearby Frank's Bake Shop, on a blanket spread out on the floor between rows of books. After dinner, Gibran took the older boys to a separate corner of the store to read scary ghost stories. Rebecca stayed with Lindell and his friend and read less scary picture books, using her exaggerated impressions and voices.

The boys lay on their bellies, propped up on their elbows with their feet kicked up behind them. Their eyes were wide and curious as Rebecca swayed back and forth in her chair, pretending to have the deep, gravely voice of a king, and then, later, the nasally accent of a Frenchman.

I moved between the two story circles.

Ford and Owen and their friends sat cross-legged in front of Gibran, and they raised their hands or blurted out what they thought would happen next in the story. Later, they came up with their own ghost stories, and Rebecca taught everyone how to do vocal impressions.

A few days after our *Night at the Bookstore*, it was Halloween. The boys got dressed in the same costumes (or noncostumes, in the case of Ford) that they had worn to dinner, and we drove across town to Morgan's house, where the neighborhood basically closes to traffic and is filled with swarms of trick-or-treaters.

The leaves on the trees were just past their peak. Most of them were a solid, vibrant yellow, and they fell easily with the gentlest of breezes. Red, brown, and yellow leaves lined the sidewalk and layered the grass. Open porches on the front side of old, square clapboard homes, set close to the sidewalk, were lit up with orange lights and decorated with fake spiderwebs.

In years past, Lindell stayed close by Dustin and me. We had to coax him to ring doorbells. But now that he was older—and much more integrated with his brothers—the three of them ran ahead of me.

I walked with my hands in my pockets and crunching leaves with my shoes. I thought about how Dustin, if he had been there, would be wearing his quilted plaid-flannel jacket. I'd tuck my arm through his elbow and share his pocket. We'd walk arm in arm and talk about how much the boys were growing up. I'd probably rest my cheek on his shoulder and hug his arm against me.

But instead, I walked alone, past husbands and wives and their children several steps ahead of them.

Just one more month, I told myself.

One more month.

Owen playing hide-and-seek in the governor's mansion

CHAPTER FOURTEEN

November

The Blaine House in Augusta has been home to Maine's governors since it was donated to the state in 1919 by Harriet Blaine Beale. The actual house, however, was built nearly a hundred years before that. I only know this because the boys told me. They've studied the governor's mansion in school. So when I told them we were invited to the Blaine House to have Dinner with the Smileys with Governor Paul LePage and First Lady Ann LePage, they were genuinely excited and curious. "The Blaine House?" Owen said. "Like the one we talk about in school? The one in Augusta?"

"Yes, the governor's mansion," I said.

Lindell started crying. He paced frantically in the living room. "A mansion like in Scooby-Doo," he said. He pulled at his hair. "Will it be haunted? I don't want to go!"

Ford wiggled his fingers in the air at Lindell. "Yeah, it's haunted with governors past," he said. He and Owen laughed.

"Oh, speaking of governors past," I said, "no showing your butt at the governor's mansion." I pointed at Lindell. "This means you."

"But I don't want to go," he said again. "It will be haunted."

Ford tousled Lindell's hair. "We were just kidding, buddy. It's not haunted."

We entered the Blaine House through the side entrance, near the circular driveway that faces the Maine capitol building. An aide welcomed us into the study, which is framed in dark wood and wallpapered with a red-and-cream-striped print that is a replica of the paper that hung in Lincoln's study at the White House. Later we would learn that this is Governor LePage's favorite room in the Blaine House. In the corner there is a dark wood desk, which belonged to James Blaine and was used by him in the US Senate in the 1800s. Encased in glass on the top of the desk is an original, handwritten letter from President Lincoln to Senator Blaine, dated April 7, 1865, just one week before Lincoln was assassinated.

The aide ushered us into a long, narrow sunroom with pendant chandeliers, upholstered chairs, and a baby grand piano. On one of the shiny end tables, there was a folded place card. It read: NO FOOD OR DRINKS ON THE FURNITURE PLEASE!

Just as I read the sign, Lindell climbed onto the rose-colored sofa. He had kicked off his shoes at the door, and his big toe poked through a hole in his dirty sock. "This place is fancy," he said. "Where's the governor?"

"The governor and first lady will be down in just a minute," the aide said. "What can I get everyone to drink?"

"Apple juice!" Lindell screamed. "No, fruit punch. Or, wait, do you have root beer?"

"No soda," I said, glaring at the boys sitting comfortably on the couch. "Tell the nice lady that you want water," I said through clenched teeth.

"Water, please," Ford said.

"Me, too, please," Owen said.

Lindell stood up and pressed his hands together in front of his chest. "Could I please have a small glass of juice, please?"

The aide looked at me for approval. I sighed and nodded.

Mrs. LePage came into the room first. She was wearing a light-

Lindell and Governor Paul LePage

---

yellow sweater set that brought out the highlights in her hair and her high cheekbones blushed with red.

"Welcome to the Blaine House," she said as she held out her arms to hug me. Her nails were perfectly manicured, and she smelled like sweet perfume. "Please call me Ann," she said. Then she looked down at Lindell's sock feet. "I see you've made yourself at home," she said. "I love it!"

Lindell ran to her, and Ann leaned down for a hug.

Governor LePage came in next. He was wearing a gray suit and a light-green tie. Lindell marched over to Governor LePage and stood in front of him as straight as the American flag next to them. Lindell looked up, his hands clasped behind his back, and said, "Are you the governor?"

"No," Governor LePage said. "The governor will be here in a minute."

"Oh, darn!" Lindell walked away. "I thought you were the governor."

"I'm just kidding," Governor LePage said. He did his characteristic loud, breathy, broad-smile laugh. "I'm the governor."

Lindell turned around and gave a thumbs-up. "Nice one," he said. "You got me."

We ate in the Family Dining Room, at the polished oval table with padded chairs and a crystal chandelier overhead. Governor LePage asked that Ford sit across from him at the other head of the table. "You are the man of your family right now," LePage said.

Ford blushed and shrugged. "Well, okay, sure," he said.

But then there was confusion among the boys about how to use all the silverware on the table.

"There are too many forks," Ford whispered to me.

Ann overheard and smiled. Her eyes twinkled beneath the chandelier's light. "Use any fork you like, Ford," she said.

The LePages planned a kid-friendly dinner full of basics: chicken, noodles, homemade bread, and a salad. Amid the silver salt and pepper shakers set in front of each of our plates, there were plastic bottles of ketchup and ranch dressing.

Between courses, Governor LePage shared his childhood story with us. When he was eleven years old (the same age as Ford at the time), he left home and lived alone on the streets for two years. His father was abusive, and he paid young LePage a fifty-cent piece to lie to a doctor and tell him the bruises on his body were from a fall down the stairs. LePage took the fifty-cent piece and ran. He never lived with his family again.

To this day, he still carries a fifty-cent piece in his pocket.

Despite his homelessness, LePage continued to go to school.

He worked several jobs in the afternoons, including cleaning horse stables. At night, he slept in the hay of the stalls in the barn.

LePage graduated high school and went on to college, and eventually he got his master's degree, too.

"You did all that without any parents?" Owen asked, his voice suddenly quiet and thin.

"Hold that thought," Governor LePage said. "I want to show you something." He left the table and came back with a handful of purple, rubber wristbands.

LePage handed a band to each of the boys as he spoke. "This is my personal motto," he said. "This is what guides me every day: ten simple two-letter words."

Ford read the band aloud. "If it is to be . . . it is up to me."

The tone of Ford's voice suggested that he was plugging the motto into his long-term memory; however, I doubted he would wear the band. It was a bracelet after all, and it was purple, too. So I was stunned when Ford slipped the wristband onto his right arm and kept it there for nearly two weeks.

Dessert was red velvet brownies served in delicate, stemmed ice-cream cups and topped with a dollop of homemade whipped cream. I whispered to the boys to wait until everyone had their dish before they dug into the brownie. When I turned around to look at Lindell beside me, he had his hands carefully placed in his lap, but he was bent over and licking the whipped cream off the top of the dessert.

After the boys' dishes were empty, the LePages told them they could explore the Blaine House for a bit while the grown-ups talked. I was embarrassed when "exploring" the Blaine House turned into hide-and-seek. But Governor LePage encouraged them. "It's great fun to have kids in the house," he said to me. And, then, to the boys, he said, "Want to see a really great hiding place?" He motioned for them to follow him into another room. Ann and I heard their giggles echoing down the hall while we stayed at the table.

Lindell at dinner with the governor

"Paul loves children so much," she said. "It really is great to have them here."

Just then, Owen ran past the doorway of the dining room. Ford followed soon after. And then Lindell and the governor. We heard a thud, so I got up to look. There, in the middle of the Blaine House entryway, with its ornate throw rugs and gold-framed art-work, my three boys were wrestling each other, and the governor stood above them, smiling ear to ear and saying, "Isn't this great?"

On our way out of the Blaine House, Lindell spotted a framed poster of all the past Maine governors. He reached up on his tip-toes and pointed at the glass. "Hey, that's Baldacci," he said. "And Angus King! We had dinner with them."

Ford patted Lindell on the back. "That's really good, Lindell.

You recognized them. So can you count how many Maine governors we've had Dinner with the Smileys with?"

Lindell turned around and counted his pudgy fingers. "One . . . two . . . three," he said. "Three! It's three. We've had dinner with three!"

"That's right, buddy." Ford put his hand on the top of Lindell's head.

The LePages sent us home with a signed copy of *Baxter in the Blaine House*, a children's book by Paula Benoit told through the eyes of the LePage's family dog, Baxter. We also had the wristbands, and Governor LePage had given each of the boys writing pens made from the wood of old logging boats. So there was a lot to gather, and we had coats and mittens and hats, too. All of our belongings were in a pile on one of those shiny end tables in the sunroom. I picked up the pile and didn't look through it until we got home.

That's when I saw it, the folded place card with "NO FOOD OR DRINKS ON THE FURNITURE PLEASE" written on the front. In the rush to collect our books and hats, I had accidentally grabbed one of the signs, too.

I set the card on the less shiny side table in our living room and smiled to myself. If it worked at the Blaine House, maybe it would work here, too, I thought.

A week later, our fiftieth milestone guest came with gold. Two pieces of gold, actually. Ellie Logan, a US Women's 8 rower, is a two-time Olympic gold medalist and also from the state of Maine. At six feet two inches tall, she towered over the boys, and especially Lindell, in our living room. In fact, when Lindell stood beside Ellie, we noticed that he is only as tall as one of her legs. Or, put another way, Ellie's legs are one Lindell-size tall.

Ellie brought her sister Jessamine, who is nearly as tall as her younger sister, but while Ellie wore jeans and a hooded official Olympics sweatshirt, Jessamine had a silk, paisley scarf tied around her neck over a long, tortoiseshell necklace. Ellie's hair is blond

Lindell with two-time Olympic gold medalist Ellie Logan

and long. Jessamine's is honey-colored and hangs in long, loose curls. Jessamine wears thin reading glasses and light eye shadow and lipstick. Ellie's skin is flushed only by the sun and her youth.

At first, the boys didn't know what to make of these tall sisters. They seemed almost shy around them. Luckily, Lindell broke the ice. "Want to come see my room?" he said, grabbing Ellie's hand and pulling her out of the living room. Ellie sat on the end of Lindell's bed, her long legs bent and tucked gracefully beneath her. She rested one foot on the side of the other foot's long tennis shoe. And she listened intently as the boys showed her their own trophies.

"We only like trophies we earn," Ford said. "We put the others in the basement."

"What do you mean?" Ellie asked.

"Like the ones they give us just for participating," Owen said. "Those are the ones we put in the basement."

"So these are all the ones you've earned?"

"Yes."

"And they're most proud of the baseball one," Lindell said.

Owen handed Ellie the championship Little League trophy from the past spring. They told her the story of winning the game in the last half of the last inning.

"That is incredible," Ellie said. "The last half of the last inning?"

"Yep." Ford stood straight and puffed out his chest.

"Did you bring your medals?" Owen asked Ellie.

"She sure did," Jessamine said. "I'll go get them."

The boys, of course, ran after Jessamine, too eager to wait for her to return with the gold. In the kitchen, she pulled from a cloth bag two round, gold medals hanging from ribbon.

"Whoa," Ford and Owen said together.

"Can I wear it?" Lindell asked.

"Oh, no, honey," I said, touching his shoulder. "The medals are very personal to Ellie. Kind of like a wedding ring."

"I really don't mind," Ellie said. "I'd love for him to put it on."

Ellie slipped the ribbon around Lindell's neck and held on to the medal as it fell against his chest. "It's really heavy," she said. "It doesn't look like it would be, but it is."

Lindell held up the medal to inspect it. Then he wiggled his hips and started to dance and sing, "Oh yeah, I've got gold." The round, gold disc bounced off his chest and flew into the air. It came down on top of his head and hit it with a *thunk*.

We all froze, waiting to see if he was going to laugh or cry. Jessamine had her hand against her mouth.

Lindell rubbed at the spot on his head, and then his eyes began to water. I took the medal from around his neck, and he ran to his room. Ellie followed to talk to him. When they were gone, I told

Jessamine, "Not many kids can say they've been hit in the head with an Olympic Gold Medal."

After dinner, the boys took Ellie upstairs to what we call the Lego Room but is actually our extra bedroom taken over by a toy chest that looks like it exploded. The boys showed Ellie all their creations, and they demonstrated their Wii skills for her. They talked more sports and asked her how it felt when she came across the finish line.

"It's surreal," Ellie said, pointing out that she had trained countless hours for that one, fleeting moment at the finish line.

"But you have the medals now," Lindell said. "So that kind of makes the time frozen. Like, you can always remember it when you see the medal."

"That's right," Ellie said. "I have the medals to remind me."

After Ellie and Jessamine left, Ford said, "That was a lot of fun."

"It was," I said. "And pretty cool that the first Olympic gold medalist you've met was a female."

Ford looked surprised, like he hadn't thought about that yet. "Yeah, I guess that is kinda neat," he said. "She seems like a really great athlete."

OUR LAST DINNER with the Smileys at our home, around the old wooden farm table, was with the children's 2012–2013 school-teachers, principals, and guidance counselors. Lindell's kindergarten teacher, Mrs. Dube, came. Owen's principal, Mr. Enman, guidance counselor, Mrs. Tlili, and fourth-grade teacher, Mr. Legere were there. And representing Ford's new middle school was Mrs. Erb, his Spanish teacher. It was our largest crowd around the table since dinner number seven with the University of Maine hockey players and Coach Whitehead. We even had to bring in the extra side table from the front porch in order to seat everyone.

The boys were excited to have their teachers at dinner, of course, but there still was an awkwardness. Teachers and parents usually stay separate. Indeed, as far as a child is concerned, a teacher doesn't even leave the school building. Ford, in particular, seemed trapped in limbo between his two worlds: home and school. I could see the fear on his face when I started to tell a family story. I imagined him thinking, *Please, Mom, no. Don't embarrass me.* But he had the same uneasiness (clutching his hands under the table, looking intently at his plate) when Mrs. Erb talked about school. It seemed as if he, more than the others, had arrived at a place in which school and home were entirely separate. I don't volunteer in his class—or even in his school—anymore. I haven't met all of his teachers. I drop him off at a curb in the morning instead of walking him inside. The most contact I have with the school is to receive report cards and courtesy calls when he is absent. Now Ford's school world—or at least part of it—was sitting in our kitchen, and the panic on his face was obvious.

Lindell delighted Mrs. Dube with his "home self," and Mrs. Dube said she had never seen him so talkative and expressive. Ford laughed, "Yeah, well, he hides it pretty well at school apparently."

The staff that came from Owen's school, besides Principal Enman, was not the same as when Ford was in fourth grade. Mrs. Tlili was new, and Ford did not have Mr. Legere for a teacher. This meant that for the first time, Owen's teachers were his own. Ford couldn't take over with stories from "when I was in _____'s class." He couldn't steal the teacher's attention. He couldn't claim to know him better or longer than Owen. So although Owen was characteristically quiet, his eyes twinkled as he looked up at Mr. Legere, Mrs. Tlili, and Mr. Enman on either side of him. He told stories about school that were unfamiliar to Ford.

"Huh, we never did it that way," Ford said.

"Yeah, well, maybe the school is different now," Owen said. "You don't know everything, Ford."

When the teachers left, Owen fell into the couch and said, "I'm kind of sad that it's over."

Owen at the 2012–2013 Teachers' Dinner

"What's over?" I asked.

"Dinner with the Smileys."

"It's not over yet," I said. "We still have the fifty-second dinner next week."

"Yeah, but that one won't be at home. It won't be at our kitchen table."

I sat down beside Owen and smoothed the hair from his eyes. Ford came into the living room with a book under his arm. "What's Owen sad about?" he asked.

"That the dinners are coming to an end," I said.

Lindell, already dressed in his fuzzy footed pajamas with bears on them, ran into the room and jumped up onto the couch. Ford sat down beside him. I put my arms around all of them.

"It's kind of weird," Ford said. "On the one hand, I'm happy the dinners are ending because that means Dad is coming home. But on the other hand, I'm going to miss Dinner with the Smileys."

"Yeah, we still have to eat dinner," Lindell said.

"And we will," I said. "Of course we will. And we'll still eat with guests when Dad is home. We don't have to stop inviting people. We just won't be—well, we won't be numbering them like we have been."

"But I like having dinners with a purpose," Lindell said. He was hugging his chest and he buried his chin into his folded arms.

"That's an interesting way of putting it," I said. "What's been your favorite purpose of Dinner with the Smileys?"

"That we get to meet lots of neat people," he said.

"And we've gotten to know them in a regular way," Owen said. "Like, it hasn't been formal and stuff."

I nodded. "It's true. We've had a lot of experiences, and we've met a lot of people. Which was your favorite?"

"Dad," they all said together, referring to our twenty-ninth dinner when Dustin came home for R&R.

"Okay, but besides Dad," I said.

"That's tough," Ford said. "All the dinners have been different. I've liked different ones for different reasons."

Owen hugged my arm and curled up against my side. "I don't want it to end, Mom," he said. "But I do want Dad to come home."

"Soon," I whispered. "Just a few more weeks now."

THE WEEK BEFORE Thanksgiving, our neighbor Earle, whom we visited as part of our seventeenth dinner, passed away. He was ninety-four years old. I told the boys when they got home from school that afternoon.

"Mr. Earle?" Lindell said quietly, staring out our living room window toward the brown wood siding of Earle's house across the driveway.

"Yes, Mr. Earle," I said. "He died this morning."

"So now we've lost both neighbors," Owen said, referring to Gloria and Earle.

Four years ago, on Valentine's Day, I made a pan of brownies and asked Owen to take one plate to Earle and one to Gloria. While Owen stepped into his snow boots, he smiled and said, "Mr. Earle lives alone, right?"

"Yes."

"And Gloria does, too?"

"That's right."

"So maybe I should take both plates to Mr. Earle, and tell him to invite Gloria over for some brownies."

I smiled as I remembered that long-ago conversation. Now that Owen was a fourth grader, however, and nearly ten years old, he disliked Valentine's Day (a "girl holiday") and anything pertaining to obnoxious things like love, roses, and glittery hearts. I knew better than to remind him about the plate of brownies. Instead I said, "You were always good about taking soup and treats to their houses when I asked you to."

Lindell pulled on my sleeve. "Remember how when you cut our hair," he said, "and you always tell us, 'Look at Gloria's house' or 'Look at Mr. Earle's house' when you want us to move our head?"

"Yes, Lindell. I remember."

"Can we still call it Mr. Earle's house?"

I pulled Lindell onto my lap and thought about the time he and Earle, with his thinned, silver hair and hunched shoulders, sat on the front step of Earle's cape and had a conversation. Earle's knees were high up against his chest as he sat awkwardly on the wooden step. Lindell's knobby knees, covered with bruises and scabs, looked like the skin of a baby next to Earle's shriveled arms covered in sun spots and dry wrinkles.

"Remember when Mr. Earle and Gloria came to my Biography Night at school?" Ford said.

"Yes, you were so cute in your Thomas Edison bow tie."

"I wish Mr. Earle could have come to mine," Owen said.

"He was already too sick by then, honey."

"What will happen to his house?" Ford asked.

"I don't know."

I thought about how sometimes, while the boys played basketball on the driveway between our houses, Earle would join them. He couldn't run, and he could barely stand straight, but he'd shuffle to the edge of the grass and toss the basketball with one hand. After a few shots, he'd sit in an old folding chair on the driveway to watch. Ever since Earle had pneumonia and went to live with his daughter across town, the chair had sat empty. In the springtime, it held a layer of pollen and occasionally grass clippings. In the winter, snow piled on top of it, until only the back was visible. The boys used the chair as "home base" during a game of hide-and-seek. They ran through Earle's backyard, leaped over his bushes, and chased the squirrels that skittered across the many bird feeders in his backyard.

I knew that no matter who lived in the house next door, it would always be "Mr. Earle's house" to us.

The morning of Earle's funeral, we were scheduled to take Anne, from across the street, to the monthly Widows and Widowers dinner at the Friars' Bakehouse since last month's meeting had been canceled. It was a perfect fall day outside. The sky was a vibrant blue, and there was very little wind. The sun cast long shadows across the street and warmed pockets of air. It was Saturday; the boys wanted to be outside. Winter was coming, and soon playing outside would require bulky snow gear and mittens. But that Saturday would have been a perfect day for hide-and-seek or riding bikes. So when I came downstairs and told the boys to be ready in thirty minutes to take Anne to the Friars' Bakehouse, they weren't jumping up and down with excitement. At least one of them moaned and sighed.

But then Ford said, "Come on guys, this is important to Mom and our neighbor. It won't take long, and we can play when we get home."

I turned around and mouthed "thank you" to him.

At 11:30, Ford walked across the street to get Anne. I watched from the window as he walked slowly back with her, chatting as they went. I thought about how far Ford had come from the November before. There were still struggles here and there, but for the most part, his mood had evened out. He was responsible more than he was childish, and he was friendly more than he was ornery.

We got into the car and drove downtown just like last time. Also like the last time, when I pulled alongside the Friars' Bakehouse, it looked dark. A sign on the window read CLOSED.

"Um, Mom, are you sure you got the date right?" Owen said.

"Yes, Owen. The third Saturday of the month, which is today."

"Okay, I'm just asking," Owen said.

I unbuckled my seat belt. "I'll go knock and see if they are in there," I said. "Maybe they are only closed to the public."

I peered into the glass storefront window, past the cement statue and hanging plants. The restaurant was completely dark. And empty. A sign taped to the door fluttered with a breeze:

FRIARS' RETREAT
SATURDAY, NOVEMBER 17
9:00 A.M.–4:00 P.M.

I looked at my phone to check the date: November 17.

Just then I realized that I never confirmed the details with the Friars. I had assumed the lunch happened every third Saturday without exception. I hated to go back to the car and tell Anne. She beamed in the passenger seat, her white hair neatly curled and her pink lipstick glistening.

"I'm so sorry," I said, sliding into the driver's seat. "I don't know why I didn't call ahead." I shook my head.

"It's okay, dear," Anne said. She held her pocketbook in her lap. "We'll try again next month."

"Well, next month is Christmas," Ford said. "So I bet it will be canceled. But what about January? Do you have any plans the third Saturday in January?"

Anne turned in her seat to see Ford. "No, I don't guess I do," she said. "It's a date."

Back home, the boys ran and screamed in the backyard. They chased each other with foam swords and dared to jump off the back porch and land on both feet. At 3:00, I called them inside. Owen was invited to a birthday party at 4:00, and the viewing for Earle's funeral began at the same time.

"I'll understand if you don't want to miss the birthday party," I told Owen. "Or, you can come with us to see Mr. Earle's family, and then I'll take you to the party a little late."

Owen nodded. He looked at me and then Ford.

"It's totally up to you," I said.

"Um, I'll go to the party late," Owen said. "Going to the funeral is the right thing to do."

Ford patted Owen on the shoulder. "Good choice," he said. And then, to Lindell: "Go put on church clothes, buddy. You can't wear sweatpants to a funeral."

On the way to the funeral home, I tried, as best I could, to prepare the boys for what they might see. I told them that if the casket was open, it would probably be in a back room, and they could choose whether to go see it.

"Like he'll just be lying there?" Lindell said.

"Um, sort of." I fidgeted in the driver's seat, unsure how to explain. The boys had never been to a funeral before. "But, well, maybe it's best if you just stay in the gathering area. I'm sure they'll have pictures of Mr. Earle there, pictures from when he was alive."

"Yeah, remember that slideshow we watched when we went to Dinner with the Smileys at his house?" Ford said. "I bet they'll be playing that."

"If it's okay, Mom, I'm not going to go in the room where Mr. Earle is," Owen said.

"That's perfectly fine," I said.

The entryway to the funeral home was warm. There were oriental throw rugs on the floor and a shiny brass chandelier overhead. Two men in suits greeted us at the door and took our coats. We moved into the lobby area, where we saw other neighbors. So far, it seemed just like a house. The boys wouldn't know any different. I relaxed.

And then—just then—as we walked past a French door to our left, the open casket was there. Earle lay peacefully, surrounded by white satin and flowers.

The boys had no idea. They hadn't noticed. Lindell ran in circles around one of the rugs. Ford and Owen continued an argument from the car about one of their video games. And behind all three of them, the casket seemed to be illuminated, elevated, and unmistakable.

I called the boys to me. "Quick, come here," I said, motioning for them to follow me toward a bathroom on my right.

"What? No," Ford said. "That's the women's bathroom, Mom!"

"Why do you want us to go in there?" Owen said.

They turned and walked away.

Lindell ran off again, too.

And it was then—that very moment when they turned around—that they finally saw.

Ford stopped in his tracks. Owen ran into the back of him. Lindell covered his mouth with his hand.

When Ford turned on his heel and looked at me, his eyes were like saucers. "Is that—?"

I nodded.

Owen's eyes glistened with tears. "I don't want to go in," he said. "I don't want to go."

"Okay," I said quietly. My heart felt like it would beat out of my chest. I was sure I wasn't handling any of this correctly. I thought of Dustin. If he weren't on deployment, he'd be there with us. He'd have on his navy-blue blazer and red tie. He'd stand straight and walk purposefully. He'd smell like shaving cream. And he would know what to do.

I found a spot for Owen to sit out of view. I told him I'd just go in and say hello to Earle's family, and then we'd leave.

"Okay," Owen said, his voice quivering. He sat in a padded chair with his hands in his lap.

Ford shrugged. "I'll go with you, Mom," he said.

"Me, too," Lindell said, grabbing my hand. I wasn't sure he really understood yet.

"We'll be back in just a minute," I told Owen.

But before we got to the French doors, Owen said, "Wait! I'll go with you."

"Are you sure?"

"It's the right thing to do," he said. "For Mr. Earle."

The room that had the casket was as cold as a refrigerator. There was a faint hospital smell. Voices around us were hushed; their murmurs ran together. For a moment, I thought I might pass out. But I couldn't. The boys needed me. If I act strong, I thought, the boys will follow my lead. So I took a deep breath and squeezed Lindell's hand. "Look, there's Mrs. McGovern," I said. "Earle's daughter."

Jane greeted us with hugs. She said that Dustin sent her a nice message of condolence and had shared his favorite memory of Earle: when he sat on the front step talking with Lindell. Jane's eyes filled with tears as she told us how much Earle enjoyed having us as neighbors.

"If only you had been there ten years earlier," Jane said, "when Dad was still healthy. He would have taken care of you and the boys every single day. He would have mowed your lawn and shoveled your driveway. He really would have."

Owen stood close to my side. He seemed frozen. His hand was up against his mouth, and his eyes were wide. He was staring at the casket. Lindell ran wide circles around the room, pretending to be an airplane. When he passed by Earle in the casket, he suddenly stopped, stood on his tiptoes, clasped the side of the casket, and peeked over. "Hey, look, it's Mr. Earle," he said.

Owen whispered to me, "I want to go say good-bye to him. Will you go with me?"

I took his hand and together we walked toward the casket.

"Looks just like Mr. Earle, doesn't it?" I said awkwardly.

"Because it is Mr. Earle," Lindell said.

"He looks so peaceful," Owen said.

"He is."

"Can he hear us?" Owen asked.

Jane came up behind us. "He's not there anymore, Owen," she said. "That's just his body. But I believe that Dad is here in spirit and that he is so happy you came to say good-bye to him."

Lindell peered into the casket and pointed at the gold band on Earle's hand. "Is that Mr. Earle's wedding band?" he asked.

"It is," Jane said.

"He's going to die with his ring?" Lindell said.

"He'll be buried with it, yes. And he'll be right next to my mother, his wife."

Lindell took my hand again. "Mommy has Dad's ring again," he said. "She wears it every day."

The boys were quiet when we got back in the car. After a few minutes, though, with the cold darkness enveloping us and only the green lights of the dashboard highlighting our faces, they began to talk.

"I thought more people would be crying," Owen said. "But people were laughing and stuff."

"They were celebrating Mr. Earle's life," I said.

"Yeah, I kind of thought everyone would be crying, too," Ford said. "I thought the whole thing would be sadder than it was."

"I thought it was fun," Lindell said.

"Why weren't more people crying?" Owen asked.

"Because Mr. Earle lived a long life," I said. "That's something to celebrate, not to be sad about. He was still sailing his boat when he was ninety years old, and he died surrounded by family and friends. Many people don't live to be ninety-four years old. So Earle's family is grateful they could be with him for so long."

"That makes sense," Owen said.

I thought again of Earle's mother, just as I had during our dinner with him in April. Her son was dead, at the age of ninety-four, and she was spared ever having to lose him herself. It was the natural order of things, and, indeed, something to celebrate.

Our last dinner was the next day.

THROUGHOUT THE YEAR, there had been so many people who helped us in large and small ways. Some of them were longtime friends. Others were new friends whom we had gotten to know better. There was Andrea O., who always included us in holiday parties, and at the beginning of the deployment was the first to leave a meal for us on the front steps.

There was Jeff, a handyman who fixed everything from the fence that fell down in our backyard to the window that leaked in the living room. Except Jeff never sent me a bill. I always reminded him, but he just said, "Oh, I'll get around to that." When pressed, he finally gave me a total—for materials, not labor.

There were the Garretts, who invited us to Thanksgiving at the beginning of the deployment when we were still in shock and finding our routine. And Jenn Khavari and Kristin Canders, who always remembered us on difficult days, like Father's Day.

There was Suchari, who in the beginning of the deployment, when darkness came at 3:30 in the afternoon, stopped by to check on us or to take Lindell to her house to play. And Ally, who helped Morgan plan my surprise Valentine's Day dinner at Fiddlehead in February.

There was Nurse Becca, who once came over in the middle of the night when Ford hallucinated with fever; Jessica and Matt, who competed in the annual Kenduskeag Stream Canoe Race in Dustin's honor; and Becky, who never let me forget a baseball practice or game.

And there were people like Jesse, Helen, Chelsey, Mike, and so many others who took time to listen, or to send me a note asking, "How are you doing?" or "Do you need anything?"

Incredibly, in twelve months, we had not been able to have a dinner with most of these friends and neighbors. I was beginning to realize that I'd never be able to repay any of them. Nor would I be able to adequately thank them. So the boys and I decided to honor them with our fifty-second and final Dinner with the Smileys.

Ann Marie, a local caterer, offered her restaurant, 11 Central, to the boys and me on the Sunday before Thanksgiving. The boys wore T-shirts with bow ties, regular ties, and suspenders screen printed on them. Ann Marie tied waiter aprons around their waists, and when Helen, Jeff, Suchari, and all our other guests arrived, the boys escorted them to a table. The warm interior of 11 Central— with its exposed brick walls and chandelier lighting—quickly filled with a community of helpers, many of whom didn't know one another yet. The boys placed the guests four to a table, and with Ann Marie's help, served them their first course: a salad. Ford and Owen filled water glasses while Lindell folded napkins and talked about the evening's meal: chicken and pasta, and then a special dessert.

Once everyone was settled, Ford clinked a water glass with a knife and called for attention. Then he and his brothers welcomed everyone and told them why they were there:

The boys dressed as waiters for dinner number fifty-two

"You've helped us through our dad's deployment, so welcome to our linner," Owen said. "That's lunch and dinner combined, get it?"

"I'm surprised the pizza delivery man isn't here because he helped Mom a lot this year, too," Ford said.

Everyone laughed.

Later, I joined one of the tables for dinner, and watched with a full and happy heart as my boys continued to serve a room full of people who had served us throughout the year.

On the way home, however, reality sunk in.

"It's really over now," Owen said. "That was our last dinner."

"No, we still have to eat," Lindell said. "We can't just stop dinners."

"He means Dinner with the Smileys," Ford said.

"I'm going to miss it," Owen said.

We were quiet the rest of the way.

The next two weeks were probably the most difficult of the entire deployment. Our dinners were done, but the reason for the dinners (Dustin's deployment) was not yet finished. I felt paralyzed with fear when I thought about the upcoming two weekends alone. No dinners. No Dustin. Just the boys and me trying to fill up time. This is what I had been trying to avoid all along.

Thanksgiving was Ford's twelfth birthday. The Cowans invited us to their house for cake and dessert, but I didn't feel much like celebrating. My feet felt like weights as I walked through the grocery store buying ingredients for Thanksgiving dinner. I placed items on the cashier's conveyer belt and looked at other shoppers with envy. I knew, because of their large turkey or bag full of potatoes, that their whole families would be together. They were probably excited about a holiday and several days off work. But when you are alone, which is how I felt, it's easy to hate vacations and weekends. If not for the kids, I might have gone up to the university, shut myself in my office, and graded papers all day.

It was strange that Dustin would be home in just two weeks, but suddenly I was feeling very depressed. I knew it was partly because two birthdays (Owen's tenth birthday would be after Thanksgiving) and one holiday stood between homecoming and us. But also, with relief in sight, I was beginning to let down my guard. My friend Amber likened it to needing to use the bathroom—it gets harder to wait the closer you get to the toilet. As Dustin's homecoming drew nearer, I had a difficult time keeping myself together. Previously, I refused to answer the often asked, "How do you do it?" How would I *not* do it? But in late November, with the end in sight, I was, in fact, beginning to ask myself, *How* have *I done this?* It was the emotional equivalent of not making it to the bathroom on time.

Dustin arrived back in the United States the day before Thanksgiving, but he had checkout procedures to complete before he could come home to us. When he called me from Norfolk, Virginia, it was the first time in months that I heard his voice intimately over the phone, rather than through a grainy Skype connection. We were finally in the same country. The same time zone even. And this new reality heralded my inevitable unraveling. I cried so hard Dustin could hardly understand me.

"I can't do it. I can't do it," I sobbed. "I can't do this another week."

"Of course you can. Just hold on a little longer," he said. "I'm almost home."

I locked myself in our bedroom and cried on the phone. The kids banged on the door. "What's wrong, Mommy?" Lindell asked through the crack.

Owen's voice was full of fear and worry as he tapped on the door and said, "Mom, are you crying? Can we come in?"

All year, I had hidden this insecurity and fear from them. I never gave them any reason to doubt that I could take care of them. But now I was falling apart, just days before Dustin would return.

Those days—the holiday and the birthdays—passed in a blur. I went through the motions, wrapping presents and baking cakes, but I felt numb. I wanted Dustin to come home. I couldn't wait. And I was beginning to realize just how much our weekly dinners had buoyed me. All along, they had been the smoke screen that allowed me to carry on.

"You've had a lot going on," Dustin said on the phone. "With Mr. Earle passing away, and the holiday and the birthdays . . ." His voice trailed off. We were both silent. Then he said, "It makes sense that you are letting go now. We're almost done. I'm almost home."

Dustin returning home

CHAPTER FIFTEEN

December

After feeling depressed from Thanksgiving and the several days following, I woke up on November 30 and leapt out of bed. I felt hungry and had an appetite for food for the first time in weeks. I was rested and felt ten pounds lighter as I ran to the top of the stairs.

"Daddy comes home tomorrow," I yelled to the kids, who were watching cartoons and waiting for me to take them to school. They ran to me, clapping and hollering.

"Tomorrow?" Lindell screamed. "It's tomorrow?"

"I can hardly wait," Owen said.

And then Ford asked, "So we don't have to go to school today, right?"

"What? Of course you're going to school today," I said.

"But Mom, tomorrow Dad—"

I shooed them all away. "Hurry, go get dressed," I said. "Let's not be late. There's lots to do between now and then."

As I hurriedly brushed my teeth and pulled my hair back into a ponytail, I went over the to-do list in my head: Get hair cut. Paint nails. Iron skirt. Shave legs. Wash sheets. Buy groceries. Move my things out of Dustin's drawers. Put my pillows back on my side of the bed. Get my hair dryer and neck massager out of Dustin's closet. Move my clothes from his hangers.

Basically, I had to make room for my husband again.

The kids hopped out of the car for school without complaining. I went to work and tried to concentrate. By afternoon, my in-laws had arrived from Seattle, Washington, so I left the kids with them while I went out to find shoes for my dress and a new shade of lipstick. I was trying to fill up time again. I felt like a kid waiting for Christmas.

As I read bedtime stories to the kids that night, I wondered how much our routine would change in just twenty-four hours. Would Dustin read the bedtime story, or would I? We were already in the middle of a book; would Dustin pick up where I left off, or would he wait until we started the next book?

I lay in my bed, unable to sleep, until after midnight. I was both excited and concerned. Would Dustin feel like a stranger? Would he be glad to be at home, or would he miss his job? What if he thinks we are boring?

I reflected on all the things that had happened since Dustin left. In some ways, the year seemed to pass quickly. Yet, when I thought about our lives twelve months earlier, it seemed like ages ago. Before the deployment, I had not finished my master's degree. Ford was still more child than teenager. Lindell wasn't in school, and Owen had several missing teeth. Before Dustin left, we didn't know Police Chief Gastia (dinner number eight), Jenifer Lloyd (dinner number five), Ben Sprague (dinner number thirty-six), Rae Wren (dinner number thirty-nine), Marion Syverson (dinner number thirty), and nearly every other Dinner with the Smileys guest. Our lives and our community had expanded in a relatively short period of time. Ford had gone from an angry and bitter pre-teen to a helpful young man. Lindell had become a little boy and lost most of his baby cheeks and the pudginess around his knees. Owen had left grade school and moved to the bigger elementary school. He had new friends, many of whom Dustin had not yet met.

I tossed and turned in bed, staring at the empty place where Dustin would be in another day. I knew that he had changed and grown, too, and probably in ways I couldn't anticipate.

Many times, military families say they can't wait for things to get "back to normal" after a deployment. I had come to find, however, that things never go in reverse. There is no normal, and even if there were, it wouldn't be in the past. Instead, I reasoned, Dustin, the boys, and I would have to meet each other where we currently were. We'd have to find a new normal. After a year spent apart, there was no other way.

I fell asleep to the gentle snores of Sparky, sprawled on the floor beside the bed.

The next morning, the kids woke me up early. Again, much like Christmas. They were bouncing on their knees at the end of the bed and chanting, "Mom, get up! Today is the day!" My cell phone on the bedside table vibrated and beeped. I turned it over and saw a message from Dustin: "Getting on the plane now. See you when I get home."

I threw back the covers and swung my legs over the bed. "Okay boys, let's get this day started!"

"Yay!" Lindell screamed as he ran out of the room.

Dustin's parents, who were staying at a hotel, came to the house early to take the kids to breakfast and give me time to get ready. When I closed the front door behind them, the house was silent, except for Sparky panting at my side. I sat down on the couch, pulled a blanket over my legs, and tried to relax. I felt like I was waiting for a first date.

I played Words with Friends and browsed Facebook, trying to keep myself from getting too nervous. Then, when I tracked Dustin's plane and knew that it was in fact on its way and not delayed, I went upstairs to get ready.

About seventy-five of our dinner guests came to the airport to welcome Dustin home. They were waiting for us at the top of the escalator in Bangor International Airport as I held Lindell's hand and we rode to the second floor. Paul's R2-D2, from dinner number nineteen, was there. He beeped and whistled when the four of us stepped off the escalator. My hands were shaking with excitement, and I could feel that my cheeks were flushed.

"Are you excited?" everyone asked, and I didn't know what to say. It didn't seem real yet.

But the kids were clearly high on adrenaline and anticipation. Lindell screamed happily and ran from one dinner guest to another telling them, "My daddy is coming home!"

Ford and Owen stood with their hands stuffed in their khaki pants, but their smiles and sparkling eyes gave away their excitement.

"The plane is landing in just a moment," someone from the airport told me. "If you follow me to the window over here, you can watch it pull up."

The boys ran to the large plate glass window, and Lindell pressed his face against it. "Where is it? Where is it?" he shouted.

The dinner guests circled around us. Doug, from dinner number thirty-nine at Mount Katahdin, gave the older boys high-fives. Becky, from dinner number fifty-two, gave me a hug. Her face was flushed with emotion, her eyes teary. Owen and Ford's third-grade teacher was there with her family. She squeezed my arm and told me she was happy for us. There were so many people—old friends and new. I began to forget whom Dustin already knew and who would need an introduction.

Jenifer Lloyd held my purse, and Elizabeth Sutherland (Ric Tyler's wife) told me where to stand for the best view. I felt a little like a bride. And, indeed, when I looked out at our dinner guests there beside me—Earle's family, Julie and Brian, the Canders, the Khavaris, and so many others—I felt as happy as a bride.

"It's time," the airport employee told me. She motioned for the boys and me to come closer to the hallway where Dustin would come off the plane. Our guests stayed behind us. Other passengers filed out of the narrow space, wheeling their luggage and walking with a purpose past us to the escalator. It seemed like the line of people we didn't know would never end.

"When, Mommy, when?" Lindell screamed as he jumped up and down.

"Do you see him yet?" Owen asked.

And then the flow of passengers slowed. There were just a few others trickling out of the hallway.

That's when the boys saw him.

Dustin came out of the shadows flashing a wide, familiar smile,

Dustin and the boys

Dustin and Sarah greeting each other as the boys look on

the one that makes lines around his mouth. He wore his khaki uniform and carried a blue backpack.

The boys ran to him, each of them jockeying for position to grab on to his waist. Dustin threw the backpack to the side, kneeled down, and put his arms around all three of the boys. Ford and Owen buried their face in Dustin's uniform. Lindell clung to his arms and jumped up and down. "I love you! I love you!" he screamed.

"It's great to see you guys," Dustin said. He never stopped smiling.

"You're just as pretty as I remember!" Lindell said, and our guests behind us laughed.

Dustin stood back up, and gently pulled the boys with him. "Let me go see Mom now," he said. He looked over at me and smiled.

I walked toward him, a lump in my throat, and when I put my arms around him, it felt exactly the way it always had. We hugged each other for a long time, while Lindell pulled at my skirt and yelled, "Mommy! Daddy!"

"I love you," Dustin whispered in my ear.

"I love you, too," I said.

We hugged again.

Then I slowly pulled away and said, "I've got some new friends for you to meet." I smiled playfully up at him. "That crowd behind me, that's just a sampling of the people who filled your seat this year."

"Daddy, come meet them!" Lindell yelled.

I hooked my arm in Dustin's and led him to the clapping and cheering crowd. Then I stood back and let him shake hands with our new community.

Dustin never—not once—stopped smiling. Lindell wouldn't

Dustin and dinner guests

let go of him either. He squeezed Dustin's face and pressed his nose against Dustin's nose. He held on to his pants pocket and swung from his arms. Ford and Owen kept their hands in their pockets, but they were still smiling and staying close by their dad. Together, the four of them moved like a unit through the crowd. Dustin greeted each of the guests and thanked them for their support.

Before he was done, a plane full of men and women in army uniforms came through the airport and down the escalator. They were an Explosive Ordnance Disposal Unit on their way home from Afghanistan. Their faces were tired, and their hair was bent and messy from hours, maybe even days, of travel. Like my husband a week ago, they were in the country, but not home yet. They were just passing through. Some of them had probably called their husbands and wives from the airport to say, "I'll be home soon. I'm almost there."

A few of the uniformed men and women looked up as they passed by. They nodded knowingly at Dustin. He nodded back. Then he started clapping. Soon, all of our dinner guests were standing and clapping, too. We clapped until the last man went down the escalator and out of view.

Then Dustin looked at me and said, "Ready to take me home?"

I was.

At home, a special note hung on Dustin's seat at the dinner table: "Reserved for . . . DAD!"

Lindell proudly showed Dustin before he could even get his jacket off. "This is where you'll sit tonight," Lindell squealed. "Our guests sat there, but now it's yours again."

"I can't wait," Dustin said.

Then he was pulled in all directions by the boys:

"Come see the pottery I made at Windover."

"Come see the book I'm reading."

"Hey, Dad, want to play Wii with me?"

"Dad, look at this Lego set I made."

Sparky followed close behind all of them as they went from room to room. His back end shook as his tail beat happily. I stayed in the kitchen to start preparing the meal.

It was just the five of us around the farm table for dinner. I made steak and potatoes and a salad. The boys picked at their food, but mostly they talked over each other, trying to tell Dustin everything at once. Lindell got in and out of his seat. He crawled under the table and into my lap. Then he stood next to his dad and stared at the side of his face, as if he still didn't believe he was there.

That night, I fell asleep on the couch listening to Dustin read a new and different bedtime story to the kids. The house felt warm and still. My stomach was full. Sparky snored beside me. And when Dustin woke me to go upstairs to bed, I opened my eyes and said, "It's true. You're still here."

The next morning, we went to church. Snow fell lightly on the stacked buildings and lampposts with wreaths on them as we drove through downtown. The city was slow and quiet. Inside the van, we were warm and without extra space. All the seats in the mini-van were filled. Finally.

Dustin let me and the boys get out in front of the church so that he could find a parking space. In my mind, I thought of all the times I had trudged up the steep hill, from parking on Exchange Street, to the church on Broadway, with the kids trailing behind me. We walked in snow, rain, and sunshine, because we didn't have the option to be let out at the curb.

When I stepped out of the van, there was ice on the sidewalk. Owen rushed to grab my elbow and steady me as I slid in my high heels. Just as he did, and without seeing Owen, Dustin said, "Hey, boys, help your mom on that ice."

Ford was on my other side, holding my other elbow. "We've already got her, Dad," he said.

The service had already started when the boys and I slid into an empty pew. The kids peeled off their winter coats, and I searched the door for Dustin. It was like I didn't believe he would reappear. I needed to see his face again. Then, there he was in the doorway, walking toward our seats.

He sat down beside me, and the smell of his aftershave filled the space. Lindell was on his knees coloring, and Ford looked behind him to wave at Ben and Malorie.

Dustin took my left hand, and laced his fingers with mine. I looked at him and smiled.

Then Owen, who was on my right, reached for my hand, too. So many weeks, the boys and I had sat there alone. We only had each other, and I had longed to hold Dustin's hand.

Now Dustin was back, and certainly I felt complete. But Owen's

The Smileys

small hand reaching for mine reminded me that the boys still needed me. The journey wasn't finished.

Ford, Owen, Lindell, and I had bonded as a unit of four while Dustin was away. We had seen and done things Dustin would only know about through our inside jokes and stories. We had formed new relationships and dependencies.

We had, in effect, gone on without him.

Our family now had two histories—predeployment and during deployment—and we were on the cusp of the next chapter: Postdeployment.

Before Dustin left, I had asked him to step aside and let the boys play ball in the backyard without him. "Soon, they won't have you," I said. "Let them learn to play together." Dustin understood. He put down his baseball glove and went into the living room alone.

That day at church, as I held Dustin's hand and saw Owen's searching for mine, I knew it was time to do the opposite. We had to let Dustin back into the fold.

I took Owen's smooth palm and placed it on top of his dad's calloused hands. Then I covered both of theirs with mine.

Dustin looked sideways at me and smiled.

Owen looked up through his long bangs and made a questioning face that said, "Um, okaaaaaay. Mom, you're weird."

And Dustin's wedding band, the one I still wore on my right hand, glistened under beams of light coming from the stained glass.

Afterword

Carol Woodcock, who accompanied Senator Susan Collins to our first dinner, brought her camera and took pictures. Until then, I hadn't thought about pictures. Dinner with the Smileys was still evolving; it wasn't a *thing* yet. So why have pictures?

A few days later, however, when Carol sent me the snapshots in an e-mail, I saw glimpses of the evening that might have gone unnoticed otherwise. I saw how Lindell pressed his cheek against Senator Collins's cheek when he sat on her lap and Skyped with Dustin. I saw the way Ford's eyes grew big when she kneeled before him and presented the flag. And I saw the way the senator made herself at home sitting on the edge of Ford's bed and looking at his baseball cards.

Friends and family were naturally curious about our dinner with the senator, so they were excited to see the pictures on Facebook. But it was Dustin's reaction that really struck me: "Looking at those pictures helps me feel like I'm there," he wrote.

Sometime before our second dinner with Lindell's preschool teacher, Mrs. O'Connor, my photographer friend Andrea Hand left a message on my phone. "I want to talk to you about an idea," she said. "Call me when you get home."

When I called Andrea back, and before she could speak, I said, "I hope your idea is to photograph my dinners."

"I don't know about any dinners," Andrea said. "But, sure."

Andrea hadn't read my column in the local newspaper about inviting people to dinner while Dustin was deployed. Rather, her idea had been to follow a family for a year and document their lives.

Andrea is divorced and has a grown daughter. She lives alone several streets away from us. She eats dinner at an empty table. This, plus her past experience as a counselor, has given her an intense interest in family dynamics. She is captivated by the ways in which the small details of family life lift up the unique characteristics of relationships between people.

"Sure, you can follow my family for a year," I told her. "But can my weekly dinners be a part of that?"

We came up with an agreement and a plan: Andrea would photograph Dinner with the Smileys, and I would give her intimate access to our family. She could photograph us shopping at the grocery store, going to baseball, sitting in church, watching television. She could follow us to parties and be there for the kids' bedtime stories.

In the end, Andrea hoped to reveal the small tasks of family life, or, in her words, to "make the ordinary extraordinary." And I hoped to document all my dinners.

Yet, what neither of us could have seen then was that Andrea's project and mine would eventually, in many ways, become irrelevant. Because what happened in our year with Andrea was that a new kind of family was created.

ANDREA CALLED FORD "Ross" for the first two months of Dinner with the Smileys. We don't know how this started or why, but it became a habit Andrea couldn't break. And it drove Ford *crazy*.

He was already having trouble with another adult being "in his way" and taking pictures, so the Ross thing was particularly offensive.

Plus, we spent so much time with Andrea she naturally started to correct the boys and their behaviors.

"Settle down back there," she'd say from the passenger seat in the car. "Your mom can't focus, and we have a lot to get done today."

Ford would glare at her in the mirror, and with each interference his face became stone-like.

"I wish she wouldn't say 'we,'" Ford said. "It's like she's taking Dad's place. She's a fifth person, but she's not a 'we.'"

Ford asked me to stop the photography portion of Dinner with the Smileys, not because he didn't like having his picture taken (although he was never overly fond of that either), but because he thought Andrea was becoming too much a part of the family.

"But I like seeing the pictures," Dustin told him through Skype. "It helps me feel a part of it." Plus, Dustin said, by opening our lives in a very public way, we were allowing military service members' absences to become more visible. "Not everyone knows what it's like to have a dad on deployment," Dustin said. "You're helping people to better understand that."

Lindell bonded with Andrea almost immediately. She is thin, petite, playful, and energetic, despite being old enough to be my mother. Her voice is vibrant, and when she smiles, she can't help but show all her teeth.

Lindell called her And-wea in the beginning, but as he matured through the year, it became Andrea. He said he loved her, and when anyone asked, "What's been your favorite dinner," he'd say, "Any dinner when Andrea was there."

Even Sparky warmed to Andrea. He barked and growled protectively when she rang the doorbell, as he does when anyone is at the door. But as soon as Andrea poked her head inside and said,

"Hello, Smileys," Sparky would flop down on his bed and sigh comfortably. "Oh, it's just you," he seemed to be saying.

Owen was not opposed to Andrea in the way that Ford was, but he didn't open up to her either. While Lindell ran to her screaming, "Andrea! Andrea! Come see what I made at school today," Owen stayed on the couch, neither disappointed nor excited by her presence.

For me, Andrea became a confidante. She stayed after our guests left and talked to me while I did the dishes.

"Do you think that went alright?" I'd ask.

"I think so. Everyone was laughing and seemed to be having a good time."

"But Ford—"

"Yes, I know. You worry about Ford. He'll find his way."

Sometimes Lindell called Andrea into his room to read his bedtime story. Or Sparky would ring the bells hanging from the back door and Andrea would let him out. She helped me decide what to wear for dinners, and when I was sick in March, she brought me homemade chicken soup.

I wish I could say exactly when Ford's feelings toward Andrea began to change. There was no precise moment. It was like she grew on him. Or, he softened and she backed off. (Maybe a combination of the two?) But what I do remember is that one night in September, when Ford was hallucinating from a high fever, he asked me to call Andrea. She showed up within minutes and sat on the side of his bed, smoothing the hair from his face.

In a story Owen wrote about Dinner with the Smileys, he said, "Ford and Andrea did not get along well at first. But then we got used to Andrea being there and she got used to coming over for the dinners. She started to seem like part of the family."

Toward the end of the year, Ford kept Andrea's number by his bedside table. In October, when the boys wanted to get me a

birthday gift and card, Ford called Andrea, and she took all three
boys shopping. Ford started including her in the "we":

"When are *we* going to Augusta, Andrea?"

"What should *we* do for the last dinner?"

Owen had warmed up faster, however, partially because he and
Andrea both share an eye for the arts and have an uncanny ability
to read people.

In his story, Owen wrote:

> After a dinner, Mom would ask me, Lindell, Ford, and Andrea,
> what we liked best about it. We always said, "It was good." But
> Andrea would talk about things she noticed about the people or
> the way we all talked to each other.

Incredibly, Andrea, who is so gifted with the camera, is even more
gifted with a pencil. She sketches portraits that look like black-and-
white photographs. Only by careful inspection can anyone see the
difference.

Owen had begun sketching throughout the year, so for his tenth
birthday, Andrea gave him a set of artist's pencils, the same ones
she uses for her portraits. Owen guarded them from his brothers,
and he found a special place for the pencils on his bedside table.

Like Ford, Owen sometimes asked to talk to Andrea when we
weren't with her. If Andrea and I were on the phone together,
Owen would say, "Oh, can I say hi?" Then he'd walk away with
the phone, telling Andrea about his art class or latest drawings.

In his story, Owen wrote: *When someone asked Lindell what his
favorite dinner was, he said, "All the dinners ANDREA was at!" And I
partially agreed with him.*

The only dinners that Andrea missed were the first (because
we hadn't come up with our plan yet) and the fifty-first, when she
was out of town helping her daughter move into a new apartment.

Another local photographer, Mark McCall, filled in for Andrea that night. He told me that he would arrive early, well before our guests, to give the kids "time to get over the shock and disappointment that I'm not Andrea."

Mark was kidding, but he was also partially correct. After the fifty-first dinner, the boys all said some variation of, "that was weird not having Andrea here."

And so, we made our unofficial fifty-third dinner, the week before Dustin came home, be in celebration of Andrea. By now, she was family, so I wasn't worried about the house or what to make. I don't think I even got out of sweatpants or put on makeup. Which was okay because for the first time, we Smileys would not be the center of the photographs. Andrea would.

I gave the boys my Canon and iPhone, and Andrea let them use her "real photographer" camera. For that one night, Andrea stepped outside the lens, and the boys were her photographers.

I never could have predicted what Dinner with the Smileys would become—what it would mean to the community and how it would inspire others to reach out and invite someone to dinner. But I also never could have predicted that Andrea's phone message—her hint at an idea—in early January, and that rocky start to our project soon after, would lead to us, as a family, having a new member who is part aunt, part confidante, and always shooting pictures.

Epilogue

by Ford Smiley

Dad was home, and now we were celebrating with all the guests from Dinner with the Smileys at a Reunion Dinner, which was actually just desserts. (On the invitations, Mom wrote, "You've had Dinner with the Smileys, now it's time for Dessert—with Dustin!")

I got into my polo shirt and khaki pants, however reluctantly, and sat down to work on the official Dinner with the Smileys Trivia game. Later that night, every Reunion Dinner guest would get a trivia card, and anyone who got less than five answers wrong would enter a drawing for the sixteen centerpieces from the tables. (Remember that; it's important.)

We arrived at the reception hall, and I was greeted by Marion Syverson, or the Food Fairy as we call her because she always brings food for us and leaves unnoticed. She was a guest at dinner number thirty, when we invited the people who helped us with our basement when it flooded.

I walked into the main room holding a stack of trivia cards. I recognized dozens of people. My mom and dad were talking to Congressman Michaud from dinner number twenty-two. I also noticed Buddy and Lily Fryer from dinner number twenty-nine, Jenifer Lloyd from dinner number five, Melissa Huston from dinner number ten, and Paul and R2-D2 from dinner number nineteen.

I decided to hand the first quiz to Buddy.

"Here's a trivia on the dinners," I told him, showing him one of the cards. "If you get less than five questions wrong, you get to be in the drawing to win one of the centerpieces."

Buddy smiled and took it. "What do I do with it when I'm done?"

"Just bring it into the room with the slideshow. I'll be at the souvenir table handing out more quizzes," I said. (Mom had put all the souvenirs we got at our dinners on a table in the lobby. She also made a slideshow that was playing on a screen.)

I noticed more people flooding in. Mrs. Savage, whom both Owen and I had for third grade, and Gibran Graham, who works at the Briar Patch in downtown Bangor.

More and more people. Oh there's . . .

"FORD!!!!!" a cry pierced the room. A kindergarten voice.

"Can I take the quiz?" Lindell asked.

"It's hard," Owen warned.

"Just take it, Lindell," I said, giving him the card.

Lindell ran away as if he had just won the lottery.

"He'll never win," Owen said.

"Let's hope not," I said. "What could Lindell possibly want with a centerpiece of Christmas greens?"

Owen and I graded the quizzes. Most people passed, but a few people got more than five wrong. The US marshal, Noel March, for example.

When it was time for the speeches, my friend Lucas, from dinners number eighteen and twenty-seven, and I went into the larger room where all the guests were mingling. Lucas and Noah (see dinner number forty-eight) are two of my friends.

"Wait!" Lindell screamed, running behind us and holding his trivia sheet.

First Ric Tyler gave the introduction. Then my mom and the photographer, Andrea Hand, talked about how Dinner with the Smileys was a great experience. Ric Tyler introduced former Maine governor John Baldacci, who gave a speech next. He talked about how Maine is a good community for giving support. Next, Congressman Michaud told some memories from his dinner, like how Lindell told him he couldn't help put flags on veterans' graves because he couldn't read. After that, Senator Susan Collins stood and told the story of brownies—with nuts. She also talked about her flag that flew over the capitol building in our honor. She even presented Dad with a special coin. And, last but definitely not least, Dad stood to thank everyone.

After all the speeches, I gave Mom flowers saying, "These are from Dad."

We took a break, ate dessert, and talked. Lucas and I went to see R2-D2. Owen and Lindell stormed the food. Mom and Dad walked around saying hello to everyone. But I just couldn't wait. I wanted to get up and announce the trivia winners.

I asked Mike Dow, from dinner number eleven, to help me set up the microphone and speakers. He did.

"Hello! Could I have everyone's attention please! It's time for today's trivia winners!" I said.

Everyone looked at me behind the podium. I called out names as I randomly pulled the trivia cards from a pile: "Lily Fryer . . . Rae Wren . . . Alyssa Ogden . . . Gibran Graham . . ."

The guests came up to receive their prize centerpiece.

I finally got to the last potted plant.

"And now it's time for the final and most important center-piece," I announced, "which is actually no different than the other centerpieces, but it's up here by the speakers, so it's special. The winner is . . ."

I looked at the trivia card. At the bottom I saw the name. I slapped my forehead.

Owen elbowed me in the ribs. "Get on with it," he whispered.

"It's Lindell," I said.

Once again, Lindell looked like he'd won the lottery. He ran with eyes wide and did a headfirst baseball slide on the carpet.

I cringed, because that had to hurt.

Lindell held the plant over his head in victory. And then . . .

"So long, fellas!" he yelled, running out of the room.

Acknowledgments

Dinner with the Smileys would not have been possible without the support, direction, and confidence of several people. This is my attempt to thank all of them, even though "thanks" doesn't seem adequate enough for the gifts, tangible or not, that have been given to me.

My agent, Cheryl Pientka, instantly understood the depth of *Dinner with the Smileys* when I first met her midway through the year. Thank you, Cheryl, for laughing or crying at all the right spots, and for being a smiling, encouraging face in the audience.

Kerri Kolen, Elisabeth Dyssegaard, Megan, Christine, and everyone else at Hyperion have offered invaluable insight and assistance as I worked on these pages. Thank you for giving me the space to tell this story in the most genuine and heartfelt way. Thank you for your patience and work and for loving *Dinner with the Smileys* as much as I have.

The physical task of writing would not have been possible without my steadfast babysitters—Kara and Becca Cowan, Brianne Ecker—and my pinch-hitters: Alyssa Ogden and Robert Fryer. I logged many writing hours while they took care of my home front.

And let it be known that eighty percent of our dinners included Morgan Mazzei's wonderful turkey lasagna and Andrea Oldenburg's homemade bread recipe.

Indeed, one of the greatest outcomes of our fifty-two dinners has been a new community of friends. By the end of 2012, nearly 250 people had shared a meal with us. Many of them have remained a constant presence in our lives. I could never thank them enough, but I hope the pages of this book are a testament to my gratitude.

But the one person, beside me and the boys, who was at almost every dinner was photographer Andrea Hand. She lived Dinner with the Smileys alongside us, and everything from her feedback and insights to her suggestions and quiet presence helped to give me more understanding of what we had all been through.

Of course, there is no story without my family, and I am forever grateful for and amazed by my husband's encouragement to tell our life story without restrictions. Dustin has never asked me not to publish something, no matter how embarrassing. It takes a confident man with a great sense of humor to do that. Dustin says he is happy to be a footnote (as in, *Sarah Smiley is married to Dustin Smiley*), but without him, there is no Sarah Smiley.

And my boys . . .

Ford, who has the gift of words and who has always understood my need to "tell the story": Today you will think you bear the brunt of negative things in this book. Someday you will read it again and recognize that the struggles you faced are universal. You had a choice to let a difficult situation bring you down or raise you up. I admire your openness to allow the latter.

Owen, who patiently waits, asks questions, and understands people's needs: You might think your contributions go unnoticed, but we all appreciate your quiet gift for making people feel comfortable and important. The dinner table is brighter because of your smile.

And Lindell, who has provided me with an endless supply of laughs and who introduces himself to others as "Lindell from Dinner with the Smileys": We saw life—politics, heartbreak, love—anew through your eyes this year. You have held the hand of senators and schoolteachers with the same amount of awe and adoration. We have much to learn from you.

To all three boys: Thank you for being (mostly) willing participants, for keeping a (mostly) open mind, and for giving me and your dad a reason to be glad about the future. Everything I've done has been for you.

Reading Group Guide

Dinner with the Smileys

Introduction

They say you are what you eat—but apparently, with whom you eat is pretty important too. Current medical research bears this out. But wellness was not what motivated mil-blogger/author/ Navy wife and mom Sarah Smiley to invite one guest every week for fifty-two weeks to have dinner with herself and her three young sons.

Sarah's motivation was to fill a void in her family life: that empty chair at the dining room table while her Navy pilot husband, Dustin, was deployed overseas for a year. But what started as a gesture meant to distract the boys from missing their dad became a joyous journey as the unlikeliest people accepted the invitations...and brought dessert. The Smiley family discovered that a surprising number of people really are available for dinner. You just have to ask.

Each dinner guest taught them about life and the importance of sharing something simple and intimate—such as a meal—to cement these valuable lessons in place.

Discussion Questions

1. Imagine you've been invited to have dinner with the Smileys. What dessert would you bring?

2. Columnist Lisa Belkin said of *Dinner with the Smileys*: "It made me want to gather my own family together for a meal." Did you have the same reaction? Why? Can you recall a special moment or a lesson learned over a casual family dinner?

3. Would you have done what Sarah did? After reading *Dinner with the Smileys*, would you consider opening your home to a community member, neighbor, or even a celebrity, given the reaction Sarah and her sons' invitations had? Who would you invite?

4. Which invited guest was most interesting to you? Which one surprised you most?

5. Sarah's candid revelations about the year as a parent, cook, and single mom are moving, funny, and eye-opening. What did Sarah's self-assessment show you about parenting? About being in the community? About the difficulties of living, as she lived, with a much-loved spouse in absentia?

6. If you could chat with one of the Smiley boys throughout the book, which one would it be and what would you say?

7. What is your definition of a good dinner?

8. The author has said that one of the things she realized during the year of dinners is that "There is no substitute for the value

of face-to-face interaction. At the end of the dinners, I realized that no guest cared about the taste of the food or quality of the dishware. They each came because they wanted to meet our family and have conversations." Is this true for you? Are there things—perceived expectations, for example—that hold you back from inviting someone to dinner? What can we learn from this? What did Sarah learn about this when Gloria died unexpectedly before her scheduled dinner?

9. Dustin Smiley is at the heart of this book, although he isn't at home for most of it. What does his presence mean to the family? What does his absence show you? Does *Dinner with the Smileys* alter the way you read headlines?

10. The Smileys are a Navy family, with all the service commitments that implies. There are hundreds of thousands of military families in the United States alone, and yet they are not the only families experiencing an empty seat at the table. Which other families are affected? Why? How is that situation the same, and different, than the Smileys' situation?

11. In Chapter Fifteen, "December," Sarah states: "Basically, I had to make room for my husband again." In this simple sentence she sums up what a year's absence can do, how far the family had come, and what so many military spouses have to learn about adjusting to absence. Did ending the book with this chapter and her description of Dustin's return work for you? What questions did this open for you after having learned so much about this remarkable family?

12. Near the end of the book, Sarah asks Lindell, "What's been your favorite purpose of Dinner with the Smileys?" (Lindell's answer is on page 321.) What is your answer?